Mr. Lean **Buys** and **Transforms** a Manufacturing Company

The True Story of Profitably Growing an Organization with Lean Principles

Mr. Lean **Buys** and **Transforms** a Manufacturing Company

The True Story of Profitably Growing an Organization with Lean Principles

GREG LANE

Foreword by John Shook

CRC Press
Taylor & Francis Group
Boca Raton London New York

CRC Press is an imprint of the
Taylor & Francis Group, an **informa** business

A PRODUCTIVITY PRESS BOOK

Productivity Press
Taylor & Francis Group
270 Madison Avenue
New York, NY 10016

© 2010 by Taylor and Francis Group, LLC
Productivity Press is an imprint of Taylor & Francis Group, an Informa business

Library of Congress Cataloging-in-Publication Data

Lane, Greg.
    Mr. Lean buys and transforms a manufacturing company : the true story of profitably growing an organization with lean principles / Greg Lane.
        p. cm.
    Includes bibliographical references and index.
    ISBN 978-1-4398-1516-8
    1. Semiconductor production equipment industry--Management. 2. Semiconductor production equipment industry--Cost effectiveness. 3. Production control--Cost effectiveness. 4. Organizational effectiveness. 5. Lane, Greg. I. Title.

HD9696.S42L36 2010
658.5'6--dc22   2009045800

Visit the Taylor & Francis Web site at
http://www.taylorandfrancis.com

and the Productivity Press Web site at
http://www.productivitypress.com

Contents

Foreword

There has never been a lean consultant who didn't consider buying his own company, to rid himself of slow-minded company managers who don't listen, to have a chance to do it the way it should be done, and to do it himself. That is, to finally do it *right*.

And there has never been a business owner who hasn't wished all the know-it-all consultants who lecture them on the obvious would put up or shut up: "Those who can, do; those who can't either teach or consult."

Mr. Lean Buys and Transforms a Manufacturing Company is for both camps — the consultant who secretly wonders what it would be like to actually lead the charge as CEO/owner and the CEO owner who simply needs the performance improvement.

Greg Lane has seen lean from all sides: as a lean specialist inside large corporations, as an independent lean consultant, and as a company owner. Greg learned the Toyota Production System directly from the source during his stint at New United Motor Manufacturing Inc. (NUMMI), the joint venture between Toyota and GM.

As owner of his own machining company, purchased on a shoestring and a prayer, Greg naturally reached deep into his bag of lean tricks. But, his company was small with few resources. He quickly realized every action he took had to be supremely practical. There could be no "lean for lean's sake." No kanban where they didn't make sense. No overblown, expensive andon systems. No extensive team of indirect employees who add no value.

As his organizing principle, Greg landed on a lesser-known Toyota approach to creating change in a workplace called "OSKKK." OSKKK stands for Observe deeply, then Standardize, followed by three stages of Kaizen. Kaizen is a lesser-known Toyota approach.

Greg first learned about OSKKK during his intense TPS Key Person training in Toyota City, Japan in the early 1990s. One of the fortunate, hand-picked few to undergo this specialized training, Greg learned directly at the hands of Toyota's most experienced Toyota Production Sensei in Toyota City. Later, as a lean consultant to his former employer Delphi, Greg was more deeply exposed to OSKKK through the work of former Toyota production control manager Yoshinobu Yamada, who was introducing OSKKK throughout many of the operational divisions of Delphi at that time.

Greg takes us blow-by-blow through the entire experience of searching for an appropriate company, completing the purchase, learning a new business, transforming it through the application of lean thinking and achieving a two-fold increase in sales during the first four years (an increase in capacity and real output of 25 percent per year), including a profit margin increase of 10 percent and finally selling the transformed business to a new, lucky, owner. Along the way, we learn about the application of OSKKK, the process of learning and improving not only the plant floor but also the office side of a small business. Author/business owner Greg even introduces a novel and cleverly simple approach to practical product costing for quicker and more accurate price quoting for new business, a little-discussed headache for every manufacturer.

Mr. Lean Buys and Transforms a Manufacturing Company is a fun read. If you've ever considered how you would go about transforming your own manufacturing enterprise or if you own such an enterprise that needs transformation — this book will definitely provide thought-provoking ideas and some guiding principles along with specific hints for dealing with challenges that your company faces today.

John Shook
President, Lean Transformations Group, Inc.
Ann Arbor, MI, USA

Preface

I am sure there are days when you sit at work thinking how things—all those things you imagine doing differently than the way they are currently done—would be different if you owned and ran the company. Maybe you imagine being at the top of the pecking order—or at least being able to advise your managers—to create a more efficient company instead of trudging along performing tasks that add no real value. How easily you could implement lean ideas to better the business if you were given the knowledge and authority. It is likely, however, that you have not been promoted to a high-enough level or your personal checking account does not contain enough money to buy the company (and if you had that kind of cash, you would probably retire to some wonderful place instead).

I made the jump from corporate employee to business owner by committing every penny I had as well as incurring heavy debt. Buying a business is not something I would recommend to everyone, especially those with a weak heart or a desire for stability via a regular paycheck.* But, you can learn a lifetime of lessons in the short term with this approach. In my case, I was able to become the owner, the boss, and periodically just another of the machine operators. I took the plunge, and my story follows. It was not a perfect transition by any stretch of the imagination and many mistakes were made, but there is a lot to be learned by these experiences.

This book tells the true story of how I purchased a stable, profitable manufacturing company and—despite having no prior experience in the industry—I was able to grow it successfully and increase its profitability just by showing up and applying a bit of common sense and the lean ideas, strategies, and philosophies I had learned.† These same ideas should be

---

* I would not recommend this course of action to others, especially if it involves selling off all your personal assets and assuming a lot of debt to purchase mostly "goodwill," as was my experience. Reflecting on it now that my situation has changed and I am supporting a family, I am not sure I would risk as much the next time around.

† I will not mention the name of the business because it continues to operate under the same name and the current owners might not want this type of publicity. When I purchased the business, I chose to keep the original name because, as I quickly found out, the purchase includes buying the "goodwill," meaning the name, the existing customers, the employees' knowledge, and any proprietary technology or processes. To change the name—especially to incorporate one's own name into it—seemed to me to be based more on ego than on a sound business decision (unless you have a really cool name).

applicable to most industries. My experience should help you to see how lean methods can lead to profitability in almost any manufacturing or service business, particularly a complex company with a high variation of products or services.

One item you will not find discussed in great detail is management culture and that is because I did not need to convince top management to change their culture in the direction of lean management. I came into the business with strong beliefs and experiences in lean. Often the more difficult part of these transformations is getting the top managers to lead by example; however, since these principals were already deeply ingrained in my style, it made the transformation much easier.

My purpose was not to implement the Toyota Production System (or lean principles) but instead to grow the business as a more profitable organization utilizing these tools. I did not explain or sell each idea to the employees as a "lean principle"; I merely implemented lean philosophies in their simplest and most logical fashion. Following a simple implementation method I began to learn while working with Toyota, a method known as OSKKK (Observe, Standardize, Kaizen Flow & Process, Kaizen Equipment, and Kaizen Layout), I was able to apply the steps in my transformation although outside influences periodically changed the order in which they were implemented. The OSKKK method was really reinforced later while I was working with Delphi Automotive during a period in which they utilized Mr. Yamada, a former Toyota production control manager, to lead and teach them continuous improvement.

Keep in mind that two things were taking place during this period in the business's history:

- I was trying to learn all aspects of the business so it could be managed successfully.
- I was implementing a lean transformation only after understanding basic aspects of the business.

It is critical to keep these things in mind because in the beginning a manager must patiently learn before he or she can successfully guide the improvements. Many managers overlook the importance of having an understanding of the tasks before trying to implement improvements. OSKKK is a methodology that helps both in learning the business and in guiding a lean transformation. All the improvements really come together as a system, and cherry-picking can lead to suboptimization—it will not maximize profits nor create a coherent business. If you require a simple, overriding transformation strategy, then I recommend OSKKK.

Most business owners have acquired experience in the industry prior to becoming owners or managers. Few assume that "lean" alone could be the answer to making that jump from employee to employer; however, the following account dispels this idea by showing that lean by itself (with its relationship to the customer's desires) goes a long way toward running a company and increasing its profitability. It also demonstrates that lean principles are applicable in a made-to-order or job-shop business.

ABOUT THE BOOK

It has been several years since I sold the business and I tell the story as well as my memory permits. Naturally, some experiences live in great detail in my mind while others are a bit foggy.

Shortly after buying the business, I was contacted about providing additional support in my former employer's lean transformation and I quickly learned that relating my own transformation experiences could benefit others. I started keeping some specific notes, which enhance the accuracy of this book. Over the years, I have often found that relating these real-life experiences has helped those wishing to better come to terms with making their own improvements. There was nothing easy about my experiences, but having a plan and sound, simple, and proven principles that I believed in proved to be a winning combination.

Although I named the chapters according to the overriding theme during each phase, the book is written chronologically; therefore, some points begin in a chapter and are developed in further detail later.

To help you in relating to my planned implementation steps and the tools I was focusing on, I have included "lean principle" boxes and "key points" highlighted throughout the text, and lessons learned at the end of each chapter. The appendices also contain examples of how I worked through some of these lean elements, and Appendix L captures what finally ended up being my implementation sequence.

This is not a technical book and it does not play "lean bingo" by throwing a lot of acronyms at you to try and impress. However, I do often use a few unique terms that are worth clarifying at this point:

- *Tribal knowledge* is when unique knowledge (e.g., the steps to complete a process, or some technical knowledge) is kept and managed inside someone's head instead of being generally agreed-to and documented.
- *CNC—Computer Numerical Control*—is a system that reads G-code and M-code commands and drives a machine tool (in this case, three- and four-axis machines for cutting metal and other materials).
- *TPS—Toyota Production System*—is Toyota's famous production system that I learned and used as the basis for improving my business though I did not continuously mention it by name or utilize much of its terminology during the transformation.
- *PDCA—Plan, Do, Check, Act*; also known as "management by fact"—creates a process-centered environment that continuously follows a loop that involves (1) studying the current situation, collecting and analyzing the data to identify causes of problems, and then planning for improvement (Plan); (2) implementing the plan (Do); (3) monitoring to determine whether it's successful (Check); and (4) implementing a permanent solution (Act).
- A tick list is a simple method to gather data and speak with the facts. Normally, an employee keeps a simple data sheet in the work place for a few weeks or months and records the occurrences.

OK   ✝✝✝ I

NOK   ✝✝✝ ✝✝✝ II

As far as I know, I am the only lean practitioner who has purchased and managed his own manufacturing company armed only with "lean experience." I hope these simple fundamentals can inspire you to formulate a method to drive continuous improvement in your business. My experiences proved beyond a doubt that lean principles will lead to successful business management even in low-volume, high-mix companies. Waste can be found and eliminated in most processes if you have "eyes for waste" and the conviction and methods to minimize it. I think my experiences can highlight and simplify this.

Prologue: The Purchase

It was 1997 when I became serious about buying my own business. I was working for Delphi Automotive (owned by General Motors at the time, but later separated from GM and became a publicly owned corporation). I was Delphi Interior's manager/sensei of international lean production implementation. I had just returned to the United States from Zurich, Switzerland, where I had worked for about four years, directing and implementing lean all over Europe in GM's Opel brand car and component plants. I was in my early thirties and—at GM's highest management level—I was on the fast track to being made a director and entering the "executive" rank.

I was not frustrated by my job nor did I feel like I was stuck in a dead end; it was quite the opposite. I was convinced that once I settled into the perks of executive life, I would likely start to thrive on the responsibility, the respect, and those wonderful benefits that came with it. But, I had started to get the itch to try something on my own, and advancement at Delphi would likely lead to putting aside my entrepreneurial desires. I also figured that since I had arrived at this point *once* in my career, I could do it again—assuming that corporate America would consider a career interruption as an acceptable diversion and would provide me another chance to rejoin the ranks if things did not work out.

Being single and having no debt, I figured this was a great time to scratch that entrepreneurial itch and give it a try. In retrospect, it is funny that the only person I knew who did something similar was my father, though he did it at a much later stage in his life. His decision carried a lot more risk, like having the responsibility of a family and the realization that, if things did not work out, it might be difficult to return to corporate life.

Being a "company man" my entire career, I was not even sure I knew how to spell "entrepreneur," let alone grasp what it took to become one. With my life savings in hand and a very specialized lean production background from Toyota, I started by purchasing my first copy of *Entrepreneur* magazine. I found that, other than articles written by successful entrepreneurs, the magazine I purchased contained many ads to buy into franchises. The franchises were mostly in the service or food industry, which did fit my vision of owning an existing business that manufactured a product. If asked "Why not start your own business instead of buying an existing one?" my answer was simple: I had no ideas for a new business. Instead, I had "Kaizen eyes" and felt very comfortable identifying waste, especially in manufacturing environments. So, why not buy a going concern and improve it? My undergraduate degree was in mechanical engineering, so acquiring a company that involved a technical product was desirable.

After *Entrepreneur* magazine did not pan out, I moved into looking through the "business for sale" section of local newspapers in northern California, my target area. I also enlisted some business brokers—the equivalent of real estate agents except they sell existing businesses.

Obviously, the biggest limitation I faced was price. My savings totaled $200K after selling my home—actually, my boat, which I had lived on for four years before moving to Switzerland to work for GM. In reality, I might have had more money to work with had I previously owned a home, which would have appreciated in value, instead of a boat, which continuously depreciates.* On top of my $200K, my father was also willing to invest a bit and act as an advisor. Between us, there was about $200K to invest directly, and another $75K in cash to operate for a month or so until some of the receivables could be collected.

Certain banks work with the SBA (Small Business Administration) to partially underwrite business loans if certain criteria are met. The criteria were not difficult and I qualified under SBA's terms. After finding a business, I also had to qualify under the bank's terms for financing.† I learned most banks working with the SBA like to see an applicant put in about 30 percent as a down payment, so I figured I could borrow between $400K and $500K.

With my criteria for choosing a business loosely defined as an existing manufacturing business that was located somewhere in California and did not cost more than $700K (and obviously, there were also profitability and longevity conditions), I intensified my search. Whether searching for a business through a broker or a newspaper/magazine, the

---

* Living on a boat was another experience that I had to get out of my system. I do not regret it at all; quite the contrary, it was a great experience. However, one saying still sticks in my mind: "The two happiest days for a boat owner are the day you buy it and the day you sell it."

† By the way, what a great deal for the banks: they were charging over 11 percent interest at the time. And, whatever risk the U.S. government's SBA program was not underwriting, the applicant was asked to sign for personally—you know the drill: your firstborn and anything else you might own.

first steps are similar: The potential buyer starts by signing a boilerplate non-disclosure contract and requesting some simple financial information. The information can vary greatly but often the first glance could include a P&L (profit and loss statement) and a balance sheet going back five years. If a broker is involved, the buyer will receive more prepared-in-advance financial information along with a write-up about the company and generally better-prepared marketing materials. At this point, the name of the company is not disclosed to the potential buyer and the seller is usually keeping the sale secret from customers and employees. Normally, as the buyer takes further steps, the seller discloses more financial information, provides copies of tax returns, and usually allows an after-hours visit of the company.

Two businesses that I considered at the time were a boat manufacturer and a coffin manufacturer. Boat manufacturing was exciting to think about because my hobbies include sailing, motor boating, and waterskiing. Plus, the boat manufacturer was located in California. However, the business had been for sale for a number of years and, at first glance, the financials looked shaky and the questions I asked about the product and market received very vague answers. That was enough to scare off someone like me because I was putting everything on the line.

The coffin manufacturer was a little different. The financials looked OK but the products were sold through a network of distributors. I learned about a problem between the company and the network that resulted in the manufacturer being blackballed. It wasn't just luck that led me to discover this problem: I remember that a recent sales decline had caused me to investigate further and uncover this information. Honestly, I was also having a hard time imagining myself manufacturing coffins. In addition to the product being a bit depressing, I imagined that, as the owner, I might find myself wishing for a local war or an epidemic to help increase sales.

A last potential worth mentioning that I became serious about was a machine tooling shop that reconditioned machine-cutting tools for airplane manufacturers. It was located in Southern California and, although not my first choice in locations, it had the type of production flow that I liked and it seemed lean improvements would be quite applicable. The numbers looked good and the owner, who had started the firm some twenty years prior, was ready to retire. The fly in the ointment was that one customer—although long-standing—accounted for over 70 percent of the business. This was a red flag.

I went through the preliminary due diligence steps that led up to my father and I flying down to Southern California to look at the business and get a better understanding. Prior to a site visit, a potential buyer is usually required to provide background information and show that the financial resources are in line with the required down payment. I guess I passed that test.

The tour of the business looked good. My Kaizen eyes identified a host of opportunities even though I was walking through after hours and no production was taking place. I had a good feeling about the owner, who seemed honest and straightforward. At this point, I also saw tax returns and more detailed financials, which I trusted at face value. Naturally, the business broker representing the business was in attendance and he couldn't help but point out all the positive aspects and how, with a few changes, the new owner could really grow the business. However, I came away with another big concern: The owner's ethnicity qualified him as a minority. Normally, this would not be a concern; however, upon further research I found that airplane manufacturers were under pressure to reach a quota for using minority-owned subcontractors and suppliers and the business's largest customer was borderline on reaching its quota. Not being a member of a minority, and knowing that the business could not survive if this customer went elsewhere, I decided this was not for me.

About the time I was reaching my decision, the owner was completing his financial statements for the previous year and was so impressed by his increased profitability that he decided on a drastic price increase. Many methods have been developed and entire books written on how to determine a fair selling price for a business. The three most typical methods are valuations based on market, assets, or earnings (or some combination of these). I had chosen to use only an earnings-based valuation, for which there are many suggestions of multipliers to use. After some research and many discussions, my father and I decided to use a multiplier of 3x EBIT (earnings before interest and taxes). We based this on an average of the previous three to five years of financial statements (i.e., fair sales price equals three times the three-to-five-year average EBIT). However, the owner of the airplane tool remanufacturing business had changed the asking price to something like 6x EBIT.

I never monitored any of the businesses I passed up to see how they fared. In reality, the only checking up I could do would be to call and see whether they were still in business, and I probably could have found the current owner's name (or the current corporation's name) in public records. But, I was too busy with the company I purchased.

Enough about what didn't come to be.

Sometime later in 1997, after close to a year of searching, I found the one I went after and finally got. Actually, I had come across it about six months earlier, but the price was out of sight at that time. I was reviewing so many Internet sites and had put the word out to so many business brokers that I don't remember whether this particular broker contacted me when the price fell into my range, or I noticed the price change on the broker's Web site.

What I found was a machine shop that manufactured parts for the semiconductor equipment industry. This industry is extremely volatile and cyclical not only because of the changes in demand by the end customer but also because of spikes in demand as new technologies are developed—and once everyone has the latest, all will go quiet again. Despite the nature of the semiconductor equipment industry, this machine shop, located in the Bay Area of northern California, had survived many of the big downturns even though only a small percentage of its business volume came from outside the industry.

A majority of development in chip-etching machine technology was taking place in the Bay Area during this period, but because of California's higher manufacturing costs, there was always the threat that any significant volume would be moved elsewhere (including offshore) and new local suppliers established. There were many similar businesses in the Bay Area because of all the development and small lot production work available. But, this one stood out because of its longevity and profitability. It had been a going concern for about eighteen years, originally started by two partners working from a garage. After a year or two, one partner had bought out the other. The primary customers were based in the semiconductor equipment industry, which basically produces the multimillion-dollar machines to etch silicon wafers to be utilized as computer chips for the likes of Intel and Hewlett Packard.

The business was small (under ten people) but looked manageable. The owner was basically a self-taught businessman with no formal education. He had some machining experience prior to starting the business and basically started with a machine or two in a garage. Although I had never even taken a machining class in high school, I figured it was a good fit with my degree in mechanical engineering and an MBA to help on the business end. Also, I am quite a handy guy and enjoy working with my hands.

Topping all of that, I thought of my lean background and my training from Toyota. Having helped others in making significant improvements to their businesses, why couldn't I do it for myself?

Although most of my training and support up to that point had been with higher-volume businesses that had a smaller variation of part numbers, I figured the principles had to be applicable in a job-shop environment. Naturally, when the time came to walk the flow through the shop and office processes, I noted many opportunities for improvements. Like many businesses, everything was learned in-house and based on experience or tribal knowledge, and without any lean experience, there were few established processes in place and plenty of room for productivity improvements.

I wasn't completely naïve to the fact that since I had no experience with machining, and especially CNC (Computer Numerical Control) machining, I was taking a gigantic risk. But, as everybody says during an interview, I am a "quick learner," and I tried to analyze the local machining industry and the semiconductor equipment market, and then I attempted to figure out how I could grow the business. Naturally, near the top of my list were goals like diversifying my customer base away from its strong dependency on the cyclical semiconductor equipment market. I also realized that the competition can be stiff in any industry where the cost of entry is not exceptionally high. However, the skill/knowledge level required for CNC machining, especially certain complex parts, is impressive, which narrowed the field of competition a bit. Also, some simple research made it clear that few of these small businesses had any lean knowledge or implementation.

So, after a lot of back and forth on price and terms, an agreement was reached, a contract drawn up, and a closing date set. Typically, the terms of sale are drawn up by a lawyer representing either the buyer or seller. I am not sure which is more traditional, but in my case I hired a lawyer to write the contract. The seller then had a lawyer review the contract and the other documents prior to signing.

Typically the terms of the sale included a provision for the seller to stay on for a month or more after the closing to help run the business and train the new owner or employees. We set this transition for a longer period—a total of six weeks—as I had never operated a conventional metal-working machine, let alone a CNC machining center. I had also asked to be allowed to hang around before the closing date to learn the business, but the seller did not want me on-site. I assumed this is frequently the case, as nothing's ever sure until "the money is in the bank," and until things were set in stone, my presence might only cause anxiety among the employees.

Next, it was time to secure financing. After soliciting some of the banks that were "SBA (Small Business Administration) approved lenders," I applied at two of them. Naturally, they were not only concerned that I had the down payment but they also wanted to see a résumé to understand how my skill sets might apply toward running a technical business. In many ways, you can compare some of the mechanics I was going through to those of purchasing a home. However, you must remember that most of the purchase price of an established business is in its goodwill, and that can disappear mighty fast if you upset a major customer or do not have the skill sets to drive the business forward. Whereas homes have a market value that is normally appraised near the purchase price, the value of a business is determined by various financial ratios, mainly its profitability. As I explained, I was valuing businesses based on their earnings and was willing to pay about three times the EBIT averaged over the previous three to five years. Naturally, many other factors contributed to the viability of the business as an ongoing enterprise. But, this helped to determine a fair price and, this time, the owner had dropped the price to 3.5x EBIT and further negotiations got him to about 3x EBIT.

Of the two banks to which I applied and received approval, I chose between the lesser of the evils based on their exorbitant interest rates and terms. I went to that traditional meeting where the banker sits behind the desk playing God and acting as if you are about to be bestowed with a great favor. After convincing the banker (who knew nothing about manufacturing, let alone machining) that I knew more than he did, and committing myself to make it work or lose everything I owned (a really compelling motivation), he graciously approved the loan on a five-year term at just over 11 percent interest. That probably makes most people feel just a bit better about their mortgage payment. I was also required to purchase a very expensive life insurance policy (sold through the bank, of course, at what I assume provided them a healthy commission) to cover any outstanding value on the loan in the event of my early demise. They really know how to cover every eventuality.

A whole host of other activities must be completed before the closing, one of which was the legal process of incorporating. At the closing, the corporation I set up bought the business assets and rights and the business name from the seller's corporation. Any lawyer will tell you that this at least affords a buyer some personal protection because the legal entity purchases the business and assumes all the liabilities. In my case, the previous owner's corporate name was different than the name of the business he was selling ("doing business as" or d/b/a). So, my recently incorporated corporation was able to take over the existing operating name the former corporation had used as a "d/b/a" for the last 18 years. After all, the "goodwill" is a big part of what justifies paying the asking price, since only taking into account the asset values would make many companies worth a lot less.

The actual closing is similar to that of buying a home except you seem to sign about double the amount of documents, if you can imagine that. Closing day for this purchase was set for Friday afternoon, and I had asked the seller to plan overtime for Saturday for two reasons: (1) although a seller may try to move as much volume through the door to maximize profits before turning the business over, there was still a backlog, and (2) as the new owner, I would need to know some important things right away, like how to unlock the doors, turn on the lights, and make the coffee. Sounds like I had set myself up for a stressful first day.

Since the purpose of this book is to tell my story of a lean guy buying a business and utilizing lean manufacturing methods to grow it profitably, and it is not a "how-to" guide for purchasing a business, I think this is enough background on the purchase. I did not highlight any of the lessons learned, as nothing pertained to improving an ongoing business. I just felt it may be interesting for you to know how it all got started. I also believe there are much more sophisticated methodologies for evaluating and purchasing a business, as there are many books written on the subject. Therefore, I would not necessarily recommend following the way I went through it.

1

The Beginning
Observation and Documentation

1.1 INTRODUCTION

It was Saturday morning, day one of owning and operating my first business and I had bought donuts to encourage a little team building. I was staying at my brother's house while looking for my own place and, on my way out the door that morning, my brother asked whether the donuts were in lieu of a 401K plan for the employees. I guess they were, in a manner of speaking.

I think at the time there were four or five employees in the shop and two in the office plus the owner who functioned as the manager. The business grew from this point although, due to the cyclical nature of the industry, it periodically fluctuated in the number of employees.

Those of you hoping to make analogies between this business and yours might be thinking that because you are part of much larger organizations, you therefore have much more complex considerations, politics, and corporate cultures to get past and will not gain sufficient insights from the experiences I am sharing. Having worked for two large companies—General Motors and Toyota—and then owning my own small business, I can assure you that most of the simple principles that I implemented are applicable to your situation. The question is how to cut through the red tape, bureaucracy, fears, and personalities involved in larger organizations to get some of these things done. In most large companies, people will offer their theories on why change is so difficult, why there is so much resistance to change, even when new management is brought in to drive this change. Spending more than fifteen years helping mostly large and medium-sized organizations with their lean transformations, I agree that the complications, politics, and culture must be addressed in the plan but the overall steps remain the same. By reading about my experience, you are sure to pick up on many improvement ideas along with proven methodologies to gain buy-in, thereby convincing the organization. However, I had one very large advantage you or your organization might lack; I am a true believer in lean and that can be a difficult conviction to acquire.

Throughout this book, I have included highlighted text featuring the "lean principles" that I focused on at the time, and I have further enhanced the discussion with "key points" which are also displayed in italics. As a business owner, my purpose was not explicitly to implement lean methods but instead to increase the business's profitability. Rather than turning the employees into lean experts, I wanted to sell the ideas to them as simple and logical steps to secure our longevity ("job security"). I assure you, many of the basics I put in place in my own company are either absent or not truly supported in other organizations, but overcoming the issues introduced by the size, bureaucracy, and personalities in various organizations is not impossible. What is required is a similar simplistic approach and an unwavering belief in continuous improvement.

1.2 OBSERVING

With only a six-week training period to learn an entire business of which I knew nothing, I went in that first Saturday morning with a plan. I was going to follow an idea I learned at Toyota known as OSKKK (Observe, Standardize, Kaizen Flow & Process, Kaizen Equipment, and Kaizen Layout; a detailed breakdown of OSKKK is shown in Appendix A) to guide my learning of the business as well as for structuring the lean transformation. I figured I would follow this sequence of steps as closely as I could. And since I needed to learn the various processes, not only as a basis for improvement but as a necessity to manage the business, this would keep me from randomly jumping in with specific improvement ideas. The beauty of OSKKK as a method of improvement is that it also closely follows the conventional wisdom that, when taking over a new position, you first observe and understand the business and its environment before implementing changes.

The week before I took over, I had written down all the likely titles for the administrative and shop-floor tasks in this type of business. For the office side, I broke them down into sections like order entry, purchasing raw materials, subcontracting, invoicing, closing the books, etc. For the shop, I had grouped items like material preparation, setting up and changing over a machine, programming, scheduling, manual machining, quality checks, instrument calibrations, and many more. I organized a three-ring binder according to these categories and figured I would gather the information as I encountered it.

Basically, I planned to learn the business from the ground up. This entailed hands-on learning for each task by going to where the work was done and the value was being added. This is often referred to as going to Gemba. Naturally, I had put myself on the fast track with only six weeks to accomplish this. Realistically, I knew I could not decide the timing of learning a particular task—that would be dictated by the demands of an ongoing business—but the three-ring binder would help guide me, ensuring I did not miss anything that I felt was important. So, I would go with the flow and learn quickly, observing and documenting.

Lean principle: *In the lean world, going to where the work is done (or where the value is added) to learn about the process before making improvements or decisions is known as Gemba. At Toyota, new employees, regardless of level, normally start their employment with hands-on learning of tasks within their areas of responsibility.*

For the time being, I was planning to keep all the employees; therefore, I did not need to immediately learn the details of every job. But, I had to determine which things the former owner/manager did by himself and quickly become competent in them. One advantage was that I had purchased the business in the middle of the month, so the six-week training period spanned the end of the next two months. This meant that I could twice observe the end-of-month process of closing the books.

When I arrived that first Saturday morning at 5:55 a.m., the now-former owner, Bob, and the shop foreman, Tom, were already hard at work. Two of the CNC (Computer Numerical Control) machines were already up and running. We had agreed on a 6:00 a.m. start, and things already appeared well underway. My first observation—or should I say concern?—was that I had either walked into a staged scene or this was one hard-working industry. I (being a slightly later riser) had questioned Bob about the wisdom of starting at 6:00 on a Saturday morning, and he had told me the guys liked early starts, especially when working overtime on Saturdays because they preferred to "get it over with." Finding the machines running before the agreed-upon start time did not jive with what I had always observed in larger businesses, where it seems that although people arrive on time, they do not necessarily get right to work. First, they might get coffee or have some discussions with coworkers, and then they think about turning their machines on and running through a warm-up procedure. A 6:00 a.m. start time in larger companies usually meant an actual production start closer to 6:30 a.m. When consulting, I frequently recommend an hour-by-hour target to avoid this lost production. However, late production starts did not appear to be a concern in my new business.

Lean principle: Managing takt time (time available/customer demand) is usually handled in low-volume, high-variation businesses that schedule a variety of products to run on a particular machine/process with a tool that is often called a day-by-hour board. This board allows planning of the various customers' part numbers against the process's capacity, and execution of that plan to be visualized in real time. This type of tool was necessary in my business but would be introduced during the Kaizening stages.

As I walked in, Tom, who had been with the business for more than sixteen years, eyed me with suspicion, as anyone in his situation would. After the papers were signed the previous day, I'd had a short meeting with the team during which I indicated that I had no intention of making any changes for the time being, and they were stuck taking me at my word. Tom, a short but solid man who looked like he could hold his own, was also a very direct sort and had stared directly into my eyes and asked about my machining background during that first meeting. I first tried to deflect the question by explaining my years of working in manufacturing and similar businesses. But, after talking around it for a while, I had to level with them: I had never managed or worked in a machine shop. All eyes drifted toward the floor, each man now considerably more nervous about his future. I could tell by the way Tom was looking at me that he was probably searching for a lifeline. But, it was not the time to explain the lean principles and how they can help to improve even in a job shop. I guess I could have responded that "I'm a fast learner." At any rate, I had to keep in mind that I was not the only one with something to lose if things did not go right.

My father—who had also owned his own business although on a much larger scale—had advised me to take the time to learn the business from the ground up, understanding the processes and the people before even considering any change. This is the wise course for anyone in a new position, and I knew I would need it continuously reinforced. I knew it was sound advice but, not being a patient man, I also knew it would be difficult for me. However, in his own way, my father was describing the OSKKK methodology I was planning to utilize to learn and transform the business. My father's advice proved to be valuable and very profitable.

Key point: Even if you are under pressure for quick-change, aggressive solutions or feel sure you know what the problems and solutions are, take the time to observe and learn the processes (go to Gemba) and gain insights from those performing the tasks. In some cases, this might even require understanding the customers, the market, and the people instead of firefighting and quickly making changes without the buy-in of those involved.

1.3 GETTING A DETAILED UNDERSTANDING OF THE PROCESSES I WOULD BE RESPONSIBLE FOR

In cases where people have worked their way up in an organization, they may intimately understand many of the processes that they have worked their way through. However, Western companies are too frequently in a hurry to make a new employee "productive" (which, by our own definition, is usually to start performing their assigned job immediately) and tend not to allow the employee sufficient time to become familiar with the business, its processes, and its people. This is especially true with either the arrival of a seasoned manager or some university graduates; we tend to fast-track them, skipping any structured process orientation. I am convinced the reason we cannot find the necessary time is because we are not able to quantify the lost revenue that this lack of training and orientation costs our organizations.

When I was hired by Toyota (NUMMI, the Toyota–General Motors joint venture) as an engineer, I spent the first ten weeks observing and then learning the business in a hands-on fashion. The first week I was sent to paint school, where I learned a lot of technical aspects of formulating and matching paint, and then I spent nine weeks on the shop floor as a team member moving through the various process steps. I worked one week in each section of the paint shop: mixing the paint, spraying it on the cars, and making repairs. This was an investment in which the payback to my employer was at least fifty-fold. It is unfortunate that many companies feel they cannot afford this time. Toyota understood the payback, and now I clearly understand its importance. And so, I planned to learn all the processes I would be responsible to oversee.

When speaking about learning many parts of the business and becoming expert in the various disciplines, I realize that this would be an impossible task in many industries. It is not humanly possible in larger organizations today, with the ever-expanding range of disciplines and the increased depth of knowledge that each is continuously moving toward, as the many "silos" of knowledge run very deep and the number of silos are ever-increasing. Each silo can require a lifetime of dedication to become proficient. But in these cases, the idea is to strive instead to understand related or connected processes. Doing this will help to better integrate and lead to improvements between the people and related departments.

1.4 A LACK OF TRAINING CAN BE COSTLY

This lack of time for orientation and learning was clearly displayed in the drawings we received to quote. The majority of engineers responsible for designing these fabricated and machined parts had obviously never worked in any of the industries responsible to manufacture the parts.

And they had no practical experience in designing parts that could be easily produced, or in the relationship between their designs and the cost implications. Being an engineer myself, I frequently understood the application of the parts we were building and what features were critical. I continually found us working with difficulties such as wrong tolerances called out in drawings. Or, drawings that made the part difficult to build. Or, there was a much easier way to build the part (i.e., making it out of two separate pieces and welding it together). Almost always when I was able to explain the problem to the engineer, he or she would ask what I suggested, and follow up on my suggestion with a "red line" drawing, implying they almost never took the time to change the original. Instead, these "red lines" kept everyone—including incoming inspectors—in the dark. Frequently, the red line drawing had to be packaged with the part so it did not get rejected when compared to the "official" drawing, which had not been modified.

What transpired more often when the drawing mistake only drastically increased the cost (instead of making the part nearly impossible to build) was to quote the part according to print and not make the effort to question it. This frequently resulted in the quoted price being twice as high to hold the tolerances called out or to manufacture the part from one solid block instead of welding two pieces together. But, it was the easiest course of action for the suppliers. I used to think that it would save the company a small fortune if the engineer had just done a short stint in a machine or fabrication shop. This will be discussed later because it often cost our customers considerably more than necessary.

Lean principle: What our customers lacked is known as DFM (design for manufacturing) or DFA (design for assembly). This is the idea or practice of designing products that are easy and less costly to manufacture and assemble. This knowledge can only be gained by spending time where the work is being performed (Gemba). Because we were not responsible for these design stages and were frequently a few steps removed from having contact with the designers, we often had little influence to improve the process. Remember: this early and critical step of involving manufacturing saves a lot. Typically, 75 percent or more of the cost is fixed by the product's design.

1.5 TRAINING AS A MACHINE OPERATOR

On that first Saturday, I started working as a machine operator while Bob managed the shop. I figured there was no use trying to manage processes of which I did not yet understand the details. I would only be setting myself up for failure and would lose face in front of my employees by making suggestions or impossible demands. I started on what turned out to be a good job from a learning standpoint. It involved a part that needed three separate machining operations before being sent out for plating; then it would come back for an assembly process. The material had been purchased "cut to size" and it had already been through one of our tumblers to remove rough edges for better hold in the fixtures and easier handling.

Tom had already set up the machine the day before and the first piece had been qualified. Qualification entailed the setup operator adjusting the CNC until he felt he had a good part. After that, he took it to another setup man, who would perform another 100-percent dimensional check. I had many questions: "Do we always purchase material to size?" "Who decides, and how is it determined which features are machined in a particular operational step?" So, I found it difficult to pay attention to the detailed explanation I was receiving about loading the machine: "Clamp the part too tight and you might stress the material or move the zero reference point." If not clamped tightly enough, it might be thrown out of the fixture during cutting. After watching Tom load a few pieces and press the start button, I was ready. I loaded a few pieces wrong and caused a little scrap, but I soon had the hang of it. I was also taught to deburr and check a few dimensions, but I was being closely watched by Tom and Bob. Nobody wanted me blowing it the first day.

1.6 DISCOVERING A LACK OF DOCUMENTATION

All the instruction on the various tasks was word-of-mouth explanations coming from years of experience. So, when I asked whether there was any documentation for these procedures, the response was a perplexed look, as if I had just asked the world's stupidest question. As is the case in most businesses, it soon became clear that there was basically no documentation (see tips on easy ways to document a task in Appendix B) and everything was tribal knowledge—meaning it was all retained in the employee's head, and when the employee left the company, the knowledge went, too. ISO- (International Standard for Organization) certified companies also usually lack any useful work standards for their respective tasks. I knew I had my work cut out for me, observing and learning by day and documenting by night. This is such a valuable point, especially regarding lean implementation and the need for standard processes (the second step of OSKKK), that I want to highlight it as a key learning point.

Key point: The easiest time to document previously undocumented processes is during the observation phase or when someone new is being trained on the particular process. This then becomes the basis for the second step—standardization.

1.7 IDENTIFYING SKILL SETS THAT NEEDED TO BE REPLACED

By way of background, the following list describes the three basic skill levels in a machine shop:

- The first level is the operator whose duties include loading and unloading the CNC machine, deburring the part, and taking some simple measurements. On a manual machine, it might entail loading the part and running the tool to a specific point following a prescribed method, and then checking the part. Operators are usually not responsible for setting up either a manual or CNC machine or for making adjustments. Usually, a setup man is nearby, keeping a close eye on the quality.
- The next level is the setup man. In addition to being familiar with all the operator's tasks, the setup man is also responsible for setting the tools and fixtures in the machine. In the case of a CNC, this might include loading the program, putting the offsets into the machine's computer, then running through and qualifying the first piece. Also, the setup man is responsible for making adjustments in the offsets and tool setups and, in some shops, making corrections and adjustments in the program (changing codes and numbers).
- The programmer—usually the third level—has normally worked his way up and is capable as a setup man and an operator. In addition, the programmer must be able to look at a drawing, conceptualize

how to make the part, decide what machine to use and what type of fixturing is necessary, design the necessary fixtures, and determine the number of operations. He must be computer-literate and capable of writing the programs and debugging the programs when problems arise. Today there is software that will write the individual lines of machine code, but the programmer must put in all the applicable information and dimensions and basically establish the priorities. The programmer must also draw up or specify any special tooling required so it can be manufactured by a tool shop.

The existing operators and setup men possessed sufficient skills for their areas, so no worries there. But, Bob had previously done most of the programming and he was leaving soon. The other skill that I would not be able to handle after the six weeks of training was the estimating, which had also been done solely by Bob. During the due diligence period, I had come to the conclusion that I could survive financially if I hired a combined "programmer/estimator," and managed Bob's other tasks myself (in addition to making the loan payments). So, my idea was to hire a programmer before Bob's exit.

The first problem with hiring someone from outside was the software that was being used in my shop for CNC programming—a DOS-based program—was outdated, and it would be difficult to find a programmer familiar with it. Can you imagine reverting back to working in DOS after working in Windows? Bob had purchased a newer, Windows-based package, but it was not being utilized because he had not found the time for training. A little research revealed that this new software was commonly used and it would be easier to find someone familiar with it than someone familiar with the DOS-based program. Naturally, I was also planning to learn to write programs, and there was no way I was about to revert back to working in DOS on a daily basis.

1.8 WORKPLACE ORGANIZATION (5S) OPPORTUNITIES

Lean principle: Workplace organization, known as 5S to lean practitioners, is a five-step process—Sort, Straighten, Shine, Standardize, Sustain—to minimize the non-value added time caused by not having all necessary tools and materials organized in the most appropriate places. Often during the observation step in OSKKK, waste caused by poor workplace organization is identified and made a priority when starting a Kaizen.

5S (workplace organization) is important any time employees struggle to find what they need, whether it is tooling on the shop floor or a file on the hard drive. As a consultant, I sometimes spend time helping companies organize their computer files, and I find the easiest time to do this is in conjunction with some other change (e.g., a new regulation, new employees, new software, etc.). It is not always necessary to spend months going back through the old files. Just set the new rules: (1) every time an existing file is used, it should be moved to the new system; and (2) every new file should be created in the newly organized system. This also allows you to understand which files can be purged or archived. Files that have not been moved to the new system after a year or two are likely unnecessary; consequently, they can remain in the old system in the rare case there is ever a need for them in the future.

After buying my business, I quickly discovered that the hard-drive directories were not set up in a simple standardized system. This problem existed in both the office and the shop, but at this point I was addressing only the shop. I was determined to suggest a new standardized filing system for the hard drive. I felt it should be started for all new part numbers that were to be programmed, and the existing files could be cleaned up, reprogrammed, and reorganized as we received repeat orders once the new programmer was on board. Although I have stated that no changes should be made until the business is truly understood, there are times when a change can be made successfully. In this case, a new, experienced person would be handling an aspect of the business that had formerly functioned based on tribal knowledge. Later, I was glad I started early on with this new structure to organize the files, and so was my new programmer.

Key point: Another lean lesson is that 5S applies to all aspects of the business and it is best to start its introduction in complicated and large systems by using a significant event like the start of a new employee. Begin using the new method going forward on all new work instead of trying to motivate people to go back and clean up all tools, materials, or data (some of which may not be represented or utilized in the future). Although this might leave you working in two systems simultaneously for some period, at least it gets you moving forward.

Sooner or later, you need to draw a line in the sand and make improvements going forward, even if you need to operate two systems for a period of time. The advantage is that soon you find some information in the old system that is not required; therefore, spending time and money to put this into a new format is a waste.

1.9 DISCOVERING DIFFERENT METHODS BEING UTILIZED FOR THE SAME TASK (NO STANDARDIZATION)

Since the crux of improving any business lies in understanding the value-adding processes and minimizing those that add no value, a detailed understanding of the processes are required to know the difference. My first full week in the business entailed a lot of learning. Everything was being taught as it transpired during the normal course of business; however, I concentrated on spending as much time as possible learning the next level in the shop, which was setting up a job. Setup was the key in this business, as the order size was small and most machines went through three or more setups per machine in a single day.

I had already set up my first job with Tom, and my next one was set up with the help of one of the setup men. As you might imagine, I discovered that things were not done the same way using similar methodologies. Each man had his own methods and experiences. As with the other tasks I had learned, no documentation existed for how to set up a machine. The methods and tricks all came from personal experience—Tom had learned under Bob and the other setup men had combined what they had learned from Tom and previous employers. As a result, the methods differed because they used different sequences, had various priorities, and put their own twist on it. Naturally, I found one method had more advantages and I documented that as the baseline. I started identifying a lot of improvements in the setup and later, by applying some SMED (single minute exchange of dies) methodology along with some training and small investment, significant improvements would be made. In a later chapter, I will discuss the setup improvements as we implemented them, but for now we'll discuss the documentation of the current best methods, which was my focus. I say "current" because, as all lean hands know, we want to continuously improve these methods; therefore, our documentation should be easy to change.

Lean principle: Standardization of work was the second step in my transformation plan (OSKKK). Where these standards are lacking usually becomes apparent during the observation period. It is critical because without standardization, there is no baseline for improvements. Standardized work is the current most efficient and safe working method that provides the desired quality.

Documenting a standard method is easy and painless these days with digital cameras, video cameras, and computers. Even if you do not have time to properly document the activity because of its complexities, the quick solution is to make a video of someone going through the steps while explaining what they are doing. In the interim, you can just store the video in a safe place, and if you need it for training, you can simply play it back. I want to capture this as a key point because it addresses the excuse of not having time for documentation. (Various options and methods of documentation are shown in Appendix B.)

Key point: There is no excuse for not having the current best method (of the standardized work) documented because making a video is fast and easy. The operator or team leader can explain what he or she is doing while working through the process.

1.10 DISCOVERING DIFFICULT PROCESSES TO STANDARDIZE

As I continued learning the various tasks, I found documenting how to write a CNC program turned out to be significantly more difficult than other processes. Bob was self-taught, so he had his own way of thinking as well as certain idiosyncrasies, especially since he was utilizing outdated, DOS-based software. I decided this would be difficult to standardize, especially since his experience was based on software I did not intend to learn. Instead, I decided I would immediately start interviewing programmers. During the interviews, I would give the applicants a copy of a drawing and ask them to list the programming steps and describe how they would estimate the part in order to determine whether any standard methods appeared. I found that few of the candidates went about it in exactly the same way but there were certain similarities, and I used these as an outline for the standardized work steps. Because programming first involves conceptualizing how to make the part and defining critical process steps, many variations for the same part evolve, some more efficient than others. Therefore, people in these roles need to be continuously challenged and educated, especially if they are "homegrown." I planned to use my notes of the various methods and correlate the similarities along with refining an ideal process flow when I had my new programmer/estimator on board.

Key point: Where processes (i.e., programming) allow different tools, programming, options, or sequences that will achieve the same end result, it is best to continuously have employees retrained and updated on new technological developments in their fields and, where possible, periodically challenge these outputs by comparing them to another "experienced" person's results.

1.11 THIS MUCH OBSERVATION REQUIRED ME TO "DIVIDE AND CONQUER"

To learn the office tasks, I had a slightly different plan in mind. To learn everything (both shop and office tasks) in six weeks was a bit overwhelming so I enlisted the help of someone who I wholeheartedly trusted to oversee financial matters and who was skilled in office administration: my mother. She was going to help by learning the key office tasks (while I was in the shop with Bob), which included focusing on all the front-office activities for which Bob was not responsible (e.g., processing a purchase order, cutting payroll, or developing a bill of material). These activities also lacked documentation so my mother would observe and document the current processes. Naturally, these tasks were learned skills and a small business owner may feel there is either no need to document them or not enough time available for documentation. Obviously, there are many opportunities to improve all these business processes but if there's no standard method, then there's no baseline from which to make these improvements. Again, video is an easy out.

Computer tasks are also easy to document using the "print screen" function along with an explanation of the steps. Most companies' processes involve many decision points; for example, do "X" if it is an "indirect material," but do "Y" if it is a "direct material." For these cases, a simple flowchart with decision boxes helps clarify things.

Step 1 of OSKKK—observation—includes the following major sub-steps:

- Take the time to see what is happening in the work area by watching multiple cycles of the same process.
- Watch more than one person performing the process and note where standardization is lacking, especially where it affects quality or productivity.
- Document by writing or videoing the individual process steps in the sequence they occur.
- Identify the origins of variation in both the flow of information and flow of materials.

Key point: For documenting office processes, you can use a combination of flowcharts, screen prints, and videos to capture the process steps for training (examples are shown in Appendix B).

You might never have been this concerned with documentation before. It might have been a nagging issue but there always seemed to be other priorities. In my case, this was an easy choice for a starting point. My lean training had taught me the need for a standard method as the basis for making improvements, and I completely understood the danger if no one experienced to perform these tasks was available. The cost of training new people is high; it is even more prohibitive if it is based on memory and a critical step is overlooked. Most accounting systems are not able to directly track the cost of training versus the considerable losses related to mistakes or the low productivity and poor quality associated with a lack of cross-training. But if they could, most managers would be able to justify and prioritize documenting and standardizing the "current best method." Toyota had learned to justify this cost.

For the time being, my mother was using a combination of all the available methods to document what was happening in the front office. At a later point, she would function in an ongoing capacity as the bookkeeper, completing the monthly statements and overseeing the accounts payable functions by reviewing and signing the checks. That would allow me to sleep better at night because I knew she was good at watching the pennies.

1.12 SUMMARY

- Step 1, the observation, had begun along with the related documentation. This served not only as the basis for step 2 (standardization), it also allowed me a structure in which to learn the processes so I could lead the business and its improvements.
- A lack of standardized processes was becoming apparent.
- A lack of workplace organization (5S) was also identified and its cost implications understood.
- Tribal knowledge was proving to be the predominant method of operating.

2

Standardizing the Estimating Process

2.1 HIRING A NEW PROGRAMMER/ESTIMATOR

I had begun advertising for the programmer/estimator by the end of my first week as the new owner for several reasons: I wanted to have the former owner, Bob, involved in the selection process with his knowledge of the business and his experience with the countless interviews he had conducted. And I needed someone in place prior to the end of my six-week training period because after that point Bob would be gone and it would all be up to me.

Although many programmers were familiar with the new software I planned to use and with the controllers on our newer CNC (Computer Numerical Control) machines, few really had much estimating experience. Many claimed to have done it, but Bob was unhappy with most of their answers when we gave them a drawing and asked them to talk us through their way of estimating setup and run times for each operation. I was unhappy, too, with what I witnessed. There seemed to be no formal structure in how the candidates approached the estimating process; their thinking and their answers in terms of the time required to complete the job varied widely. Although I was not sure what the correct answer was, I knew it had to be determined by something more reliable than a wild guess. This was driving home the point of how critical and difficult estimating is.

I realized why so few programmers had acquired the necessary skills when I discovered that most owners of small-to-medium-sized businesses either did the estimating themselves or closely supervised the process and adjusted the numbers before submitting the quotation. This was basically tribal knowledge that most business owners learned through the school of "hard knocks" and had never put any thought into systematizing. And this was true in my new business, where nothing about the existing estimating process had been documented. It was more like black magic that took place inside Bob's head, and even he was perplexed by how to standardize the process. "You just have to know what you're doing. Every situation is different."

After two weeks of conducting interviews with about eight candidates, Bob was just happy to find one who described approximately the same operational steps for manufacturing and who finally arrived at the setup and run times that Bob had determined for a particular part. As for me, my lean experience would not allow me to believe that a flowchart or a few check sheets could not help to standardize the processes for the different types of parts someone was likely to quote. As I learned how to quote, I later put a lot of standardization behind it.

2.2 WRITING THE FIRST DRAFT OF STANDARDIZED STEPS FOR PROGRAMMING AND ESTIMATING

We finally had found our man—John, the candidate who had come closest to suggesting a sequence similar to the one Bob had used previously to manufacture the part in question. He was also in the range of Bob's setup and run times for each operational step. I was just happy when I asked him how he arrived at these conclusions and he explained a clear and logical process that he followed.

During the short shop-floor walk at the beginning of the interview, John had assessed our various fixturing and tooling, and he was familiar with the newer CNC equipment we had (although he had no experience with any of our older machines). His thought process started with how he would fixture the part for each operation with what was available, and he thought through what features would interfere with which other features when machining, which helped to determine the best sequence of operations. Then, he thought about how many tools each operation would use to determine the setup time and how much tool change time would be required while the program was running (e.g., he actually knew our machines had a seven-second standard tool change time). Finally, based on the types of tooling we had and the available RPMs on the machines, he could determine the approximate cutting time for each tool. In other words, he could sum the times for each tool and approximate the total run time for each operation. He had quickly done his calculations on a scrap sheet of paper while Bob and I waited; however, when he walked me through his notes, there was a certain logic to it. I figured that this scrap of paper was the basis of a process that could be standardized. Obviously, he was only quoting the labor portion of the job as he could not pull material prices out of the air. But, he clearly knew what materials and outside operations like plating and silk-screening would be required to manufacture the part. I had the beginnings of a "standard" process flow and quickly captured it. (An example of how I first standardized the quotation process is shown in Appendix C.)

2.3 CONSIDERING THE COMPLICATIONS WITH QUOTING

There are many cost factors to include in the quotation, even for a simple job shop that does not design the products. The basics are material and labor. Although materials would seem easy, you only need to quantify the requirements and then get pricing from your suppliers. Even in this simplicity, complications exist. In my case, for example, either I could buy materials cut to size or I could buy some standard sizes and cut them to size myself. So, there are decisions to be made at each juncture in the estimate; therefore, the process starts to look like a flowchart with a lot of decision boxes.

The labor estimate should vary for the different processes, based on their respective work content, and should be in line with market rates. For example, a part that requires extra deburring time should not have this manual task (which is a lower skill rate) charged at the same rate as CNC machining time (unless it is very critical deburring and requires a higher skill level). Usually, assembly rates are also lower because they do not require capital investment, or likely require extremely high skill levels (again, rates will be higher for more skilled and critical assemblies). The machining rates should also vary depending on the type of machines required, their cost, and their difficulty to operate. Other considerations are the type of material being machined and the related tooling (and other consumable) costs associated with it. Harder machining materials and/or more expensive materials demand a higher rate because of tool wear, etc. So, labor needs to be divided between the various tasks, and hourly rates need to reflect a competitive cost within the local market. Things like tooling costs can be established by gathering data (not taking wild guesses). None of this had evolved into a system of various costs/rates during Bob's tenure, and I only began to improve the system when reaching the Kaizen Flow & Process" phase of my OSKKK transformation strategy.

As John began his work, I tried to learn and document as much as possible. He seemed confident with the new software and appeared happy to improve the organization of files on the hard drive. He was familiar with the numeric controllers on the newer CNCs in the shop, but I had two older CNCs that were unfamiliar to almost everyone we interviewed. This always helps prioritize where to document first. Outdated and specialized equipment are by far the hardest to find experienced people to operate, so this is always a better starting point for documentation and standardized procedures.

Key point: Far fewer people in any industry are experienced with the special requirements of older and outdated equipment and processes. Therefore, this is a priority when documenting because it is unlikely that you will find many people within your organization or outside of it who are familiar with the specifics of older equipment and its idiosyncrasies.

2.4 MINIMIZE TRAINING AND START-UP TIME BY UTILIZING SIMILAR EQUIPMENT

The other thing to keep in mind when purchasing new equipment is that if you stay with the same equipment manufacturer or at least the same type of software or controllers, you are likely to end up with minimal training requirements and the programming will be the same or similar. I think if companies could quantify the time lost training people on all the various control systems in a plant, more effort would be put into minimizing the variations.

As my business grew, I bought the same brand of equipment with identical controllers whenever possible, and we were always able to run those at full production the day after the machine had been commissioned.

2.5 CONTINUING TO DETERMINE WHERE SKILL SETS WOULD BE LOST

Once John was hired, I went back to concentrating on learning Bob's specific responsibilities. Although John was handling all estimates as we received requests for quotations, I had Bob review each one while I looked over his shoulder. We had hired John because his estimates had come closest to Bob's in the test part of the interview but I was now seeing significant differences between them in estimating costs. These differences highlighted the need for standardizing the process as much as possible. In some cases, Bob would pick up something John left out, like a stress relief that would help guarantee a certain flatness, or a tight tolerance on one specific dimension that was sure to take extra time and likely to cause some scrap. Again, I felt that check sheets and flowcharts would be necessities, especially when Bob would no longer be around and it was going to be my responsibility to look over John's shoulder.

After getting through the first and second steps of estimating—the material and labor costs—the next step is to factor in the current market conditions, the particular customer, the required delivery time, and a host of other considerations before converting the material and labor costs into a final price. It is complicated enough to determine labor accurately, but the distribution of overhead costs like administration time, programming time, packaging costs, etc., could further complicate each estimate.

So, Bob used the simplified method of a standard shop rate—$60 per hour—that had all our overhead costs and profit margin rolled in. There were some exceptions, but that was the norm. Bob felt it was representative of the area and the market in which we competed. However, he also felt this number should be adjusted in some cases depending on the customer, how desperate they were, the likelihood of the part receiving a repeat order, etc. Nothing as easy as $50 of material plus two hours at a rate of $60 per hour for a final price of $170. This sales/marketing twist of adjusting the price required knowledge of the customer, the current market conditions, identifying likely competitors for the quotation, and a few other considerations. And, of course, all this had been previously considered and analyzed in Bob's head based on his experience. To me, utilizing one flat rate with some vague rules for adjustment at the end of the process did not appear to be a reliable system. So, to my way of thinking, standardization would be a necessity.

Most sales people say the market, not the supplier, sets the price unless there is some type of proprietary product or special patent. Therefore, there is always a requirement for knowledge of the market. And there are various viewpoints on whether to use standard profit margins, cost plus pricing, or simply an adjustment made by the sales person based on market conditions at that time. In our case there was not a "market price" since these were customer designed parts; instead establishing a price was a responsibility shared between the estimator and salesperson, as is the case in most make to order businesses. Therefore, my focus was to quickly understand the customers and their habits, and start applying a markup or markdown as required. At a later point, I would revisit this to see what type of standardization could be introduced.

2.6 MEETING THE CUSTOMERS

During my second week, Bob had started taking me out to meet the customers and explain the ownership change. I had seven major customers and others that made less-frequent purchases. Bob called the customers first and asked for a bit of their time, and he mentioned that I was coming along to be introduced and he had an announcement to make. Naturally, customers become nervous anytime there is an ownership or management change because dealing with the unknown affects their comfort level.

As I met the customers, I assured them that there were no major changes planned and tried to discuss any current concerns or issues they had. Some had a few comments on price but, overall, everyone was very satisfied with the quality, customer service, and on-time delivery. Naturally, I assured them that this would not change.

I had noted during the due diligence process that although the company I purchased had a nice sales distribution among its larger customers, most of the customers were concentrated in the design and manufacturing of semiconductor etching equipment, which as I previously mentioned, was a volatile market. During these meetings with the customers, I continued to think about my diversification plans. When first reviewing the company, I had questioned Bob about why he had not diversified into other industries as his equipment was very flexible, and he indicated it was possible but he had not put in a lot of effort. This is a typical response during the sale of a business as the seller obviously wants to dangle the carrot for the prospective owner. But I was pushing Bob to get his specific ideas, even though I first needed my own experience observing and leading the business as it currently operated.

Lean principle: *Customer focus is a lean principle that might appear intuitive but is often not well-executed. In product development, it entails understanding the customer's needs and the market. With regard to quality, it requires understanding what quality level the customer desires and is willing to pay for, and then ensuring those needs are met. With regard to delivery, it is necessary to understand the customer's expectations and what others in the market can provide. Finally, applying the focus to cost, it's imperative to understand how cost-sensitive the customers and the market are.*

As Bob explained the peculiarities of each customer, I found I needed to further subdivide and categorize the habits of each individual buyer with whom we dealt (often the customers had more than one buyer). They all had their unique personalities and methods, which dictated how they needed to be handled. It quickly became my responsibility to take the estimate, which assumed a standard hourly rate, and adjust that according to the customer.

This was further complicated by how the request for quotation was received. A rush job would often support a higher margin (or rate). But, a standardized quote sheet that appeared to be sent out to a few other companies deserved a "sharpening of the pencil," usually equating to a lower margin. I also had to factor in how busy the shop was and how desperately I needed the work. Naturally, this always posed a bit of danger because it was hard to know which parts were candidates for repeat orders and how busy the shop would be when that order came in. So, a low price during a slow time could come back to haunt me as a repeat order during a busy period. Although I have said that I did not know which parts would repeat, there were a few tell-tale signs that separated one-time orders from repeaters. The type of part, the revision level on the drawing, the type of customer, the end product with which the part was associated—all helped in determining whether the job was prototype or production work and where it was in its life cycle. Previous experience with the customers as to how they liked to work and which types of parts repeated most often was also invaluable.

2.7 STARTING SOME MEASUREMENTS

Regarding the quotations at this point in my deployment, the underlining assumptions I was forced to accept were that the labor had been correctly calculated, the necessary materials had all been accounted for in their correct quantities, and all necessary outsourced processes had been included. We all know the danger of assumptions, but what choice did I have? At that point, I did not have enough experience to question my estimator. But then, the simple solution hit me: measure the actual against the estimates. This would be straightforward to do for the time required inside our shop. It could also be done with the materials by measuring what was actually used and comparing it to the estimate. But my priority—and overriding suspicion—was that the greatest differences would likely lie in the estimated versus actual labor times. It was not going to be complicated to make a comparison since the estimator now followed the standardized quotation form. All I needed to do was add columns—to be filled in by the employees—for the actual times (see the example in Appendix C). I also added a column where any problems that were encountered could be noted, providing a place to explain why the expectation was not met. I would then circulate the quotation sheet with the documentation package that followed all work orders throughout the shop.

Lean principle: Visual management, which often entails monitoring status compared to the expectation (the actual vs. the goal), will only yield results if the leader frequently monitors the visual (instead of gathering this information from the computer, through meetings, or in discussions), observing and questioning the deviations, and working with the team to resolve the issues. Visuals should begin slowly as leaders need to change their style and the culture as to how they obtain information. In addition, it takes a lot of support to make improvements, and most organizations can only support a few areas simultaneously. The team using the visual must also understand its purpose and will only see its value if management supports this by helping to resolve problems.

2.8 VISUALIZING THE MEASUREMENT

It is always important to show respect and involve people in process changes so they understand the overall context—the significance—within the company. I explained to the entire team the importance of recording their actual times: These hours were multiplied by a figure that covered all costs related to the business. If we hit or improved on the target, we would be on time to the customer and within the budget, which would allow us to make sufficient money to pay wages and secure jobs. I also explained that if a job took more time than what was estimated, it was OK, but we needed to understand why and learn from this. Everyone seemed to understand, though I think John felt the most pressure since we were measuring against his estimates. This pressure to learn and improve is another advantage of visualization.

I noticed estimates were now taking a little longer, and I assumed John was taking more time to review his numbers. He and I had agreed we would go over the feedback together on Friday afternoons—not to pick through it, looking for mistakes, but to see whether we could continue to improve the estimating process.

So, as each work packet was introduced to the shop floor, I stapled the newly formatted estimate sheet to the front. John had already filled in his estimated times on the sheet, and next to the actual hours column was a column where problems could be noted.

As I began running around, anxiously checking how these sheets were getting filled in and how the numbers compared, everyone complied and completed them to the best of their abilities. We had essentially established a feedback loop for our estimates.

Key point: *If a new measurement is introduced (which I did, by recording actual vs. estimated hours) and it is not important enough in the leaders' mind to drive him or her to continuously be seen monitoring it, it is guaranteed to fail.*

A manager needs not only to monitor any new visual measurement but also to understand the root cause of the problems that keep a goal from being achieved. Often, how the data is input and the way in which the measurement is calculated will likely require further refinements.

2.9 PLAN, DO, CHECK, ACT (PDCA)

Six years after selling the business, I continue to be amazed as a consultant to repeatedly find few estimating processes with feedback systems. It seems most managers have never worked in this end of the business and do not realize how many assumptions are used, how much pure guesswork goes in, and the opportunities they are missing in terms of continuous improvement to the process without some feedback system. They seem to be content with explanations of complicated quoting methodologies and studying the big spreadsheets they are shown, along with a belief that the responsible people have enough experience to determine the correct costs. If managers had some feedback and better accounting methods, I think they would really be surprised at the error rate. I encourage many of my clients to diligently track actual costs incurred for just one or two difficult jobs and compare them to their estimates. Those who have done this with any kind of resolve have realized there are a host of opportunities.

Another method I encourage as a reality check is to choose an estimate that includes a lot of labor hours and ask the estimator (usually during a review with the estimating team) to look over the breakdown of labor hours. Then, target an area that has a lot of labor hours, one in which you feel there is likely to be inaccuracies, and suggest that the estimated labor hours should be reduced by 15 percent, for example, and see if you invoke discussion or disagreement. If you find no strong disagreement and are not challenged, you likely have a lot of guesswork going on and

Figure 2.1

should question the process being used to determine the numbers. Always remember not to make it personal but bring the questioning and improvements back to the process utilized to establish the numbers. Always center on improving the process.

Lean principle: A fundamental principle within Toyota's management system and necessary in all lean transformations is to instill PDCA as a necessary way to behave for all levels in the organization. This very simple principle becomes only a theoretical idea within "firefighting" organizations that are always moving full speed into the next problem. It is not only a way to solve problems; it should also be part of all actions and processes we support.

I had identified a process in desperate need of utilizing a PDCA loop (see Figure 2.1) to drive improvement. The estimating process only employed the "Plan" and "Do" parts by prioritizing estimates and then going through the process to arrive at a cost. But, there was no "Check" for the accuracy of the estimate versus the actual costs incurred and nobody "Acted" to learn and standardize improvements as part of the process before utilizing the process for the next quotation.

Up to this point, I had only implemented a method to verify the accuracy of the direct labor hours and the direct materials. I will come back to this because I found I was only scratching the surface of how complicated this process really is, even for a small company. These estimates are vital since they are so closely linked with profit margins and how well you comprehend where you are making money versus breaking even or even losing money. My remaining time with Bob was ticking away and I had only a few more weeks to complete my education (pulling the "tribal knowledge" out of his head) before he was off fishing and manufacturing fishing reels, which was his real desire after he retired. It seemed his way to combine his work experience of running a machine shop and his hobby of fishing was to design and manufacture reels. Who was I to question this? I guess once machining is in your blood you never want to be too far from it.

Had I not later learned the details of each process step for which a time estimate was required, I do not think I could have ever have arrived at realistic estimates. A good basis for estimating depends on having someone with an intimate understanding of the processes for which he or she is responsible to quote. Afterwards, estimators need a feedback system with specific data to reinforce where they were correct or incorrect so they can continue to improve their skills.

Key point: The quotation process is key in every business and every step of the process should be standardized and continuously refined. To have a good system, it is necessary to continuously provide feedback on how quotations compare to actual costs and learn from this to improve the accuracy (a PDCA loop for making continuous improvement). This also has a strong link to activity-based costing, which will be discussed later.

2.10 SUMMARY

- Prioritization of processes to document and standardize should be based on the tasks for which you have only one or two qualified team members trained within the organization. In my case, it was easy because I was aware of Bob's imminent departure (so programming and estimating were at the top of my list), though often we do not know who will leave the organization and are frequently caught off guard.
- Complicated processes are often a high priority for instilling a PDCA loop. In my case, the estimation task was one of those.
- Measurements are unlikely to improve if they are not important enough for frequent follow-up by managers.

3

Learning the Office Processes

3.1 INTRODUCTION

With only a few weeks of training left, it was time for me to learn the office processes that the former owner, Bob, had always handled and my mother had not begun learning or documenting. I had been focusing on what I considered critical skills in the shop that had previously been handled exclusively by Bob, and now I needed to shift my focus to the front office. (I continue to call it the front office because we also had a small office in the shop where the programming was done along with other tasks—attendance records, completing critical measurements, filling in quality sheets—that were performed by the foreman.) I knew that before I had enough background to make any decisions or improvements, I needed to understand the processes in sufficient detail to ask reasonable questions and make educated choices.

In addition to certain purchasing, planning, and accounting tasks that Bob regularly reviewed and made decisions about, the front office also did some part number marking, label adhering, packaging of the smaller parts, preparing shipping labels, scheduling the shipping, and invoicing. Because nearly half the orders were for new part numbers (parts we had not previously manufactured), there always appeared to be a lot to set up in the computer systems and a lot of materials that required specifying and ordering. I knew there were bound to be a lot of non-value added steps being performed within these processes, and my mother had already indicated that both documentation and standardization were lacking.

Before we could begin making improvements and changes, we would have to apply a simple OSKKK strategy (Observe, Standardize, Kaizen Flow & Process, Kaizen Equipment, and Kaizen Layout).

3.2 INPUTTING ORDERS

Although it was not one of Bob's responsibilities, inputting an order into the computer was my first task of the morning. My mother had already documented the task and written a standardized procedure, but I would also need to understand it for overseeing the day-to-day operations. As I said, I was not learning how to input orders because I might be expected to do it; rather, I needed to understand where the pitfalls were in the process so I could later make improvements and handle the task if necessary. Using "Kaizen eyes" means understanding the detailed steps and questioning whether or not each step adds value. Toyota managers usually know how to perform the majority of tasks performed by their direct reports (naturally, this does not apply to highly technical/complicated disciplines). I doubt that can be said across the board for the majority of managers I have come across. They usually feel they control too diverse or large an area for this and their function is to get employees to do things by motivation and organization, forgetting they need to bring out the operator's natural problem solving abilities. I would have preferred that all my employees had "Kaizen eyes" and would find the waste on their own, but I knew they had not been taught or given the responsibility to suggest and implement changes. That would come. In the meantime, it would be my responsibility to identify the opportunities and teach through example.

Our version of an order entry and MRP (material requirements planning) system was an old DOS-based program in which all details of the orders—except for the BOM (bill of material)—were entered. (Just to be clear, I *did* say "DOS," that terrible old operating system of the past.) The program had been locally developed for job shops, and my business had been one of the test sites. Almost eighteen years of data had been entered into it. Unlike most MRP systems, the program only included a blank screen for inputting and tracking of materials in a free format, and it was not capable of monitoring incoming materials and linking their arrival so that the corresponding job could be scheduled. Therefore, I was inclined to wonder how helpful it was as an MRP system (although MRP is not as critical to the made-to-order functionality of a business like mine as it might be elsewhere). It simply scheduled orders based on due dates without taking material or manufacturing lead time into account. It might have had additional functionality—but if it did, nobody was aware of it.

A new Windows-based version of the software was available for more than $15,000; however, money was a little tight at this point, as you can imagine. And because I needed to better understand the business before making any investment decisions, the old program would have to do for the time being. Although my comments in Chapter 2 indicated I did not want to return to using DOS, this program seemed friendly enough at first glance and it served the purpose of tracking customer orders, invoicing, and providing materials and parts histories. Actually, inputting data into the system was fairly simple and it seemed you could pull out most necessary reports, which was ironic, in my opinion, for a DOS-based system.

Lean principle: MRP systems were not a fundamental principle within the Toyota Production System. Instead, the tendency was to use Kanban systems where appropriate for material replenishment, which is linked directly to the customer's actual consumption patterns and helps in visualizing material levels allowing everyone to participate in a PDCA (Plan, Do, Check, Act) cycle and constantly refine the min/max levels. Job shops like mine—where the product is made to order—could only order most materials after receiving a customer order, so MRP systems are less applicable. I put in place some Kanban systems for standard materials (those that we could stock with low risk) and for consumable items.

One small change I implemented early on was that all new part numbers had their estimated setup times and run times entered into the program. Naturally, these became the basis for costing and for shop-floor planning. Since the first established times (in hours and minutes) were only estimates, we required that part of our PDCA cycle also included entering the actual times into the program. Once the actual times were entered, we could decide which time—estimated or actual—was to be used as the standard basis for costing and planning on any future orders.

3.3 PROBLEMS WORKING WITHOUT A PDCA CYCLE IN THE ESTIMATING PROCESS

Three problems I found without any actual feedback on our estimates were (1) Bob's estimates did not have any structured feedback on the accuracy of his estimated labor hours (as discussed in the previous chapter); (2) if the hours were not correct, we could not accurately plan and determine available capacity; and (3) if the hours were not correct, then the profit margins were also not correct and all business decisions were likely based on poor costing data. If we got this wrong too often, we would randomly be overcharging for some parts while undercharging for others.

Although some might think this balances itself out, I had previously witnessed managers in other companies not accepting new orders for products they felt had too low a margin or pushing products they believed had a high margin. That might work if the data is correct. But, I found the labor times in some cases to be far enough off that some managers were not making the margin they thought on those "cash cows" and other products were really making a higher margin than shown on paper. This is further obscured by standard costing and allocations, subjects that deserve a lot of attention and will be discussed throughout the book. For now, I will summarize this as a key point.

Key point: If you do not have some type of feedback or verification system for labor hours and are not continuously learning about inaccuracies and adjusting them, you likely have many errors and a poor basis for costing and planning. It is also possible you do not have a clear picture of your profit margin for each part number or family of parts.

I found a number of occasions where I improved the accuracy of this data and feel it helped me make good decisions; other times, I suspected we made rather poor decisions based on the lack of accurate data. Profit margins are further and sometimes more strongly influenced by accounting methods—but that discovery was to come later.

3.4 REPRICING DISCUSSIONS ARE EASIER IF BASED ON ACCURATE DATA

Later, when I found customers pushing for price reductions (or asking us to match a "target price") for certain parts that had started to receive more regular orders, armed with more accurate labor and material costs I now had a basis from which to make a good decision. Periodically, the customers asked for price reductions of anywhere from 10 percent to 25 percent, or threatened to try to find another supplier to meet their target price. As our feedback system for quotations continuously progressed, we were better able to understand our true labor and overhead costs as they applied to each product and part number. Combined with accurate material costs, this put us in a much better position to analyze and respond to these requests. With sufficient confidence, we could now understand exactly what profit would remain if we agreed to these new prices. In almost 50 percent of the cases, we were able to come close to the target price (and maintain enough profit to justify the order); in the other cases, we confidently stuck with our price and took our chances by not offering the customers a new price, as we knew our hourly rate or margin would be unacceptable.

Lean principle: "Kaizen eyes" are something developed over the long term. This involves the ability to recognize/identify all types of non-value added activities through structured observation. One basic part of having Kaizen eyes is being skilled with "motion Kaizen"— where you learn to focus on the employees' hands, feet, and eyes as they are performing a shop-floor or administrative activity—to identify the traditional seven wastes within the task's work elements. This includes identifying the wastes of overproduction, correction, motion, material movement, waiting, inventory, overprocessing, and the recently added waste of not involving/engaging the mind of the operator. To complete my training with Toyota, I was continuously tested by being asked to observe a task and in a few minutes identify ten wastes (or provide ten ideas for improvement).

3.5 LEARNING TO PURCHASE

The office was managed by Sandra, who had been with the company for more than ten years. She seemed the picture of efficiency as she bustled around the small office, working with her assistant who did a lot of the repetitive tasks and the grunt work. It was Sandra who taught me the next task: how to purchase material. What I found pleasant in the office, and I later learned some of the customers also enjoyed, was Sandra's accent. She was British and although she had lived in the United States for many years she still spoke the "Queen's English." Whatever it takes to keep the customers happy, I just hoped that when I answered the phone with my plain voice and simple Midwestern drawl, I did not send anyone running to the competition.

Sandra would periodically wait for a day or two before ordering to see whether we received multiple POs (purchase orders) requiring similar materials. Purchasing materials in large quantities qualified us for volume discounts as our suppliers generally priced by the total weight of the steel or aluminum we were buying. Sandra felt the savings frequently justified the delay. Naturally, if the PO had a short lead time, the order was placed before the end of the day, and this was often the case, as we worked in an industry that demanded short lead times. Being a lean practitioner, I was constantly thinking about lead time, so I wanted to better understand the cost versus savings related to this delay—but that would come later.

A simple PO format was used. Each blank form was filled out by hand and had a unique PO number on it. (It was usually not necessary to first complete a purchase requisition and then have it approved. As a made-to-order business, we were mostly purchasing direct materials for a firm, short-term customer order.) For each different supplier involved, one PO form was completed with information like material type, quantity, job number, due date, etc. Only the supplier's name was omitted since determining this was the function of purchasing (Sandra or her assistant). The completed forms were filed according to the promise date on which the material was due to arrive; however, they were put into a file drawer—out of sight—and only referenced as material arrived.

My idea was to use a simple visual system as a start. I asked Sandra to keep the completed POs in our receiving area, out in the open in a simple file that had a slot for each day of the month. Each PO would be filed in the slot that corresponded to the promised delivery date. When the material arrived for that order and all was accounted for, the form was to be moved to another file to be reconciled with the invoice prior to payment.

Moving the POs from the receiving area file to the reconciliation file gave us an easy, visual method of identifying outstanding POs—late orders. We could now follow up on these late materials easily, and I did not have to check with Sandra each day about them. It was safe to assume that POs that had been moved from the receiving file had either been fulfilled or Sandra was following up on them.

I also suggested we could use these POs to track which suppliers were frequently late. I wanted to see how we could become more proactive with a late order, not just recognizing it after the due date passed. But, for now we had a simple visual system that showed abnormalities. Sandra indicated she had a good "feel" for which were our worst suppliers, but I suggested that we always speak based on data in the future.

Key point: Visualizing abnormalities as early as possible for all administrative and shop-floor processes should be every manager's focus. This requires defining the difference between normal and abnormal and showing this visually and in a timely fashion.

Key point: Here's a good yet simple business tactic: If you find yourself talking in circles because you do not have data available to make good or clear decisions, then stop and put a quick method in place to gather some simple data. Often, a simple tick list kept on the corner of someone's desk is sufficient. You will learn a lot, and nobody can argue with hard data.

Another good point to highlight is that, for many processes, it is fairly easy to put a visual in place to track whether things are running on time or behind, or whether or not things are functioning normally. Since my job as a business manager was to understand when a process was in trouble, to detect this as early as possible and then provide help or guidance, it was key to make this apparent as early as possible for every task. Then, if everything was running according to plan I could sit around drinking coffee all day…right?

3.6 SCHEDULING THE SHOP BASED ON TRIBAL KNOWLEDGE

After the orders had been entered and POs issued for the necessary materials, we could print out a shop-floor priority chart through our very basic computer system. The problem: our system only sorted the orders by customer due dates and it did not contain their routings, required labor hours, or the status of whether materials were available. Sandra informed me this had not been a problem since Bob had an idea in his head about how many hours each job required, and once the material was available he could prioritize the jobs by how long he felt they would take to get through the shop. (It was no surprise to me that all this had previously been managed in this way.) She also seemed to think that a quick glance at any drawing allowed Bob to understand all internal and external process steps (i.e., he could visualize the entire routing for the part). Once again, alarms were going off in my head: Bob's tribal knowledge was critical for yet another step and I questioned how well he could manage the five to twenty diverse part numbers that moved through our shop each day. I needed to quickly find a way to put some system in place as I had no system in my head that could balance these five to twenty part numbers each day, and since I wanted to grow the business, this would only become more difficult. Also, as a newcomer to the machining industry, I had no tribal knowledge, and instead of the confidence that I could properly prioritize all this in my head, I had only questions and concerns. I also questioned how effectively this could be performed in Bob's head and what effect his mistakes would have on lead time and on-time delivery. On the positive side, the new orders now included the estimated times on each work package (as previously discussed) and the routing through the various operations. But, repeat orders—which accounted for about 60 percent of our volume—did not currently include these time estimates and, to further complicate this, the priority list (when it was printed) showed none of this information. Again, all these issues were being discovered by first observing and documenting, and then working toward standardization.

3.7 JOB-SHOP PLANNING

As a general theme, job-shop planning is not only an interesting subject, it is almost an oxymoron. Think about it: Nothing is consistent. There are no forecasts and no standard orders. And I basically did not know what the customer would ask for, but I knew they would likely need it immediately. The positive side of this from a lean perspective is the concept of working "just in time"; you only build what customers want when they require it.

Systems like MRP or ERP (enterprise resources planning) cannot offer much help since they work on two assumptions that likely do not hold true in this type of business (and rarely hold true for any made-to-order company). These systems assume accurate forecasts and are unaware of changes in lead time (unless you are constantly updating the lead time within the computer). In my case, forecasts did not exist, and if they were available, they would likely be inaccurate. It should be noted, however, that periodically we received an order with split delivery dates, although even those dates frequently were changed.

Constant lead time is another oxymoron within most businesses. Demand for each machine or process usually varies hour by hour or day by day based on customer demands, and in the case of a job shop, you have little influence on customer demand (other than not accepting the order). So, lead time is constantly changing based on the queue of work waiting at that particular process or the amount of work the external plating or painting shops have waiting. For example, at the beginning of the week you may have only one day of work waiting in front of a certain machine, but by Thursday you may have received enough orders to fully utilize this machine's capacity for the entire next week. In this case, lead time will have gone from just more than one day to more than one week. Therefore, it appears these MRP or ERP systems were created for another type of business, predominantly those that build in either large batch production, have fewer part numbers, have stable forecasts, or their capacity is more evenly balanced. I think this is the reason people in made-to-order businesses often refer to MRP as "More 'wRong' Parts."

So, what can a job shop do to plan and accept only orders for which it can meet the customer's delivery date?

In my case, Bob had always worked all this out either in his head or on a scrap piece of paper, which presented a few problems for the new guy on the block. I was not as familiar with all the jobs as Bob appeared to be, and I might not be around every day to develop the schedule or confirm whether we could accept an order for the date the customer was requesting. (My master plan was to develop a business that would allow me some freedom from the day-to-day operations.) Therefore, the simple print-out from our system—which only sorted the jobs by due date, did not relate their lead times to the various routings though the different processes, and showed no relation to working time—was not a method I could use going forward. Also, I was finding it nearly impossible to standardize Bob's thought process. For the short term, my task was to quickly learn the methods through observation and then standardize them, though this one would have to wait until I better understood the related processes and could develop my own standardized method as the baseline for improvement. In made-to-order businesses, materials planning is often more straightforward than capacity planning, which is more difficult because of the continuously changing lead times. My interim plan was to visualize the current workload for each process and to display this in real time while quantifying where the available capacity resided, essentially helping to determine the ever-changing lead time.

Lean principle: JIT *(just-in-time) is an inventory strategy to improve efficiency and minimize waste by receiving goods only as they are required for the production process, thereby reducing most of the costs associated with inventory. This method requires that manufacturers are able to accurately forecast demand, which in our case was also easy as we performed no forecasting and only built to a firm order shortly before the required ship date. Since we only ordered materials once we had an order and had the available capacity to produce it, we were already working to JIT—one of the advantages of working in a made-to-order business or a job shop.*

3.8 SIMPLIFIED SHORT-TERM PLANNING

Short-term shop-floor planning should involve ensuring you have the materials and capacity available before you start the work, based on its routing through the various processes and the lead times associated with the required steps. Hopefully, this style of planning allows the part to be completed in time to arrive at the customer on or before the due date. Again, it doesn't sound difficult when I sum it up in a simple sentence but there are many nasty little surprises—or should I say "variables"—that complicate things. As a consultant, I encounter many companies that only "material plan." Often, this means that by the time they receive sufficient materials to start on an order, they are behind schedule, and so they immediately release the job to production and do not perform any capacity planning. This means they cannot proactively analyze where the bottlenecks will be and work to minimize them—thereby becoming only reactionary firefighters.

Obviously, the first concern is that the materials arrive on time so that the work does not have to be expedited within your own process. Experiences with poor suppliers have led some planners to inflate delivery times in the computer systems, thereby trying to avoid being caught out. This just adds to inventory. In my business, I basically had no idea what type of material would be required until I quoted the job. I could keep some basics in stock that could be cut to size to reduce lead time (though this had labor and inventory costs/risks associated with it), and there were actually many suppliers that could provide most standard materials cut to size within one to two days. So, that was not my biggest problem. The problem was the more exotic materials that came longer distances with fewer choices of suppliers. That aside, I found historically there had been no tracking of the suppliers' "on-time delivery," but I figured that, with my new system in the receiving area, it would be easy enough to visualize when things arrived late. From previous experience, I had learned that the really detailed planning (process by process) should not be performed for a period of longer than twenty-four hours. Therefore, the best answer was a "planning board" at each critical process that displayed the work planned and showed the actual status periodically updated by the operator. Later, I implemented this system, and it is discussed in this book.

3.9 A MORE COMPREHENSIVE WORK ORDER PACKAGE

Leaving the discussion on the planning system for a later point when I arrived to "kaizening of the process" in my OSKKK strategy and also achieved a better understanding of all the factors involved, I decided to move on to learning other tasks. One of the other functions performed in the front office was putting together the shop-floor work packages, which consisted of only the customer's drawing; a copy of the purchase order for the materials; and a short form showing due date, any additional outside processing, and any special instructions (like "part to be supplied without hardware" or "group with job number X for outside plating"). These were pulled together a day or more in advance and Bob would then decide which machine they went on.

The work package did not indicate whether it was the first time we were producing this part. Early identification of a first-time build was critical because it might require programming the part first, increasing lead time. Existing parts, on the other hand, already had developed programs along with tooling and special fixturing when required. Naturally, this affected the number of steps and the lead time through the system. For example, a new part that required programming could add a half day or more to the lead time depending on the programmer's workload and the number of programs (operations) the part required (typically, each separate CNC [Computer Numerical Control] operation required a separate program). Normally, any special tooling or additional process steps were identified during the quotation. But, from time to time a non-stock tool or an additional external stress relief might be identified during programming. Therefore, the earlier all processes were identified (e.g., the programming step previously discussed), the fewer the chances for last-minute delays due to some unforeseen requirement, thereby making it easier to determine an accurate routing and lead time and thereby maintaining high on-time delivery performance.

Either Bob or Tom (the shop foreman) generally managed these planning/programming details in their heads. I did not want to change the process at that point, but I felt that I could at least add a step. On the work package form, I wanted to add a place for the front office to indicate whether or not a program already existed, plus any additional external process steps that may be required. Further, to allow a quick check for any potential tool shortages, I asked for a preprint of the tool list from the program. At least now I would know whether a program existed and which outside processes were involved. That information would allow me to more accurately determine the lead times and then organize priorities for scheduling.

3.10 POOR WORK ORDER PACKAGES
CAN INCREASE SETUP TIME

I was also thinking about how a poor shop-floor work package can increase setup time. In many cases, half of the setup time was used for adjusting and checking the part. Ideally, we should have been able to return as quickly as possible to the parameters of a previously manufactured part (which had been built to an acceptable quality standard). To do this, some notes regarding the previous program, tooling, or the fixturing modifications—all the subtleties—would be required in order to take advantage of the information and profit from it. Naturally, a small amount of time would be invested after a production run in capturing these details. In our case, we manufactured thousands of different part numbers and although about 60 percent received repeat orders at some point, the repeaters were so random and unpredictable that the operators could not readily recall the specifics of any particular set of parts. I did not feel it was the proper time to tackle this issue, but when the time came to focus on setup time reductions, this was high on my list.

I continue to work with companies that have made the same part hundreds of times, but because they did not document the peculiarities and fine adjustments of previous production runs, they always find themselves starting over. They pay the price each time they set up. Instead, they should be racking up the profit from their previous experiences.

There were many other small tasks performed in the front office such as the weekly payroll (another area my mother was overseeing during this transition period). Paychecks were issued on Mondays. Bob had implemented this policy to ensure everyone showed up to work each Monday, traditionally the poorest attendance day for hourly employees. Other small tasks like invoicing, chasing late payments, and accounts payable were jumbled in the mix. Then, there were the financial aspects: closing the books and the nonexistent budget.

3.11 CLOSING THE BOOKS

My experience with most large companies is that people live and die by the closing of the books. The exception was Toyota, where I never heard the typical question, "How are the closing numbers shaping up?" Instead, I saw everything focused on waste elimination by those who controlled the processes.

I know for certain that I do not fully understand discussions or statements dealing with standard costs and all their related variances. As I look around meeting rooms when the discussion centers around a standard cost variance that has increased or decreased, I always think that nobody else appears to understand the root causes behind these variances either. There always seems to be a controller or accountant in the room trying to translate these statements so somebody can decide what to do about the numbers. For my part, despite all my MBA courses, I am almost never sure how to take a "negative variance" and directly turn it into an appropriate action that will transform it into a "positive variance" on the standard cost without acquiring a lot more information on what might be behind that particular variance.

On the other hand, in my own company when I reviewed one of our end-of-month closing statements, it was so straightforward that I could ask intelligent questions and draw conclusions that I had some faith in. I had concerns that in its current state, it might be a little too simplified to draw detailed conclusions. For example, we looked at the sales resulting from the current month's shipments, but we simply compared those to the current month's costs by taking totals of all checks issued/paid out during that month (this is also practical for many items like direct and indirect labor, which are usually paid out in the period accrued). However, we were really paying for last month's material purchases during the current month, and depending on whether we consumed more or less material last month, the profit and loss could be misleading (although our profit and loss determined for time and materials on each job was more accurate). Utilizing an average percentage of material costs could also be misleading in our business as this varied depending on the features of the job. Our accrual system for certain costs was also simplified and would likely require a better understanding before suggesting any improvements.

The advantage was that it only took a few hours to close the books. My mother was temporarily handling this process and had taken responsibility to document it and make suggestions to improve it. I also figured that in order to really understand profitability in a job shop, I would need to look at it on an order-by-order basis. So, for the time being I decided to stick with this simple closing of the books and then let an accountant explain things like depreciation to me at tax time. The important point was that I wanted to be in the position where the end of the month numbers held no surprises, all of our other real-time measurements ideally would focus our activities, and closing the books would simply confirm what we already knew.

3.12 COLLECTING THE MONEY

Like all businesses, receivables were critical, though I had the feeling that in a small business they were even more so. Bob kept a close eye on any invoices that went beyond the standard thirty-day terms. Thankfully, our computer system printed a simple report and grouped outstanding invoices by those over thirty days, those over sixty days, and any that might hit that dreaded limit of over ninety days. Apparently, those reaching forty to forty-five days outstanding initiated phone calls; after that, Bob usually told Sandra to be a little more forceful and he would start getting involved. Since we were typically dealing with the same seven or eight customers, we were usually working on a newer order and could always threaten to delay delivery as a last resort. Here I saw no need to change any of the current practices other than simplifying the measurement unit to DSO (days sales outstanding) and planned to keep the payment terms and the collection methods the same for the time being. DSOs also take into account the time it takes to prepare and send the invoice, a process I felt could use some improvements.

Lean principle: It's critical to focus on key measures and present them in a simple format so that everyone can understand what influences the numbers. When measuring receivables, the recommended unit of measurement is DSO: days sales outstanding. DSO is typically defined as the average number of days it takes to collect the payment after a sale has been made. The unit of measurement is "days"—which is easy to relate to payment terms that are also in "days"—thereby quickly making a determination whether a business is operating within a normal or an abnormal range.

Obtaining quotes for raw materials and subcontracted process steps was also a responsibility of the front office. I have already explained some of the limitations in the quoting system that was in place at the time I purchased the business, one of which was that Bob did not use a clear format to indicate what materials were required and what further processing was necessary. I have discussed the new quoting sheet that John (the programmer/estimator) was starting for each part he quoted (shown in Appendix C), and which Sandra then completed by adding the material and subcontract prices and determining the awarded supplier's name (based on quality, delivery, and price). The only flaw in the system was that Sandra and her assistant had all the suppliers' names in their heads and some of the phone numbers programmed into the speed dial. As usual, I was thinking this needed to be standardized, and my overriding concern was the possibility that I would be required to complete the task myself in the event neither Sandra nor her assistant were available (i.e., absent or quit). I put together a simple table—including the type of material, the typical suppliers we would use, who to contact, and a place for additional notes—and they began to populate it.

These were the majority of critical front-office tasks in which Bob was involved. And although the plan was for Sandra to continue working with us as the office manager, she had a close relationship with Bob, and I felt she worked there mostly to support him. Therefore, she might leave at any moment now that Bob was almost out of the picture. Just one more reason to quickly learn, document, and standardize. Having my mother become familiar with all the processes was a good backup.

3.13 SUMMARY

- Made-to-order businesses (and job shops) are already working to JIT standards; therefore, systems in the front office must support short lead-time orders (i.e., MRP systems often do not directly support the predominant characteristics of these companies).
- PDCA again proved critical in the administrative processes, with most tasks requiring a feedback loop and measurements to support continuous improvement.

- Developing standardized work for business (administrative) processes is just as critical as having standards for the shop-floor processes.
- Although the OSKKK process indicates standardization is the step prior to starting any Kaizen, I feel there are instances where implementing an improvement should be done instead of standardizing a poor practice and then improving it. Though in most cases I was just imagining the improvement at this time or adding an enhancement to the existing process, the majority of ideas would only be implemented when I reached the "KKK" point in my transformation plan.

4

The First Days Alone

4.1 INTRODUCTION

At the end of October, the former owner, Bob, was leaving so we closed the books together with help from Sandra (the office manager), who typically handled this. It had been my first full month owning the business and it was the acid test for me to gauge how I was doing. It is similar to being a manager and getting rewarded if the monthly targets are met except it is a whole lot more personal. It was especially critical for me as my $75,000 of seed money to carry the business through until our receivables starting coming in was basically bottomed out. We had a reasonable month in shipments but I was unsure of the total expenses, especially during the last week. After the numbers were checked and double checked, I had good news—not necessarily great news but good enough: despite making the monstrous loan payment and the added expense of a new programmer, we still had a positive cash flow. I had only paid myself a $2,000 monthly salary, which could not last forever, but I was surviving and damn proud of it.

With Bob's last day and a hearty handshake, I was now on my own and, although content for the time being, next month's numbers would really separate the men from the boys. I figured if I could make it a month on my own and still be profitable, there might be an entrepreneurial future for me. I was aware, however, that I could not live on a monthly salary of $2,000 for long and if sales had been a bit lower or expenses a bit higher, I would have either drawn no salary or written the company a check. So, there was not a lot of room to sit back and relax.

The obvious solution was that I needed to increase sales and/or proportionally reduce expenses. As a "lean guy," I was thinking of productivity improvements for all processes. Since Bob already kept expenses to a minimum—in other words, there were no big corporate perks to cut—I just wanted to get to the point at which he had arrived and have a few company cars floating around while paying myself a decent wage. For the time being, with a big loan payment and a new programmer on the payroll, that was not in the cards until we increased sales.

Although I was still single, I was involved in a serious relationship and was contemplating the idea of popping the question some day soon. Not knowing much about the opposite sex or having a lifelong partner, I was just sharp enough to assume I needed a more stable financial situation before anyone could comfortably commit. I had done some mental gymnastics and figured if I could get six profitable months under my belt and I could pay myself enough to live comfortably in the San Francisco Bay area, then I could more seriously consider popping the question.

It was now Monday morning of week seven as the owner, which meant the training period had ended and I was on my own. Bob had indicated I could call him if I had questions. I had my mind made up to only call in an emergency. In no way would I say I felt confident to take over. Six weeks of training had finished and I now knew how to turn on the lights and had a rough idea of a few other tasks. But, competently performing all that Bob had been responsible for was another matter. This first day alone had some similarities to starting a new job when you reach the point where you are starting to make your own decisions. The major difference with a job is the greatest downside could be unemployment and possibly stalling your career. When you own your own business, you could upset a few large customers and bankrupt the business, which in my case meant losing my life savings and becoming indebted to the bank for a long time to come, not to mention putting other people out of work.

4.2 MY FIRST PRICING DECISION ALONE

Monday morning, my first day alone at the helm, and everything was rolling along fine—well, fine by machine shop standards, which seem to be defined as OK if you only have a few minor problems simultaneously on each machine. The first item of the day—a request for quotation—had been received. John (the programmer/estimator) had gone through and completed the labor hours and required materials. The front office had quickly added in the material prices, and in short order it came to me for approval. The moment of truth had arrived. But, par for the course, it was not an easy part to manufacture, and with a quantity of thirty pieces and a high material value, roughly 38 percent of the total price (which is high for a company that averaged 18 percent material costs), it was not an easy decision without Bob. I had learned we could usually add a 15-percent margin on top of our standard hourly rate for this customer and the particular buyer. Since it appeared there was no rush for this part, I decided to take the conservative route and only add a 7-percent margin. Then I submitted the quotation and the waiting game began.

Historically, we had somewhere between a 60-percent and 70-percent hit rate on receiving orders on our quotes. This number seemed reasonable to me as there was a cost associated with each estimate. We wanted a relatively high hit rate but too high would indicate we were undercharging. So, I set my personal target at 70 percent. For the time being, I still lacked the experience to challenge John's labor and material specifications but felt I would continue to track them against actual hours and costs and review this every Friday (a complete PDCA [Plan, Do, Check, Act] loop). We received the purchase order for this quotation and hoped it would yield the margin we expected and would not turn out to be a loss because of a poor estimate. At least we would measure and confirm this.

4.3 CREATING EXTRA CAPACITY WITH 5S

Creating extra capacity was naturally a theme to start on quickly. Workplace organization (known as 5S to lean practitioners) is a simple but effective tool to kick this off. This is especially true where time is lost looking for items, which results in decreasing the effectiveness of a process or an employee (especially where employees rotate between workstations and jobs). Bob had traditionally run and organized the shop like his own basement, meaning he knew where everything was and the others just had to figure it out. The fact that things were not always in the most practical and easily accessible places was just accepted. So, I figured this would be an easy win but wanted to let Tom (the shop foreman) and John handle this after I asked just enough questions to let them draw their own conclusions about the current state. One advantage was John had previously worked in other shops so he brought a new perspective that Tom did not have, and I was sure he had observed superior workplace organization with his former employers.

During my first six weeks, I had noticed a lot of time being wasted by the setup men looking for the right cutting tools for the CNC (Computer Numerical Control) machines. It was almost comical as all tools were kept in mostly solid-colored plastic cases (to help protect the cutting edges from being damaged) and grouped into cardboard boxes only according to their basic diameter. This meant a lot of different types of tools were mixed in a single cardboard box (e.g., a quarter-inch, two-flute high-speed steel end mill was stored with a quarter-inch, four-flute carbide end mill). The plastic cases for specialized tools were labeled a little better, but the setup men had to open many plastic cases to locate the tools called for on the tool list.

I did not want to dictate my solution to John or Tom; instead, I mentioned the frustration and wasted time involved in looking for tools. They agreed. So, I asked John whether the other shops where he had worked had stored tools in the same fashion. He indicated he had seen various methods but none as "cheap as this." So, I asked what these other shops did instead. He indicated most organized them in drawers within their tool rooms, where different drawers contained dedicated sizes, and they were further sorted within the drawers by specific type. Also, they were stored in slots within the drawers so everyone could easily identify the specifics of the tool. It was the type of answer I was looking for, and Tom seemed to grasp the advantages but pointed out Bob's reluctance to spend money on things like tool cabinets. I did not view it as spending money but as wisely investing money that would quickly be paid back. Now was my time to get even for all those years of working with larger companies where even small investments required many approvals and the delays were endless. I immediately ordered $1,500 worth of specialized tool drawers and had them delivered within two days. Tom was surprised by the swiftness of my actions, and I told him that as long as there were sufficient benefits and the cost was not great, we would move quickly. Organizing the tools into these drawers suddenly had everyone excited and it seemed they almost forgot about running the machines as they offered to start helping. I asked for a little thought to be given to determining which tools got used most often so that they would be given the most logical placement with the easiest access. Now we were on a quest toward better workplace organization.

Although many businesses are not currently throwing things in cardboard boxes, there are always items that accumulate in mysterious places and much time is lost in trying to locate them. The trick is awareness and prioritization.

Lean principle: Poor workplace organization (5S) had now been shown as a source of non-value added time during a changeover. I consider making this improvement part of the standardization step in OSKKK (Observe, Standardize, Kaizen Flow & Process, Kaizen Equipment, and Kaizen Layout); therefore, it is an appropriate first step that often leads to productivity improvements. The productivity improvements are most applicable in organizations that have cross-training and job rotation (i.e., different people performing the same job).

Naturally, workplace organization became a topic we continuously pursued. It is not worth going into considerable detail as I think the concept is easily understood. I can only say that to get it ingrained in the culture took a bit of patience on my part as well as asking questions every time I observed time being wasted looking for items. Also, when I noticed operators losing time because they were sharing a fairly common tool like a fixture, a wrench, or deburring tool, I would ask how often this happened and how much time they imagined was lost either waiting for it, going to get it, or looking for it. Often, we came to the conclusion that each workstation should have its own tool, and without hesitation I told Tom or John to order what was necessary to eliminate this "forced waiting time." After a few weeks, I found the team making suggestions on its own. I only had to ensure the time that was being saved was used productively. Time being used productively would be further ensured in the future with the addition of scheduling boards helping to make certain that everyone always had enough value-adding work being planned. Tom had also been trained in a culture where employees never sat around or worked slower to appear busy, so I was lucky that each minute of productive time we gained was making me more money as long as I kept bringing in enough work to keep everyone busy.

4.4 ESTABLISHING NORMAL VERSUS ABNORMAL

My real challenge continued to be defining normal versus abnormal for all aspects of the business. If I could accomplish this, then I could concentrate on quickly applying my problem-solving skills to minimize the effects of the abnormalities.

In the shop, I relied on Tom's experience to help clarify abnormalities. It was not as easy as simply asking him "What is going on here that is abnormal?" Unfortunately, this would not make any sense to him. Instead, as events took place—for example, an end mill would break—I would ask, "Does this happen often?" I would get responses like, "This usually happens when we work in stainless steel." Therefore, I could determine that we needed to replace an end mill after it cut a certain amount of stainless. Of course, it was much better to replace the end mill before it broke because if it broke while cutting a part, it was also likely to damage the part and cause scrap. The problem was the wear was not always apparent when looking at the tool. However, most tools have a tool life (in terms of time or the amount of a particular material they can cut). In shops where you continuously run the same parts, it is easy to determine. For example, after machining 100 pieces, the tool should be replaced based on cutting time. Our problem was that our average order was only for a few pieces and we could not afford to replace all the tooling after every stainless steel job. Therefore, I proposed each tool be given a number and replaced in the tool tray according to that number, and each tool tray had a place where the total cutting hours could be tracked by shading in a calibrated line (see Figure 4.1 for an example). The line was only as long as the total available cutting hours for which the tool was rated.

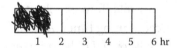

Figure 4.1

Lean principle: Standardization is what helps in clarifying what is normal and abnormal in the administrative and manufacturing or service processes. Instead of accepting excessive firefighting as the norm, try to determine a standard expectation and visualize when you are meeting

the standard (i.e., a normal condition) versus when you are not meet-
ing the standard (i.e., an abnormal condition). Remember: your job
as a manager is to quickly realize when a process has crossed into the
abnormal range and to help to rectify the causes with a permanent
countermeasure.

We knew from the program the total cut time being utilized by each tool, so the operator only needed to multiply by the number of pieces he had manufactured and this was only required for stainless steel and a few other hard materials. This also drove home the point that stainless steel parts should not be priced (in other words, not have the same hourly rate) as easier machining materials like aluminum. I was already beginning to see all the pitfalls of Bob's simplistic $60/hour flat shop rate. This is an example of where we identified a problem because there was no standard, so the process was Kaizened (the first "K" in OSKKK), which drove us to create a new standard process for the operators.

I decided that as each problem was encountered or when I was required to make a decision, I would try either to develop a process that helped minimize the problem or simplify the decision making. I also wanted to work to understand when any process encountered an "abnormal" condition and try to move firefighting to the lowest level possible. In my case, this basically meant that I wanted either my shop foreman or programmer to handle most of the shop-floor problems but this would require some training in problem-solving skills.

Previously, I noted that in many cases when Tom encountered a problem, he would involve Bob before fully understanding the root cause. I basically wanted my foreman to act as a team leader. Then, as either the setup men or operators encountered problems, Tom (acting as a team leader) would solve them with little or no involvement from me. I did not want each operator to struggle for some period of time and then call Tom. Instead, I wanted him to be in the position to immediately respond and quickly resolve the problems, and while he was working on the problem, the operators could be assigned to other tasks like deburring, tumbling, or preparing the next job's material. I knew this would require some problem-solving training—nothing as in-depth as Six Sigma (we did not have the volume to apply statistical problem-solving methods)—but some simplified one-page problem solving (also known as A3 problem solving) and simple thought processes like the five whys and fishbone diagrams. Basically, Tom just needed some confidence and a few simple, structured methods, and I was sure he could work through it.

Lean principle: *Within a lean context, a team leader does not have management authority over the team members but is challenged to keep processes running, resolve problems, perform root cause analysis, fill in for absenteeism, etc. Many of us who deal with the categorization of direct versus indirect employees think that direct employees add more value and are therefore easier to cost justify. Some managers view the team leader as an indirect employee and this is unfortunate. Toyota realized it is better to have directs only doing the direct work and specialists available to handle problems and irregularities. This allows the directs to have productivities in the high 90-percentiles and skilled problem solvers resolving the issues at their root cause, yielding a better overall productivity when executed correctly.*

The second line of defense was my new programmer. In his position, John already possessed the ability to think more abstractly in terms of what was happening at different points in the program as the part progressed through its various steps. I figured if John and Tom received a little theory and structure, they could handle most of the technical issues, though it first required coaching them through the reasoning behind root-cause problem solving. Bob had always handled the problem solving and he had not developed those skills within the organization. I did not want the business to rely solely on my skills. Instead, I wanted everyone to develop these abilities, which would free me from this as a daily responsibility.

Lean principle: *Problem solving can be accomplished in as few as five steps:*

1. *State the problem as specifically as possible.*
2. *Analyze the problem (other perspectives).*
3. *Formulate a wide range of solutions.*
4. *Evaluate solutions.*
5. *Choose solution to trial.*

It can also evoke more complex methodologies like Six Sigma depending on the nature and characteristics of the issues. Another, often better option is A3 problem solving, a structured approach used to engage those involved and to help in developing future leaders.

4.5 PROBLEM SOLVING VERSUS FIREFIGHTING

I really believe that some people thrive on firefighting, especially when they solve a problem that is delaying a process and walk away as the hero. This is not a personality trait that I possess. Instead, I always thought that, with a problem-solving process in place for identifying problems early on, it would be better motivation for all involved if the team leader led them through the problem solving and then had the time to put a more permanent countermeasure in place. Although this sounds simple, it takes a lot of time to evolve and it requires a manager who asks questions that lead employees to their own solutions (instead of just telling people what to do). I was not born with a lot of patience, so asking questions to allow employees to draw their own conclusions is something I had to learn. My Toyota training helped me along in developing these skills. This is a key point since I feel it leads to more successful problem solving, which helped to reduce a lot of our lost machining time.

Key point: When encountering problems, coach employees through root-cause problem solving instead of assuming you already understand the cause and/or the solution. This is much better than dictating what should be done since evidence shows most of us are wrong about half the time. It may take longer but you are engaging the brains of the entire organization, and in the long run you will develop a team of problem solvers who will ultimately minimize lost time by reacting quicker.

4.6 IDENTIFYING THE NEED FOR SHOP-FLOOR VISUALS

Defining normal versus abnormal for many processes was another priority for me, but I knew this would take some time and require observation followed by standardization. The more non-standard a process is, the more difficult it is to say what is normal. Typically, when you ask, "What normally happens next?" the answer is often, "It depends on this or that." Therefore, I wanted to identify the most critical processes first and concentrate on those. I knew some of them would be on the shop floor and others would be in the office. Although both our quality level and on-time delivery rates were reasonable, I knew based on our short lead times that our on-time delivery was always vulnerable. Therefore, I decided to start some visual management on the shop floor, not just to ensure we were running in a "normal" condition and would deliver on time, but also to develop a simple process that ensured the front office could decide when an additional order could be rolled into the schedule. This would provide them a tool to easily commit to a delivery date (in other words, creating a job-shop planning system). Previously, this was all done by Bob and most of it took place in his head.

I started with the idea of a simple scheduling board for each machine. The board was to be used by the foreman, programmer, and me to indicate whether we were on schedule (normal) or not (abnormal), and to help the front office to determine the lead time for new customer orders. I felt the boards needed to display the current day's plan in detail and ideally have this short-term capacity well utilized, plus have the option to display the approximate workload going out for the next week. This was discussed in the previous chapter and an example of the type of board we first used is shown in Appendix D.

We normally worked with such short lead times that anything requested outside a two-week window was an exception and consequently rarely a problem. I felt the scheduling board should function in hours because that is how we estimated and planned each operational step. I also wanted the office to consider pulling ahead some of the work that was not immediately due and to plan the schedule allowing sufficient lead time for any external processing steps (plating, painting, stress relief, etc.). This would provide the opportunity to group orders with other materials going out for the same external processes, reducing cost and transportation.

I chose a simple dry-erasable board for each machine and planned to start only on my critical machine (the Haas VF-4) as a pilot. Since most of the CNCs had the same capabilities and were only differentiated by the size of the material they could handle, the largest machine was the one most likely to become the bottleneck as it was the only one with the capacity to manufacture the complete range of parts. Consequently, it was frequently in higher demand.

Before purchasing the pilot board, I wanted to first discuss the idea with Tom and John and get their buy-in. I was not sure of John's background with visual management. But, I knew that during Tom's eighteen years at the company, visual management had not been embraced. Instead, his experience was the frustration of trying to read Bob's mind for what should be done next. I wanted his support in making things more transparent. I explained the advantages: Tom and the operators would always understand the plan for the day and the quantity of upcoming work. The expectations would be clear and I felt we could minimize any schedule changes. Also, Tom and John could have input to improve the sequences, helping minimize changeover time as long as it did not impact the on-time delivery, and we would all quickly see other abnormalities.

It seems my sales pitch went well as they bought into it, and Tom felt confident the operators would also see the advantages. I basically wanted Tom to handle scheduling on the boards and told him I would make a simple flowchart to help him in following a standard process for determining priorities, ideally based on FIFO (first in, first out) between processes. I wanted to push the order in at the front end (based on its lead time) and then keep it flowing/moving. I also asked John to review the boards at least once a day and give Tom any input if he saw a better changeover sequence or felt Tom had not allowed enough time for the external processes or other potential problems with the complicated parts. Starting with only the first board, the entire plant would not be completely optimized as many parts could be built on various machines; therefore, the best sequence for changeover could only be determined at a later time when all the machines were viewed together. Although I was starting with a bit of suboptimization, it is always better to pilot ideas on one process, make a few improvements to the concept, and then ensure those involved see the benefits before rolling it out across the plant. Imagine the buy-in to the schedule now that Tom and John were going to be developing it each day.

Lean principle: FIFO (first in, first out) is a process usually associated with material control, though it is also recommended for scheduling work-in-process, especially in manufacturing where parts are routed through second, third, and fourth steps, etc. This is critical in maintaining lead times for all work-in-process. Since I was allowing my team leader limited flexibility to change the sequence based on optimizing

> setups, it might appear I had disregarded FIFO. I clearly only allowed reshuffling within one shift's worth of production; therefore, the lead time to move though a particular process would be the current queue time plus a maximum of one shift. A particular part could only be shifted backwards one time, always allowing me to quantify when it would arrive at the next step.

Appendix D shows the idea behind our pilot board with the in-trays for the shop's information packages (quote sheet, routing sheet, tool sheet, setup, page, etc.). This was only the beginning, and this board changed in format as we found better ways to plan our work. I found it critical to start with a "pilot," which is owned by those who use it; therefore, my role was to coach and facilitate by providing a starting point and the guidelines as to what should be accomplished, and let them create and customize the tool.

> **Key point:** When starting any visual process, it is better to set the guidelines, clarify the purpose, and start out simple. The entire team should have input on taking the "pilot/prototype" (i.e. of the visual) through its various improvement stages. You never get it right the first time.

In all honesty, the reason I began visual management with a planning/attainment board was to ensure I was made aware of all available capacity. I could then try to sell it in the short term, thereby increasing my profitability. Selling unsold capacity brings in more profit and whether it was sold based on Bob's $60 per hour rate or some discounted number within reason, it still made us more profitable than letting a machine sit idle.

4.7 CONVERTING SMALL PRODUCTIVITY IMPROVEMENTS INTO PROFIT

One of the biggest problems with making small productivity improvements in large businesses is that they get lost either within a poor management system or by a lack of understanding of how to transform these small and sporadic amounts of additionally created capacity into profitability. Often, poor habits like not adjusting a standard process time after an improvement has been made can cause the planning system to continue to schedule in the unnecessary time on the next occasion this part is manufactured. The great part of my experience was I knew the necessity to adjust these times and that I could continue to push more work through the shop, even if I took it at a lower margin. Even at a lower rate, it was still going to increase my overall profitability. Naturally, a productivity improvement has to do with getting more volume through in a shorter time, assuming the additional work contains the same range of profitability. Here lies one mistake I have often observed and did not plan to make myself: the inaccurate profit margin per part number. It sounds like an impossibility to understand each individual part number's true profit with any level of confidence. And I knew I would not get it exact, especially with as many allocations as we had in our overhead costs. But, at least I planned to get my direct labor hours and material costs as close as possible and then group some of the other more costly indirect activities into categories. I figured I might start with more than one standard shop rate depending on some characteristics or the activities required for the particular part being quoted. I was not looking for precision, just more accuracy than what I had observed we were applying.

Most finance departments do not appear to have a PDCA cycle to ensure any accuracy in their allocations and do not appear to work at continuously improving the process. If I could hold someone's interest, I think I could write an entire book about the mistakes I have witnessed in leaders assuming the finance department's "profit margin" per product is reasonably accurate without challenging it. To sum up, the biggest problem I have observed, overhead allocations aside, is the fact that so many companies do not have feedback systems for their quoting (comparing quoted to actual hours), indicating the chances of their direct hours being accurate are minimal. You should not be thinking that your direct labor is only 7 percent or 10 percent of the total cost and dismiss this point because the direct labor is only the tip of the iceberg (since it is often the basis for allocating most of your overhead costs, which are significant).

Think of it this way: you start a weekend project at home, and while driving to the hardware or garden supply store to pick up supplies, you might try to guess how things will go and how long it might take to get it done. At least that way you can plan when you will be finished. Will the job take just a few hours, the entire afternoon, or the next few weekends? If you are like me, things rarely go as planned and no matter what time you promise your significant other you will be finished, it usually does not work like a Swiss watch.

Now, imagine that you were to do that same job again—what would be different? First, you would have learned a few tricks, so likely the job would take less time the second time around. Also, you would have a much clearer idea of the exact time and steps involved because you performed the job yourself, in which case you are directly providing the estimator (yourself) with the feedback.

Apply this experience to the work environment. The first complication is you usually have one person estimating and another performing the work. Without a feedback system, how is the estimator to learn about inaccuracies in the way you learned about them during your weekend project? The second thing to consider is that if the work were to repeat, how could you be better prepared after having gone through it the first time? Even in the case that you had originally estimated the correct time, imagine how you would be able to make improvements for your second run that would make you more competitive. A smart business person would be aware of these savings in terms of improvements, would document or capture the learnings for the next time, and not plan for the unnecessary time and waste. Naturally, if your customer is still willing to pay for this extra time, go ahead and let them. But, you need to understand the true time (in other words, the true profitability) so you can make the best business decisions. Therefore, a system without feedback or a method to continuously update the time it takes to perform the job as you constantly introduce improvements is comparable to having someone else perform your weekend project the second time around, and not sharing with them what you learned on the first occasion. Likely, they will make the same mistakes and you will end up paying for this one way or another. This analogy can be extended to more than just direct labor hours; it also applies to indirect tasks and all processes in which you are engaged.

4.8 CHALLENGING THE REPORTED PROFIT MARGINS

The advantage I had was I did not plan to make the same mistake that I had seen others making for years. I have sat beside many managers when asked by the big boss, "What is our profitability on this job?" In many of these cases, I had been on the shop floor and observed the actual time, materials, and effort required, and compared those to the available standards (routings, bills of materials, etc.). Therefore, I knew the times were not correct as noted in the routings and there was no system in place to continuously update this. Consequently, when these managers answered something like, "We have a 17.5 percent profit margin on this job," I knew that this was inaccurate since it was based on some poor data and lots of assumptions in allocations of the overhead. But, everyone else seemed content to take this number at face value. What if, in reality, they only made 2 percent because they did not account for additional overhead costs (i.e. extra Q.C. effort) and then further orders for the same part/service were received? Ignorance can be bliss but if this happens too often, real financial jeopardy can follow.

I have already explained my Excel spreadsheet that was being utilized as our format to ensure standardization for quoting the jobs (shown in Appendix C). The sheet was then attached to the shop-floor information package that traveled with all jobs. The gray boxes were completed to show actual times, problems, and later the actual material that was consumed. My concern was now to capture improvements and encourage us to continually improve the times. Setup time is the traditional starting point to be pursued during a lean journey, but I also wanted to look at the cycle times (the machine operating time) for each operation. I wanted to drive this continuous improvement and always capture the savings without encountering a lot of paperwork or extra documentation costs. However, this would come a bit later as the OSKKK method indicates to first Kaizen flow and process because they are the least costly to change and have the most impact. The next step is to Kaizen equipment (fixturing, cycle times, etc.) as this involves incrementally more cost. The final step is to Kaizen the layout as this usually has higher cost implications and a longer payback.

Lean principle: Runners, repeaters, and strangers are segregations for various types of parts when implementing lean (also referred to as ABC analysis or stock and non-stock). This is even more applicable in high-mix plants. Runner parts—typically, the 10-20 percent of your part numbers that account for approximately 80 percent of your sales volume—are the ones on which you first apply many of the lean improvements. This is where you will obtain your best payback.

Simply put, you need to continuously monitor and improve the times for parts that are produced over and over. You need to understand and document these improvements, not necessarily passing the savings onto the customer if the market does not demand it. Also, never forget that profitably selling any additionally created capacity is the best scenario.

4.9 SUMMARY

- 5S is a tool that improves productivity, especially where you cross-train and have job rotation (which are critical elements).
- It is crucial for managers to quickly distinguish between normal and abnormal conditions. Well-executed visual management can aid in quickly determining the status.
- Team leaders are vital in problem solving and resolving issues at their root causes.
- FIFO is important when managing work-in-process as these jobs route through the various process steps ("push" at the beginning and then "flow"), and without FIFO the lead times will fluctuate.
- Determining more accurate profit margins for each part number requires a PDCA cycle as the basis to direct continuous improvement.

5

Creating and Selling Capacity

5.1 ONLY THINKING IN TERMS OF FULL ABSORPTION COSTING

I might not be the "sharpest tool in the shed" but I completely understand that the more volume you move through a manufacturing plant, the more likely you are to be profitable. I can't argue with those of you who are thinking, "Yeah, but it has to be work at a decent margin." But, in the case where you have already covered fixed costs with baseline volume, it is basically hard to lose money on additional jobs as long as they absorb more than just the variable costs. The problem most companies encounter is their quoting and accounting systems are stuck in the mind-set of full absorption costing (includes all manufacturing costs: i.e., direct materials, direct labor, and both variable and fixed manufacturing overhead), instead of having the aptitude in certain cases to apply only variable costing (includes only variable manufacturing costs: i.e., direct materials, direct labor, and only variable manufacturing overhead) plus a bit of profit. In those special circumstances where you look at only variable costs, it would lead to arriving at a lower quoted price and might put some work in your shop that you might not otherwise have been awarded.

Luckily, I was not burdened with such a difficult system. I was able, not only to judge each job on its own merit with real numbers, but to look at it also in terms of incremental costs compared to full absorption costing and make an educated decision: Did I want to make money (assuming the customer was unwilling to absorb a fully burdened rate containing excess allocations) or be burdened by a rigid pricing system that did not take into account the realities of my available capacity versus demand? Naturally, it was always a gamble that this particular part (quoted at a lower rate) could come back later to haunt me if it were to receive repeat orders (in particular for larger quantities), especially at a time when my demand was exceeding capacity and I could instead be selling that capacity more profitably. I was willing to take some calculated risks because lean methodologies offer many possibilities to increase capacity. I also knew that as I reached the Kaizen stages during my OSKKK (Observe, Standardize, Kaizen Flow & Process, Kaizen Equipment, and Kaizen Layout) strategy implementation, I would need some money to fund these improvements, especially in the areas of Kaizening equipment and layout; therefore, any extra profit could be quickly reinvested in the business.

5.2 OVERTIME AS A POSITIVE

I find it amusing that some companies view overtime as a negative. I agree that it is a major concern if you do not manage your daily business, and overtime is driven by poor productivity, poor uptime, or employees manipulating the system for a bigger paycheck. In my case, almost all of our overtime was the result of additional demand that exceeded our capacity, this was ensured by controlling nearly every minute of straight time with planning boards and time management. This made almost all my overtime very profitable, even when paying one and a half times the normal hourly rate. I could still put money in my pocket since about two-thirds of the standard shop rate went to cover my overhead, which was basically already fully absorbed in our standard forty-hour work week. The weeks that we had a full shift running on Saturdays even encouraged a tight guy like me to buy a round of coffee at Starbucks on the way to work. My formula was simple—my rent remained the same, my loan payments remained the same, my insurance remained the same, and those extra hours billable near $60 per hour or more earned a lot of profit. I was not about to overlook that by putting some incorrect metrics in place, always applying full absorption costing, or thinking of overtime as a "negative." Even the jobs I sold at less than $60 per hour to secure the order were still profitable when estimated and managed correctly.

Before going on, I want to capture this point about overtime, as I feel it is often misunderstood.

Key point: Overtime is a negative if you do not manage your daily business, and this additional cost is necessitated due to poor productivity, poor uptime, or employees manipulating the system for a bigger paycheck. On the other hand, overtime is a positive and is profitable as a short-term solution to meeting temporary increases in demand if you profitably manage your straight time.

5.3 SETUP-TIME REDUCTIONS

I do not want to give the impression that I willingly paid overtime. On the contrary, I was continuously looking for productivity improvements to create that extra capacity, achieving more output without overtime. Being a "lean guy," I naturally focused on setup time as one of the first steps within the OSKKK strategy—setup falls under the second "K," Kaizening of Equipment—therefore, any extra profit could be reinvested when fixtures and tooling were required thereby further enhancing profitability.

Our first successes were low-hanging fruit. For example, originally we did not have complete sets of tools and fixturing at each machine, causing the setup men to walk away to find and periodically wait to share a common tool. These were mostly inexpensive hand tools so the first steps were some small investments. Some items like cutting tool holders for the various machines were a bit more expensive, and we had to gather a little data first to see how often a particular operator had a delay caused by not having sufficient tool holders or a particular type of tool holder. After identifying a concern, a simple tick sheet—requiring minimal time to complete—was put up on each machine for a few weeks. Using the tick sheets, we quickly quantified how often either a few minutes were lost due to searching for a tool holder or how often significant time was needed to configure an alternative tool holder. We further noted how often it was necessary to revise the program to use another cutting tool, and we also tracked how often we used various fixtures stored close to the machines. The results showed that we needed some sorting to be done (5S, workplace organization) so that infrequently used tools could be stored further from the machines or even disposed of and vice-versa the runner tools were located close to their point of use. Once the data regarding delays was in front of me, I applied an average time lost for each occurrence, and from there it was easy to justify some investment and determine the particular type of tooling to purchase to minimize forced waiting times. Real-time Pareto charts were the method we employed to quantify the amount of time lost for every occurrence when a tool was not available (see the example shown in Appendix E). The advantage of the operators putting the data directly into this real-time Pareto chart was that I did not have to spend time transferring the data into a different format to interpret its meaning and draw conclusions. I could do that in real time as the data was entered by the operators.

Lean principle: *Kaizening of Equipment—the second "K" within OSKKK—consists of:*

- *Reducing setup time using SMED (single minute exchange of dies) methodology.*
- *Improving machine feeds and speeds.*
- *Measuring and improving OEE (overall equipment effectiveness).*
- *Balancing operator workload to machine cycle times.*
- *Making improvements in TPM (total predictive maintenance).*
- *Simplifying machines to improve OEE.*

The importance of basing decisions on data acquired through observation is another key point because, without data, I often find people talking in circles or making poor decisions or not able to draw firm conclusions.

Key point: *When a decision requires some investment (either time or money) and not all parties clearly buy-in, it is easy to have some simple data gathered over a few weeks or months by the people performing the processes, then regroup and review the facts. Usually, the data—especially in the format of a real-time Pareto chart—will speak for itself and make the choice clear, one way or another.*

Many other setup reduction ideas presented themselves, some to do with improving our work order package by including better tooling lists, others to do with standardizing locations for certain expensive, high-usage tools that were shared among the operators (further simplified as we purchased more of the same types of CNC [Computer Numerical Control] machines that permitted us to share more common tooling). We standardized some fixturing that would remain set up on certain machines and some of the bigger machines were standardized with multiple types of fixtures left permanently in place spread across the larger machining tables. One advantage in any machine shop is that once you get everyone focused on improving the setup, you engage everyone's mind and people get creative. Machine shops have a further advantage in that they can manufacture most fixturing in-house; not only can someone come up with an idea for fixturing, but he can also usually produce it if it is not available in a catalogue.

5.4 CONTINUOUSLY MEASURING SETUP TIMES

Most changeover time-reduction efforts flounder because of a lack of support or because there is no measurement or incentive put in place. Fortunately, this was not the case for me.

As previously mentioned, the estimate sheets for all new jobs (or the previously achieved times for repeating jobs) were now being attached to each work package and the operators were required to fill in their actual setup and run times for each operation. Therefore, the measurement system already existed, and we were not going to have the problems that I have encountered at other companies: they run setup reductions or SMED workshops but do not continue to focus and follow-up on them, or they do not constantly measure the results. It was far too important an area for me and we already had our monitoring system in place. The monitoring had been functioning for about two months by the time we focused on the setup, and now this data would help to confirm the accuracy of our estimates, highlight problems with setup times, and allow us to capture improvements by reducing the allocated time.

The incentive for my employees might not have been directly financial; but, since I had explained that the longevity of the business would be jeopardized if we were not achieving or beating the estimated times, their motivation came through job security. Also, I announced that I planned to develop a bonus system that would take productivity into account. Productivity was important to me—and what is important to the boss should be important to the employees—and that meant I was going to be constantly monitoring and trying to improve it. This is probably one of the biggest reasons lean transformations are not successful: the managers do not significantly change their behavior (or their standardized working methods).

Key point: What is important to the boss should be important to the employees, and continuous monitoring, reviewing, and supporting improvements can only lead to success. In lean terms, you must always "Plan, Do, Check, Act" (PDCA) in a continuous cycle.

As far as incentives for the entire team, I was working to create a bonus system driven by these productivity improvements. At this time I did not have enough background in the financials and had not put the proper metrics in place. But I promised that once they were in place, some form of bonus would be paid. I had yet to figure out how, but I was confident it could be done. And after seeing some poor bonus systems in other companies that frequently promoted behaviors contradictory to what was intended, I felt I would not make the same mistakes. I later learned that this was easier said than done and that designing a reasonable bonus system was beyond my abilities.

Lean principle: A formal suggestion system encourages employees to submit ideas to address waste, safety concerns, and environmental improvements. Naturally, it supports a structured way to channel, evaluate, and track ideas. It also encourages continuous improvement by providing the motivation and form to evaluate and discuss these ideas, instead of encouraging only a few at higher levels in the organization to provide the majority of suggestions for improvement. These systems can become unruly if not thought out and supported with resources and management involvement. I was discussing a bonus system with the employees, but a suggestion system is also important.

Returning to setup-time reduction, I was really looking to separate the internal and external setup elements, using the SMED methodology pioneered by Shigeo Shingo. Keeping in mind that we typically changed over a machine between three and six times a day to one of a few thousand part numbers, few if any of which were familiar to us, we had our work cut out for ourselves. I had a few further concepts to implement in conjunction with this theme, the biggest being that I really wanted my foreman to function as the team leader.

The great advantage of having Tom (the shop foreman) as team leader was his work ethic. He was a "working machine," and those who could not keep up fell into his bad graces and I learned later that they would not survive working with him. I wanted Tom to be freed from running a machine and instead to be dedicated full time to solving problems, preparing setups, and minimizing any machine stoppages. Bob (the former owner) frequently had Tom running a machine, feeling that the highest productivity (or profitability) was achieved when Tom performed this direct labor function in addition to his other responsibilities.

I was not hung up over the traditional separation of "direct labor" and "indirect labor," and did not view the latter as having a negative cost impact. I had been trained by Toyota, where there was no such mentality. Most businesses are willing to accept lower uptimes or OEEs (overall equipment effectiveness, defined in more detail in Appendix F) and let everyone solve his own problems; however, they do not demand a higher OEE by providing the resources to solve the problems and keep the machines running at or above 80 percent. I knew the superior solution was to have one skilled problem solver running around instead of relying on the various problem resolution skills of all my setup men and operators to deal with the various abnormalities.

So, before I liberated Tom from the day-to-day running of a CNC, I gathered some data in order to compare the before and after, and determine whether we achieved a productivity improvement. For almost two weeks I had everyone attempt to record every time his machine was down and the duration of the delay. Again, the simplified, real-time Pareto charts (shown in Appendix E) were utilized. I figured I was about to have one less part-time machine operator, and I needed to justify this cost by having the other five or six machines running more productively. This team leader concept was one of Toyota's proven successes, so I figured I could get it working in my little world. When a machine is involved, OEE is a critical measurement for improving productivity. We began with the operators capturing the downtime data and placing it into categories while I was able to calculate the OEE based on the good parts we produced.

Lean principle: *OEE is the ideal measurement for monitoring and indicating where to improve manufacturing processes (ideally, auto cycle machines or cells containing auto cycle machines). More details can be found in Appendix F.*

5.5 CREATING A TEAM LEADER

Although most would think anyone would be glad to be more or less free from running a machine, I had discovered at Toyota that many people who were promoted to team leader would later ask to go back to working as an operator on the assembly line or running a machine. All that running around and dealing with everyone's problems can sometimes be too much pressure and some feel it is mentally and physically easier to just operate a machine or work on the line and call for help when there is a problem. (A list of traditional team leader responsibilities within the Toyota system is captured in Appendix G.)

Tom had been the shop foreman for many years and was used to coming in early to start things up and get prepared. But, most of the day he struggled to keep a machine running while simultaneously performing his other duties—realistically, he was only leaving his machine to firefight. Instead, I now wanted him to continuously try to reduce any reason the machines might not be "cutting chips." So, it was time to take Tom out for a beer or two and present the idea to him, to share the reason for suggesting a change, and to see how he felt about it.

Tom seemed to like the idea and the challenge; he also felt he could learn to be a better problem solver. I started to explain a few theories on how problem solving could be applied but thought the conversation might go better at the shop rather than at the bar. We agreed not to implement this new role immediately but over the next few weeks we would clarify the responsibilities and discuss how things would work differently. I also indicated that there would be no hard and fast rule that Tom would not go back to running a machine if the business case required it or if he needed to fill in for an absent operator.

Key point: When choosing a team leader, not only do you need someone like Tom, who had earned everyone's respect and knew all the jobs in the area, you also want a leader who is trained in problem solving and sets an example in working methods/ethics and dedication. For me, it was an easy choice because Tom was one of the most dedicated workers I have ever met. He knew the jobs and had earned the trust and respect, all he needed was some training in problem solving.

While we were planning for Tom to move into the team leader role, we started discussing all the setup tasks that would be externalized (prepared while the machine was still operating) and how we would best leverage the other setup men (who functioned as operators when not performing a setup). The simple fact of externalizing setup activities implies that either the operator must have the time (outside of keeping the machine running) to perform these tasks or a team leader (or similar individual) with the available time must handle them. For example, you cannot just say that we will have all the tools prepared in tool holders prior to the beginning of the setup without a plan for who will be doing this and making time available. (While the machine was running in our shop, the operators were often busy running a second machine, deburring, measuring, etc.; therefore, they did not have a lot of available time for preparing tools.) Keep in mind, though, as with most companies I was selling my machine time at a much higher rate than the cost of the employees' hourly wages, so the more time the machines could be producing, or in this case "cutting chips," the more chance I had for profitability.

5.6 INCREASED PRODUCTIVITY THROUGH VISUAL MANAGEMENT

The scheduling boards I had put in place about a month before were also beginning to help in improving the available capacity. I found just by setting a targeted completion time, then monitoring against it and being proactive in reducing problems was motivating the team. (Naturally, there is a danger if you set the target too low, but PDCA helps to verify the times and minimize this).

It took a lot of work on my part in the beginning to monitor these boards and try to get everyone to see it as a positive. But, I think it was successful because I always tried to focus on what went wrong within the process instead of making it personal. Everyone could then look to improve the standard processes instead of feeling they were being personally attacked. In all honesty, there were times when someone had just screwed up and often I suffered the financial consequences of the lost time or scrapped material. I tried not to lose my cool very often; instead we would discuss what should have been done by the operator and I would document the serious instances. The upside was that if I decided an employee had too many of these problems, I could let him go without being accused of unfair treatment or being challenged for a poor labor practice. Often, supervisors do not take the time to document infractions related to quality or productivity but it is a necessary part of the job.

Instead of setting explicit expectations with relation to time, Bob had always just given out the next job. It was matter of prioritization, and he was just spoon feeding Tom. Nevertheless, I noted during my training period that Bob periodically told me a job seemed to be taking too long (based on his experience). Then he'd either ask Tom if he knew what the problem was (though frequently Tom was unsure of the reason because he had returned to running a machine) or he would ask the operator himself. The problem with this random system was Bob had not set the expectation with the operator, and the machinist obviously was not trying to achieve anything other than staying busy. He did not know if he was ahead or behind and only looked at the clock to determine how far off break time or quitting time was. When I began setting time-related expectations, there were instances when an operator did not agree with the scheduled times; but it is always better to discuss this and set the expectations up front.

About this time, I had owned the business nearly six months and had closed the books for four months since my training period had ended. Overall, things were still looking good. I had continued to earn enough to cover the loan payments and was even able to pay myself a decent salary. I felt I was getting a little closer to financial stability though I was not in any shape to "weather a storm," and it would only take a few months of poor sales or some major quality issues to throw me into a downward spiral, losing money instead of drawing a paycheck. The unwritten rule among business owners is that you need to survive for five years (apparently the magic number) and to have your debt level significantly reduced before feeling there is any breathing room or longevity for the business. However, I was not getting any younger and I knew I could not wait five years to pop the question. And if I had to bet, I was sure my girlfriend would not want to be strung along for that length of time.

5.7 PDCA OF THE ESTIMATING PROCESS

I was continuing my weekly reviews with John (the programmer/estimator) regarding the accuracy of his quotes. I realized that any actual times that were within ±10 percent of the estimate were not worth dragging into our Friday reviews, and there were weeks I left out some that were 15 percent above or below the time estimates. The various hourly rates we had begun using (accounting mostly for the type of material we were machining) to better account for our tooling and direct shop costs were also beginning to better align actual costs with estimates.

I wanted us to improve as much as was reasonable and I was also trying to learn and improve the processes as quickly as the organization could absorb. So, the more quotes we reviewed each Friday, the more I was able to learn, and periodically I was able to further evolve or refine our quoting process. I had even started doing some of the simpler quotes myself and then John would look them over and give me pointers. I had good days and bad days but I learned something from each of John's reviews. I was even more interested if we got the job to see how the actual times compared to my estimates. It basically becomes a point of pride when you get it right. On some occasions I was even getting some acknowledgments from Tom, who wasn't exactly free with a compliment. I was also tracking our hit rate on quotes from week to week and month to month. In the early days, you may recall, I had set a goal of winning orders on 70 percent of our quotes. With our type of business and the short lead times, we either heard back quickly by receiving a purchase order or it was not meant to be. Our hit rate was averaging anywhere from 50 percent to 65 percent and was utilizing a reasonable level of the shop's capacity on one shift.

I was still learning different buyers' habits, how to read into the seriousness of the quote, and how much price flexibility there might be. I was also trying to compare this to the profit margin per job and look at an average margin per customer. Bob had given me a gut feeling for which customers were more profitable, and my simple data analysis had basically proven him correct. It was also interesting to track the hit rate by customer and for each particular buyer. There were wide swings, and in some cases we were getting over 80 percent of quotes for a particular buyer turned into orders; others were as low as 15 percent. These numbers indicated which buyers shopped around or just used us for a second or third price quote and which buyers were too busy or too lazy to get alternative quotes and just regularly sent us the order. I guess the other possibility from those buyers from which we had a high hit rate was that the alternative quotes were always more expensive or our on-time delivery and quality level ensured us a lion's share of the work. In these cases, I needed to ensure we had a good profit margin from these jobs and we weren't just getting orders where we made mistakes on the quotes and underbid. Remember: "winning a job" was only a good thing when it had been correctly quoted and yielded a good margin.

Just when all seemed to be going well, John did not show up for work one day—no show, no call. The second day, I tried to reach him as I could not let the difficult quotes wait any longer. His wife would only tell me he was not at home, and so I assumed I had lost my estimator. Although John had not been late or absent in the previous three months, I would have to terminate him if he failed to show the next day on the basis of the strict attendance policy I had implemented: mandatory termination for a combination of three late arrivals or unplanned absences within a rolling ninety-day period. I had learned this attendance rule when working for Toyota and it was part of a larger program that kept absenteeism down near 2.7 percent during my tenure.

5.8 BECOMING THE ESTIMATOR

I had feared something like this happening since I took over the business and had been planning for it by learning and documenting all the critical tasks. However, the quoting was one of my greatest fears as it was a high-level task that required an in-depth understanding from the perspective of both a machinist and a programmer. I had no other choice, so I started working through a difficult batch of drawings and working up the quotes. The first day John was absent I had taken the first step of sorting though the drawing packages and deciding which parts we could not build because they were not within our capabilities or they were sheet metal or fabricated parts. When Bob owned the business, he would try to subcontract some of these parts to other machining or sheet metal companies and then add a markup (though he did not let the customer know that the parts were manufactured elsewhere). I noted that most buyers were not concerned or involved enough to understand where the manufacturing took place. They just wanted a good price and good quality for all the drawings in the package and it was easiest for them if the entire package could be placed on one purchase order with one vendor. I had further capitalized on this outsourcing and generally tried to quote all drawings within the package, which required digging around and finding additional subcontractors to those that Bob had used. But, I hoped that the average 15 percent markup that some of those orders brought in was worth the effort. I later learned that sometimes the difficult parts were more trouble than they were worth and outsourcing work with some new suppliers could periodically damage my reputation in terms of quality and on-time delivery. Bear in mind that I was not outsourcing to reduce my costs. I was only going outside when I did not have competitive capabilities internally.

Of the quotations I was working on that morning, I had already sent out for subcontractor quotations all the drawings I had determined we could not manufacture in-house. I had resolved that I needed to do the in-house estimating, at least in the short term, while I worked to replace John. So, I began to conceptualize how to manufacture each part; in what form I would request the raw material (i.e., bar stock, cut to size, etc.); what the first, second, and third operations would be; and I began filling out my standardized quotation sheet. This sheet was a real help my first time alone at this process. It helped keep my thinking structured and worked like a check sheet to ensure I did not overlook anything. I was really glad that I had not only learned the process but had also taken the time to document and structure it. All those Friday afternoons spent reviewing the quotations were really paying off, especially when we found something had been overlooked and we went back and improved our standard quotation form. I would not say I liked the position I had been thrown into but I was much more comfortable and better able to handle it because of having a standardized process in place and having pried all the tribal knowledge I could from both Bob and John. I really had a good standard process instead of just following Bob's words: "You learn it as you go and then you'll know what to do."

I worked through the two drawing packages that were waiting for pricing and put my final numbers together. A little follow-up and I had all the numbers in from the subcontractors. Then, I had to decide what margins could be used with these customers. This all happened within the day, and before 5:00 p.m. I was ready to fax back the quotations. Again, the proof of how well I had done was not whether I won the bid for the job because that might just mean I missed some important items and underbid it. The bottom line was in comparing the real costs to my quoted costs. I was typically quoting individual parts that ranged from $20 to $2,000 each—just think how critical estimating is for companies quoting large, expensive systems.

For one customer, I had quoted eleven different parts and received the orders for six at the smaller quantity levels quoted (periodically, customers asked to have parts quoted at various quantities, which usually meant they were looking at inventory management or they did not yet have an order themselves). Only getting part of the order sometimes indicated that I had overlooked something that my competitor had foreseen and included in his price. But, after a quick review of the six parts for which we received the order, I did not see anything obvious I had overlooked. From the other quotation, we received the order for all nine parts we quoted. I had expected this as we usually received what we quoted from that particular buyer. She was my favorite type of purchaser—not familiar with the commodities she was buying, always overloaded, and always in a hurry. Normally, I did not have to "sharpen my pencil" too much with her. She frequently laid her cards on the table, indicating how desperate she was for the parts by the way in which she sent the request for quotation: a hand-scribbled note sent via the fax machine with some hastily conceived drawings, a due date of ASAP, and asking how soon she could have the quote back. It was a clear indication that if I could quickly get the quote back with a short delivery time, price would not be the determining factor. I think this is another key business point to capture.

Key point: It is critical to have measurements in place that indicate when the purchasing or estimating departments are overloaded or only given a short period in which to place an order. Under these circumstances, you will not have sufficient time to obtain the best prices and quality, thereby not providing competitive quotations to your customers. This normally results in significantly increasing costs or using poor quality suppliers. If your real-time purchasing workload indicates an overload, you should have other people trained to temporarily support the purchasing and estimating departments. Another tactic to pursue is to reduce departmental workloads. For example, in purchasing you can put some frequently consumed parts onto Kanban reordering, utilizing blanket purchase orders that will reduce the daily workload, and creating more available time to obtain the best prices on other purchased components.

After we built the jobs for which I had prepared the quotations and I reviewed the actual versus estimated costs, I found I had done well and decided I would still look for a new estimator, but I did not need to rush. Again, my goal was to be freed up from day-to-day operations as much as possible, so I wanted an estimator. But, I did not want anyone to be able to hold me for ransom because he or she was the only one that had that specific skill. I was on my way to proving that no one could pressure me into thinking I could not live without an estimator.

5.9 SUMMARY

- Full absorption costing is not the only option; to better utilize your capacity in certain instances, variable costs plus adding some profit could be utilized when quoting.
- Reducing setup times is a critical and early step in lean improvements, and when you are able to profitably sell the additional capacity you have created, you have a win–win situation.
- You must continuously monitor setup times to truly benefit and continuously improve.
- Team leaders can be some of the most productive employees if they are assigned the correct responsibilities and receive proper support from management.
- Putting a PDCA loop in the estimating process is a vital step for any made-to-order or job-shop type of business.
- Monitoring the purchasing department's workload to recognize when they are overloaded is critical to maintaining cost control. This is especially important when you have a high percentage of your spend on either raw material, purchased components, or outsourcing.

6

Getting Everyone Motivated for Improving the Machine's Output

6.1 INTRODUCTION

I had been drawing a regular paycheck, enough to live on but nothing to brag about. So, I was periodically giving myself a small bonus at the end of the month, assuming it was in line with our monthly profit. The good news was the monthly bonus was becoming steadier—which was great because when I had popped the question during a surprise visit to my girlfriend in Spain, the answer was a big yes. The surprise visit to Spain was two fold: I partially wanted to astonish her, but it was also important that I do it on her turf and in her mother tongue. On the flight over I was busy digging through an English/Spanish dictionary trying to figure out the necessary words and put them into proper sentences. The Spanish woman sitting beside me asked if she could be of some help. I was a little embarrassed, but once I explained to her what I was attempting to do, she appeared to be so taken with the idea, she couldn't do enough for me. I found it very strange practicing and repeating the phrase "will you marry me" with a complete stranger. Though prior to landing she told me that my pronunciation was fine and apparently it worked. Can you imagine what the others on the flight were thinking as I repeated over and over again "will you marry me"? Now, attaining a bit of financial stability and slowly developing a cross-trained workforce, the idea of marriage was feeling a little more comfortable from my working perspective. Maybe even a little time off for a honeymoon would be possible.

6.2 MANAGING EACH JOB VISUALLY

I continued looking for a new programmer/estimator while sharpening my own skills in these areas. With only about six months experience under my belt, I was outsourcing the more complicated parts; however, with each passing day I was able to estimate and program progressively more difficult jobs. When I reviewed my estimates against the actual times, I found there were good and bad days. In reality, I did not even need to wait until Fridays to know how I had performed. I was visually scheduling jobs according to the estimated time. Tom (the shop foreman), the operators, and I were immediately aware when certain jobs began taking more time than planned, and we started observing/monitoring and asking questions. Of the jobs requiring extra time, it seemed about a 50/50 split between those that had encountered operational problems that caused the overrun and those that I had incorrectly estimated. It wasn't as bad as it sounds because, although the errors frequently were underestimates, periodically I overestimated the time, and it put a smile on my face to see a very profitable job moving through (although I still wanted to get the quoting right). Also most of the incorrect estimates were only off by 10 to 20 percent. As they say, "You win some, you lose some." I just hoped those very profitable jobs would be the ones to repeat.

Lean principle: This visual scheduling of jobs is really how a made-to-order business accounts for its takt time (the customer demand). Remember: takt time helps set the pace/beat based on customer demand, and this must be compared to the cycle time, which is how long the process itself takes. So, the time estimated for a job is basically what the customer has agreed to pay for; therefore, this is as close to takt time as you have available. The visual board was measuring this time against how long it actually took (the cycle time). Since this helps to improve the machine's output, it is a further form of Kaizening of equipment, the second "K" in OSKKK (Observe, Standardize, Kaizen Flow & Process, Kaizen Equipment, and Kaizen Layout).

6.3 THE DESIRE FOR INDEPENDENCE FROM DAY-TO-DAY OPERATIONS

No viable candidates had responded to the newspaper ad I had run the week after losing John, the programmer/estimator who had quit. I had been holding off running another ad for a few weeks when I received a call from my former employer, Delphi Automotive, asking if I could come back and support them. Their first priority was to evaluate a particular plant's current lean status before a visit from the CEO of General Motors. Following this engagement, they needed support for some other plants on a lean consulting basis.

As challenging and exciting as it was running my new business, it was also intriguing to think about keeping my hand in my former profession. I had not even mouthed the word "consulting" until receiving this call. I had wanted to get the business to the point where I could step away from the day-to-day operations for a holiday, a practice I had become accustomed to while living in Europe. Though the thought of part-time consulting was well worth considering, the business was not at a point that I felt comfortable enough to pursue this idea. I explained this to my contact at Delphi, who felt the offer would still be open in the future; in the meantime, could I spare a day or two to help them get ready for this extremely important visit, especially since I had overseen the lean transformation at this plant? I made this trip, but in reality I was busy working ten-to-twelve-hour days refining and putting new processes in place. I was also functioning as the estimator/programmer and handling other functions that I had taken over from the former owner, Bob, and still had not had the time to cross-train others to perform. Therefore, I felt six months was about the best I could do before I would feel confident to leave the business for a week at a time. So, with the possibility of consulting as a sideline, finding someone to handle the estimating and programming responsibilities once again moved up on my priority list.

We—Tom and I—started interviewing again. One of the most important reasons I wanted Tom involved in the interview process was that he had more experience in the industry and he had some "street smarts" that I was lacking. Another key reason was that he was going to be working more closely with the estimator than I would be. Actually, I wanted the estimator to report to Tom (even though the position would likely pay slightly more than Tom's) because I trusted Tom to always get the job done. I also wanted the interviewee to be clear that the estimator position would report to Tom—who never smiled and was very direct. I felt it was only fair for the interviewee to consider who he would be reporting to, and for Tom to know ahead of time who he'd be working with.

After more than a month of searching, we found Jake. He brought over twenty years of experience and had worked with various materials and machines. Again, I wanted to pick his brain to learn what we did different than other shops and where he thought we could improve. I wanted to hear his opinion on everything, but I preferred he tell me his ideas prior to sharing them with everyone else in the shop. I had to keep in mind that the others had been working in the industry significantly longer than my seven months of experience, and if I were to let the new guy influence too many changes without letting everyone else voice an opinion, I was sure to make a few waves.

6.4 PREPARING FOR FURTHER SETUP REDUCTIONS

I was now ready to further intensify our efforts at reducing our setup times. It seemed to me that now the average quantity of pieces per order we were receiving had decreased from what they had been when Bob had owned the business. As I looked back through the history of past purchase orders, it seemed to be moving slowly in the direction of decreasing lot sizes per order. During recent weeks, Tom had been moving into the modified role of shop supervisor/team leader, which would enhance our setup methodology. The big change was that I really only wanted him to operate a machine after all the other machines were up and running; the tools, fixtures, and programs were lined up for the next work order on each machine; and our most significant recurring problems had been resolved or at least received attention. We had been working through guidelines and issues with his new role just as Jake came on board. The advantage was that Jake was faster at programming than John had been so he often had a few spare minutes. It became Tom's responsibility to understand when Jake had time available and keep him busy preparing tools and fixtures. This created the opportunity for Tom to get ahead of the game and start to either run a CNC (Computer Numerical Control) machine or start a manual job on our more traditional lathes.

Lean principle: *Runners (A), repeaters (B), and strangers (C) are terms used to classify various parts (sometimes referred to as ABC analysis or stack vs. non-stock). Runners (A) are usually the top 10 to 20 percent of the part numbers that typically account for 80 percent of total sales. Repeaters or B parts are the next group of part numbers representing the next 15 percent of total sales (i.e. from the 80 to 95 percent range of total sales). Finally strangers or C parts are all those remaining part numbers accounting for only the last 5 percent of the total sales. It is critical to group parts this way so you can manage them differently. Runners might be applicable to controlling with some type of pull system (Kanban), meaning you will likely keep a small inventory (usually as WIP(work In process) before the process step where significant variation is introduced, not in finished goods) to balance the supplying lead time with the customer's required lead time; on the other hand, strangers would always be built to order.*

6.5 CONTINUING THE KAIZEN OF EQUIPMENT BY IMPROVING THE ADJUSTMENT PHASE OF CHANGEOVERS

Since we had already purchased additional setup tooling and tool holders, things were beginning to move along faster. Jake was able to show us how to premachine some jaws and fixtures, allowing faster changeovers. I was trying to create a competitive environment encouraging us to always improve on the previous changeover times, which had been noted on the estimating sheet that followed each job through the shop. The danger in making things too competitive, however, was the possibility of quality being sacrificed, along with it being difficult to keep that motivation up in the long term. Though where I saw our biggest opportunity was in the adjustment phase of our changeovers. I had a short brainstorming session with Tom, Jake, and the two setup men to determine how we could quickly return to the previous point where we had been manufacturing a quality part. We concentrated this adjustment phase improvement to our "runner" parts. It became clear that we needed a way to capture even more notes and details of where we left off during the last production run regarding offsets, adjustments, and specific tooling. Since this documentation added a cost to the business, I only wanted to perform this on parts for which we expected repeat orders. I indicated that this was something on which we could make an educated guess during the estimating phase and should indicate which jobs were likely repeaters by adding and marking a box on the estimating form. This determination would be based on the customer, the type of part, the current revision, discussions with the purchaser, and some other general hints like certain customers' part numbering systems that were designed so the number indicated whether they were designated as production parts or only tooling/fixturing, etc.

For these new parts that were expected to repeat, a standard setup sheet would be attached to guide the setup man through documenting the important items, thereby saving some time during repetitive setups. This setup sheet was to be designed with input from everyone in the team and was to be continuously updated when we had improvement ideas. The concept was to utilize the tool sheet as the basis with certain columns to be added after each tool to cover offsets, specific tool references, and comments. It would also contain a sketch area where the part orientation could be shown along with other details and notes written in it (or digital photos attached). Jake had only seen a similar sheet used at one shop where he worked, but he was able to add a few more improvement points.

6.6 RUNNING A MACHINE WHILE CONFIRMING THE QUALITY OF THE FIRST PIECE

Since my previous experience had demonstrated that over 50 percent of a changeover's time was consumed in the measurement and adjustment phase, I knew we were on the right track. I also explained to the team that for repeating parts on the setup sheet we would highlight the dimensions that would likely be affected by a mistake during the setup, and I would indicate whether material was inexpensive and/or additional pieces could be cut in-house. If these conditions were satisfied, then the setup man could quickly check the highlighted dimensions (those likely to be incorrect due to a problem caused during the setup) and, if everything checked OK, he could start running the next part while he finished qualifying the other dimensions. This would buy us anywhere from a few minutes to about one hour additional cutting time—assuming all other dimensions were correct when completing the check on the first part. And it would only cost us some material the few times we might have missed something. Remember: on these repeat parts we already knew our CNC program was good so we really only needed to check for correct tooling and offsets. Naturally, our internal quality system and our agreement with our customers required a full dimensional check for each batch or order but that did not have to be completed on the first part. It might sound a bit like gambling (a Las Vegas approach), but every minute of machine time was worth at least $1 and often it could take ten minutes or considerably more to completely verify all dimensions on a part. We still completed the necessary quality checks; we just did this while the machine was producing the second and third parts of that batch—presumably manufacturing good parts—and we were going to contain and scrap these first pieces if we found a deviation from the allowable tolerance. Overall, I found we won much more often than we lost, meaning the first part passed so the next few were also good.

Lean principle: *Fifty percent or more of changeover time is typically utilized for verification/measuring and adjusting (quality control). This provides a significant opportunity to improve the time by being able to quickly return the process to the exact point (parameters) where you left off the last time you produced the exact part to the correct quality standards. This requires observing the process and documenting where all variables are set for the particular machine/process so you can quickly return. This is frequently done by the operator keeping certain notations (in a standard and organized format); these notes are usually reissued in the work order package. Physically scaling and marking machines is also a common technique.*

I found with this setup sheet continually being improved upon that we were reducing our setup times during the first few production orders for a particular part. I think this a learning point worth highlighting.

Key point: *After focusing on improving the physical changeover, you should work to reduce the measuring and adjustment phase, which usually accounts for more than 50 percent of the total setup time. This should* *be done by working to document (or marking the reference points on the machine) and quickly return to the same conditions that allowed you to produce a quality part during the previous production run. Taking the time to complete this documentation in an organized format can have huge payoffs.*

I thought I could further link these improvements in setup times to an employee bonus system. When I refer to a bonus system, I am really referring to some type of profit sharing instead of an incentive system. Incentive systems usually fly in the face of lean ideologies because they encourage standards be set that can be exceeded, and then workers are naturally encouraged to exceed those standards (i.e., a pieces-per-hour target). This does not encourage standardized work or continuous improvement.

6.7 DIFFICULTIES IN CREATING A PROFIT-SHARING PLAN

I did not have the resources or the wherewithal to design and monitor a bonus system that linked each employee to their daily performance. However, by monitoring items like the OEE (overall equipment effectiveness) of the machinery (for which the reduced setup time would play a part), I could really motivate the team to continuously work toward these improvements. Although I told them I was going to work toward linking these machine improvements to profit sharing, I later found that in a high-variation business where thousands of different parts could be randomly ordered, there was too large a range of variables that affected OEE. Some of these were outside of the employee's control; therefore, I was not able to link this level of detail to the bonus system.

Other problems were that some share of profits should be allocated to the bonus system, and logically this system would be used to distribute those profits fairly. There were a lot of reasons we did not show profit some months and those were not always related to the team's working efforts or even our sales figures. It also related to what constitutes "profit": one simple definition is "when operating income is greater than adjusted operating expenses." In my case, this was not always a black-and-white issue. In addition to my large loan payment (an operating expense), there were investments in new equipment and tooling that increased operating expenses, and my compensation was likely to be whatever was remaining. Therefore, I did not have a rigidly defined accounting practice, making it hard to base any bonus on "profit."

Lean principle: I was attempting to design a bonus system or at least implement a more Western-style suggestion system, which stresses the economic benefits of a proposal and also provides an economic incentive. A more idealistic approach stresses the boosting of morale through positive participation from the employees. There are usually three stages: encouragement, education, and improving efficiency. I wanted a simple system for its economic benefits, but I had previously experienced how labor-intensive they can become if not well planned out.

In the end, after playing with some different mathematical formulas I gave up on creating an ideal bonus system based on items like quality, cost, and delivery. It seemed in all cases that a critical element of my various proposals was the monthly or quarterly profits, which was not workable in my case. Although clearly defined by the IRS (Internal Revenue Service), tough decisions were necessary when so many necessities called out for money and a lot of "profit" was being reinvested in the business. The final bonus system—in place by the end of my first year—was based solely on an individual's attendance. It was based on a fixed percentage of the employee's wage, being paid in full if they were late less or absent less than a prescribed limit during the prior six months, and for each occurrence that exceeded this limit a small portion of this amount was deducted.

Another factor often brought to the forefront when working to implement a bonus system is whether or not the base wages are competitive with local industry standards. It was pointed out to me that the wage scale established under Bob's tenure was a little low, so I did a bit of research and established comparable local wage rates for our various skill sets and provided milestones so the team could move up to those rates. I listed the criteria for what an operator and setup person should be able to handle and then pointed out where I felt the individuals needed to improve. Each employee was to pick one task at a time to work on, then Tom and Jake would try to support them in practicing and learning that skill. This development plan was included in our cross-training (or skills) matrix (this is also shown in Appendix H).

Lean principle: A skills matrix (cross-training matrix) for either a department or team quickly shows how much cross-training is in place for different tasks (and can also display a future training plan). They are used to help in identifying and assessing shortcomings in skill sets as well as in aiding managers and employees in planning employee development. Naturally, these higher skill sets are openly encouraged with a skills matrix and are frequently linked to pay rates. See an example of a visualized skills matrix in Appendix H.

So, motivating the team to work on setup time improvements through the bonus system never came to be. Instead, I had to provide the motivation. Going back to what I mentioned in an earlier chapter, if it is important to the boss, then it should be important to the employees. Since things like setup time and schedule attainment were always important to me and never reached a "program of the month" status, the motivation remained there for the duration of my tenure. My continuous monitoring and helping to improve these measurements (PDCA [Plan, Do, Check, Act] in lean terms) is what really made it important for everyone. I've explained my shortcomings with respect to creating an ideal bonus system but if someone ever designs the near-perfect manufacturing bonus system, I would sure like to hear about it.

6.8 STAYING HANDS-ON SINCE "THE DEVIL IS IN THE DETAILS"

I found my time was split between the office and the shop floor, although with Tom supervising and Jake in the annex office programming, estimating, and helping prepare setups, I could have spent more time in the front office with the administrative or sales tasks. But, I wanted to continue to learn the business from the ground up and I could not sit in the office making decisions without having a true feel for the details.

We all know the phrase "the devil is in the details," and in a technical business where you build or assemble a completed part from a complex drawing, it holds a lot of truth. Therefore, I spent time on the shop floor observing as well as setting up, running, and programming jobs. Especially being necessitated when we were behind or working on a rush order, I would take over running a machine during the team's breaks or lunch time. Naturally, this led to me continually coming up with my own improvement ideas along with all the suggestions that were coming from Tom and the others. This hands-on approach also helped me hone my skills with front-office tasks like reviewing quotes, purchasing tools/materials, and really confirming where investment was required.

One example that comes to mind from early on: We had two rather small, old-style band saws for cutting material to size. Each had an add-on coolant system that functioned miserably on a good day. One morning, I noticed we were slightly behind on a job (which included operating one of these saws) and I offered to run it during the morning break. Tom indicated to me that keeping the saw running to cut the steel bar to size was part of keeping this particular job going. The cycle time on the saw was a bit longer than the machine's cycle time. So, it was a bottleneck and Tom was planning to set up the second saw after his break. I ran into a problem with every piece I tried to cut: the saw blade would pop off a guide, the coolant system would plug up, etc. Naturally, the guys came back from their break laughing and asking how I was enjoying my time with the saw.

My standard procedure in a case like this would be to coach Tom or another team member through problem solving and—hopefully—eliminate the biggest problems without making a major investment. I estimated that during my fifteen minutes of operating the combination of the CNC and saw we had incurred about four minutes of lost run time on the CNC. Relatively speaking, the saw is an inexpensive piece of equipment compared to the CNC and is not much of a profit center itself. But, it caused such a distraction of valuable resources that I found myself losing critical time on the CNC machine (the profit center). The bottom line after a short investigation was that the saws could not be brought up to an acceptable standard because of their inferior quality and age, and a new saw that could exceed the capacity of the two old saws required less than a $2,000 investment. Plus, it gave us some additional cutting capabilities (relating to size and accuracy) so we could keep more work in-house instead of outsourcing (keeping this cutting in-house also allowed us to better control our lead time). A quick calculation indicated payback would be between three and four months. The point: had I not been working hands-on and able to quickly assess the overall cost impact of this poorly performing saw, it would have been more difficult to convince me and the team would likely have gone on struggling with it. It highlighted that we still did not have a good system in place to identify and quantify where we were losing money within the individual processes.

As a consultant, I have often observed operators struggling with insignificant parts or pieces of equipment and managers either looking the other way or accepting it as a given. It always comes down to how often it is happening, multiplied by the cost impact, versus the cost of the simplest and least expensive solution.

I found similar things happening with tools, fixtures, and even a poorly functioning mop bucket being used to clean up oil spills. If you are getting the impression I am easy to convince to spend some money, you only need to speak with my friends and they will tell you that it is usually necessary to pry those dollars out of my wallet. This desire not to spend money foolishly is the exact reason I spent money to eliminate these ridiculous little problems that were really costing me much more money. I really view all these non-capital expenses as wise investments with great returns. The trick is that you must be involved with the details to understand the effects and the savings. Once again drawing on my earlier analogy related to home projects, when you buy a new, superior tool to replace an old, infuriating tool at home, you think of it as a great savings. It can be harder in the work environment if you are not involved in the task and only seeing it from the angle of signing a purchase order instead of really understanding the full impact. In the case of just signing purchase orders for equipment or tooling, you are also forced to assume that whoever proposed the solution is a good problem solver, that he or she has done some root-cause analysis, and this is really the best and least expensive solution to eliminate the problem at its "root" level.

6.9 COST JUSTIFYING A TEAM LEADER

One thing I still had left to do was justify (mostly to myself) through a cost–benefit analysis that changing Tom's role essentially to a team leader was a wise investment. Under Bob's direction, he had functioned more then half the time as a direct employee by running a machine; under my new plan, he was operating a machine less than 25 percent of the time. It is like I turned a somewhat direct employee into an indirect employee. Most of us have been brainwashed into thinking of direct employees as the real money makers and indirect employees mostly as overhead or burden cost. I had learned while working at Toyota that they did not have this direct versus indirect mentality or vocabulary. Most companies are content to let their employees intermittently perform most supplemental tasks related to their primary job. In manufacturing, this frequently involves getting your own materials, making small repairs, and basically handling other problems with little guidance or support and only asking for help when "you" have determined it is beyond your means. With this comes, most managers' unconscious acceptance of about a 70- to 80-percent uptime or effective operating time for their processes. On the other hand, Toyota targeted an uptime in the mid-ninety percentile, recognizing this could only be achieved if operators could remain at the workplace focused only on performing their direct tasks. They further understood that not every-body had the same problem-solving skills and it was better to have some-one trained and skilled to solve a problem at its root cause than having an individual operator band-aiding it. Toyota also knew these team leaders were critical to resolving sufficient problems, thereby allowing them to set up connected processes that operated with a respectable efficiency without significant WIP to hide problems.

Since most of my sales dollars—and therefore, profit—came from man-ufacturing parts on the machines (I provided other value-added services like assembly, deburring, painting, plating, etc., but they were not my bread and butter), I had to keep good parts coming off the machines. The best way to measure this and to assess the additional value being added by Tom as a full-time team leader was to compare the OEE before and after Tom had been in the position for a few months (and was likely to be having an influence). Previously, I indicated that when Tom and I first discussed his interest in taking over, we agreed to define the "team leader's respon-sibilities" before we made the change. The biggest reason for this was that I wanted to gather data on the current OEE level of each machine. I knew that if this number increased, it would be simple to convert it to dollars and compare it to Tom's wages.

Lean principle: ROI (return on investment) measures how effectively the firm uses its capital to generate profit and for machining processes this can be determined by measuring OEE (overall equipment effectiveness) improvements. I have found it best when companies convert what a 1-percent OEE improvement means in terms of productivity or potential profit for each machine or process. There is normally an investment made when improving OEE and that should be openly compared to the benefits. In my case, there was a cost in making Tom the team leader, though the ROI more than justified this cost.

After a few months of Tom assuming most of the responsibilities of the team leader (summarized in Appendix G), I compared the previous and the current OEEs. As it usually goes with data analysis, it took a little bit of interpretation, but basically I was seeing an average of a 7- to 8-percent OEE improvement on our critical machines after the first few months. A rough translation of this to dollars from our five main machines, which at the time were unfortunately only averaging thirty hours scheduled production per week, was

$$\frac{30 \text{ hours/}}{\text{week}} \times 5 \text{ machines} \times \frac{8\%}{\text{improvement}} = \frac{13 \text{ additional hours}}{\text{of production per week.}}$$

Multiply the additional thirteen hours per week that I gained (assume I was able to sell most of that time, which was realistic for us) and multiply by the average of $60 per hour for which we sold our machining time, for a total of an additional $780 per week of sales (with no other additional costs). This almost covered Tom's wages (without benefits). But remember: Tom also still ran a machine up to 25 percent of the time and performed many other value-added activities like functioning as the supervisor. It proves the correct decision was made and implies that you should not get hung up on the number of direct and indirect employees; instead, focus on the value each position is adding.

Key point: Do not be concerned with whether an operator is classified as a direct or indirect employee; instead, measure the value added and quantify the productivity through a measurement like OEE improvement.

Having a team leader in place allowed the operators and setup men to always be at their machines, which not only kept the machines producing more good parts, it also made it easier to manage. Now, if people were observed not to be at their machines, Tom or I would instead think of this as an abnormality, instead of just accepting that they were probably looking for material, looking for tools, or working on a problem. I shared my calculated savings with Tom, showing him the thirteen hours per week we had gained. Naturally, I wanted further improvements and asked for his input. In reality, he threw out a few small ideas to fill in the silence, but I think he had been too busy to give it much thought and seemed satisfied with what we had already achieved. I asked him to scribble down any ideas he came across during the next few weeks. Unfortunately, I had no suggestion plan to financially reward individual ideas; but, for the most part everyone was motivated. My team had not become so accustomed to overtime that their lifestyles depended on it, so they were not motivated to slow things down during their normal shift to create the need for overtime. This led to being open-minded in helping the company develop and implement improvement ideas. Also, I was too involved with the day-to-day operations to let wasted time go unnoticed, and we had a measurement where we continuously compared our actual times against either our quoted times or our previous build times.

The offer to increase pay in line with local industry standards was serving two purposes with relation to improved productivity: (1) it motivated the employees to better themselves by acquiring skills they were lacking, and (2) it benefited the company as I had a better trained workforce, which minimized manpower shortages (creating flexibility to better balance capacity in line with demand). With the planning boards being utilized, the operators could not slow down their work pace when they noticed the workload diminishing; instead, they would either work on my ongoing miscellaneous task list or cross-train—and since I paid based on abilities, this could put money in their pockets.

All of these ideas as well as others I have likely forgotten helped get more parts out in a shorter time, one of every manufacturing manager's goals.

6.10 CLOSING THE BOOKS BECOMES ANTICLIMACTICAL

The monthly closing of the books was becoming a non-event for us for a few reasons. We were monitoring productivity and material consumption so closely that we knew, job by job, whether or not we were profitable.

We also monitored weekly spend on indirect purchases, payroll, etc., and our accounts receivables were continuously updated. Further we had improved our accounting system to include accrued liabilities each month to cover items like equipment maintenance, new capital purchases, etc., so continuing to show profit was even a more significant event. Therefore, we had our fingers on the pulse in real time and the end of the month was as simple as tying up a few loose ends.

6.11 SUMMARY

- Managing each job visually is one way to judge things in smaller time intervals and react quicker, which is the backbone of lean.
- The measuring and adjusting phase of a changeover frequently accounts for over 50 percent of the total changeover time; therefore, it is critical to improve this part of the process.
- To minimize the time necessary for the adjustment phase of a changeover, quickly return the process to the point where you left off the last time (with a quality part). This requires documentation and reference markings.
- Profit sharing is often difficult, though a good suggestion system that rewards implemented ideas is a step in this direction.
- Team leaders are often cost-justified positions with very high rates of return. You should not dismiss this idea, especially on the basis of the position being considered that of an "indirect" employee.

7

Seeing the Administrative Processes from a New Angle

7.1 INTRODUCTION

I was on the downhill side of making it through my first year as a business owner. I would also like to call myself an entrepreneur because the word has a nice connotation. But, I have always felt this word describes someone who starts something from scratch, comes up with a new idea, or invents a new product. I had essentially taken a profitable business and further improved its profitability using the OSKKK (Observe, Standardize, Kaizen Flow & Process, Kaizen Equipment, and Kaizen Layout) strategy. Sales levels remained flat, which was tolerable only because the industry had been suffering a slowdown at the time and many of my competitors had seen sales decreases near 40 percent. Therefore, I deduced that maintaining my sales level in and of itself was an accomplishment while simultaneously learning the business and starting to improve profitability. I was also envisioning what would be possible during the good times within the semiconductor equipment manufacturing industry, plus I was starting to get a feel for where I might be able to generate sales in new markets.

I had just returned from Spain, where I tied the knot. Other than a few embarrassing moments with Spanish mispronunciations, including one in front of a packed church where I apparently said a word that came out sounding like a sexual organ, the wedding was great. This was the first time I had been completely away from the business for more than a week.

A key goal in buying the business was that robust processes would allow it to function without continuous on-site management. The former owner, Bob, had never been away from the business for more than a day or two. In my absence, Tom (the shop foreman) kept the shop floor running while Sandra managed the office. So, the fact that I was able to get away proved that standardization of the shop and office processes was paying off.

7.2 VISUALIZATION CONFRONTS OBTAINING INFORMATION EITHER FROM COMPUTERS OR IN MEETINGS

I needed to get refocused on growing the business, partially through its lean transformation. The OSKKK methodology was helping to reduce the time necessary both for office tasks and shop tasks, though the best way to profit from this lean transformation was to sell the additionally created capacity. The shop was functioning better, and with the few visuals I had in place I was able to quickly grasp where problems were being encountered when I was on the shop floor. I cannot tell you how many businesses I walk around in as a consultant and feel sympathy for the production managers. Although they are typically made aware of the larger catastrophic problems, there are typically no indicators as to what should be happening—no visual plan to establish "normal"—I am always forced to assume that these managers just get historical (after the fact) information in meetings and reports and cannot quickly discern "abnormal" conditions in the workplace. The first problem with using historical data is you have to be able to pay for previous problems and the related losses because by the time you learn about it in a meeting, "the money is already spent." Or, the manager is left to assume he or she would not have had any valuable input while the problem was unfolding. Second, you have to be content with only offering potential solutions for the smaller problems whenever they might occur again or learning about the large problems when they are already into their later phases.

Since I did not have the money to support unproductive machines or people and felt my problem solving was better than average, I wanted to know about the problems from the start. Most organizations have trouble defining exactly when they began encountering a "problem" and become accustomed to all the daily firefighting of the small issues. It is not always easy to determine when a task or process can be said to be in an "abnormal" condition. But to arrive at this point you must have clear boundaries for normal and abnormal, which are usually clarified through visualization. Most organizations feel they have so many "problems" that they can only respond to the big ones. So, everyone is left to his own devices to determine when a problem is big enough to call for a resolution. Consequently, most "abnormalities" are swept under the carpet. Therefore, throughout my tenure I spent considerable time defining and refining what we considered "abnormal" and then began processes to quantify and deal with the significant issues.

7.3 NOT ALLOWING EXCUSES FOR A LATE START

Another change that I made after putting Tom in the team leader position was to have him start preparations somewhere between fifteen and thirty minutes prior to the start of the shift. During this time, he made sure the air compressor was started, he turned on all machines and let the older CNC (Computer Numerical Control) machines warm up—it seemed that if the older machines were started with a "dummy" program, running the machine through movements similar to those for which they were first scheduled, they would hold better accuracy. I guess it is like people getting older, needing more time or coffee in the morning before we can function properly. Depending on the part the machine was to run, it often seemed that fifteen to twenty minutes of warm-up sure helped in quickly obtaining good parts. Tom was able to start a few machines and let them run simultaneously while he prepared other tools and materials. As a result, there was no need for the entire team to be delayed waiting for machines, looking for tools, waiting for compressed air, etc.

Lean principle: TPM (total productive maintenance) is a philosophy to integrate maintenance into the manufacturing process and involve machine operators. The goal of TPM is to eliminate downtime losses caused by equipment stoppages that are restricting the production of good parts within the cycle time. An indicator of how successful TPM is can be seen in the OEE measurement (overall equipment effectiveness). Although Tom handled many parts of our TPM program, the operators were also trained to be proactive in supporting it.

During this preparation time, Tom also put out any special measuring tools required, checked their calibration, and made sure the machines were in mechanical order and were topped off with coolant, lubricating oil, etc. He also stayed after the shift to perform anything he felt he would not have time for the next morning, like more involved TPM activities. This machine maintenance is part of the second "K" in the OSKKK strategy: Kaizening of equipment. I felt this was some of the best overtime money ever spent; there were rarely excuses for late starts other than those Tom encountered, like periodically having a machine or material problem. In the cases where he could not correct the problem, he would call me (prior to 6:00 a.m.) and ask what to do. My wife and I both dreaded those calls, but we agreed they were necessary since some of this saved time would end up increasing profitability. Also, we were working to permanently resolve these issues so the same ones would not be encountered again. This also helped in our measurements. For example, the hour-by-hour planning was simplified because we could arrange for production to start at full speed by 6:00 a.m. and did not have to factor in any "start-up time." I learned this technique during my training period at Toyota while they had me supervising an assembly line. All four team leaders on my line were paid to come in early and get everything prepared. Toyota knew it was more expensive *not* to do this; for example, to stop an entire line while waiting for one operator to warm up a sealing machine could cost thousands of dollars. I recommend this to most manufacturers; therefore, I want to highlight it.

Key point: Having a team leader or supervisor come in early to prepare all workstations is money well spent. It not only eliminates the excuses, it also lets you plan your production better. It is better to have one person paid a little overtime rather than to have the whole team milling around looking for tools, or waiting for a machine to warm up or a problem to be resolved.

7.4 SMALL BUSINESSES LOOK AT THE RECRUITING PROCESS DIFFERENTLY

I recall that during this period my attendance policy (a combined total of three times late or absent in a rolling ninety-day period meant dismissal) had caused us to lose two operators. As I ran ads to replace these operators, I received a lot of interest. It was not hard to find trained operators. Between the San Francisco Bay area and San José, there were nearly 3,000 machine shops, and a lot of trained operators already lived in the area. There was a lot of development work for high-tech industries that supported this, although most of these industries were also cyclical.

The basic rule I had learned from Bob's experience of running a small company for eighteen years was to avoid hiring those who had worked for large companies. This probably sounds harsh, but when speaking to other small business owners I found a general consensus on this point. The basic reasoning was that many employees in large companies were used to an easier working pace, and they thought about things like unions, cigarette breaks, and how they could get overtime. They were often not accustomed to being so directly tied to profitability and to handling the wider range of skills and tasks required by each employee in a small business. Naturally, generalizations are always dangerous, but I can attest to a different type of worker within the small shops. Having observed horrifying work habits and bending of the rules while working for General Motors, with certainty I can say that nothing similar happened in my little world. Tom and the other setup men I inherited with the business had always worked in small shops where you were expected to be a team player and do a fair day's work, handling everything from running a machine to sweeping the floor. And a small shop meant the boss was more involved and concerned with the results. Tom had actually worked for Bob for the previous sixteen or seventeen years so he had really been mentored and molded into a responsible and hard-working machinist.

During this period, I had made the mistake of overlooking this advice when we hired a setup man who had worked for a large machine shop in a semiconductor equipment manufacturer's plant—a "large company." Since big businesses frequently have larger training budgets and undertake more formal schooling, this man had achieved a great pedigree including many courses and certificates he had completed. With all his training and his experience in a large and varied machine shop, I really felt that he would bring a lot of insight and new ideas to my little world.

Because it is better to make such things clear during the interview to ensure you are not wasting each other's time, I explained the environment of our shop: We did not have a one-man-to-one-machine mentality, and a setup man might find himself operating more than one machine simultaneously and would even be required to take his turn at certain cleaning tasks. He indicated that he understood what I was telling him. After about two weeks, however, I began noticing his pace was much slower than the others and he was taking many additional breaks to have a smoke.

The deal breaker, so to speak, happened during his third week. His work habits—the slower pace and the cigarette breaks—and his know-it-all attitude were already getting on Tom's nerves. Then, Tom overheard him telling the others that a fifteen-minute morning break and a ten-minute afternoon break were really not enough—at his previous job, they had twenty minutes in the morning and twenty in the afternoon. So, I cut his last check and quickly walked him to the door. It is just that easy in a small business, especially within the first three months of a new hire's employment. The last thing I wanted was a bad apple poisoning a good team, and we all know it frequently only takes one.

More regulations apply to terminating an employee in larger companies, but I find the rules are not the reason many managers put up with the underperformers. The reason has to do with indecisiveness and a lack of documentation in the employee's file. Again, not documenting each case in which an employee is not performing as expected is either a problem in the process or a lack of disciplined management. Whether or not you have had similar experience or agree with this suggestion of a preference for hiring employees with their previous experience in only small- to medium-sized companies, I want to capture it as a key point.

Key point: When hiring, assuming you find candidates with similar backgrounds, the preference should go to those with previous experience in smaller firms as they are likely to have better working habits. Documentation of all instances when an employee is not meeting expectations is also key to successful termination of these workers.

7.5 FOCUSING TO IMPROVE THE OFFICE PROCESSES

While the shop was running well, I wanted to focus some more on our administrative processes. I felt I could further cut some costs and lead time, especially before soliciting work from new customers in other industries.

I wanted to better understand our processes and refine them, and then I could use these points to convince potential clients that they would want to work with us. I also wanted to look into getting some accreditations from regulatory organizations to distinguish us from others. The accreditation that I was fairly familiar with was ISO (International Standards Organization) 9001. ISO was not as critical for second- and third-tier suppliers in the industry we served, but it was becoming more common to see the larger machine and fabrication shops promoting it. (Most customers individually qualified us by having representatives from their quality departments periodically assess our quality systems during on-site visits.)

Lean principle: OSKKK is an ideal process for improving both the shop floor and the administrative processes. Deciding where to first focus your efforts (and limited resources) should be based on where the major bottleneck resides with respect to getting products out the door. Remember: a shop floor can only function effectively when all the support (administrative) processes provide the information and materials on time and tasks are performed in a timely manner.

One of the first areas I looked into with a view to administrative process improvement was the speed and ease of locating information, which I felt caused several bottlenecks. With only three of us working in the office, the lack of a computer network may not seem like a big issue, but without it there had been no easy way to share many tasks and have everyone working from the same data. For most of us, computer networks are a given, but when I took over the business all the PCs were stand-alone. I had finally gotten all the computers networked, including the shop computer which was further connected to all the newer CNCs, allowing programs to be sent back and forth throughout the entire network. I could even access the network remotely, and any programming I did at home could be sent directly to a machine. This had been completed for some time but since I had not begun cross-training or taking advantage of the network, few benefits had been realized and everyone still kept all the data they managed on their respective hard drives. Setting up a network is not worth discussing in more detail, but it is important to note that without properly organizing this "taken for granted" infrastructure, the optimizing of many tasks and information is significantly more limited.

The perfect time to organize data is when you start fresh with a big change like a new network. I knew any effort spent looking for information was costing me time and money. Because everyone was now networked, they needed training on how to properly store data files—it would have been counterproductive to lose time looking for data in a randomly created structure and file-naming system. For lean practitioners, this would be considered 5S—workplace organization—in the administration area. Since we had an eighteen-year history of everyone saving their files on their individual PCs, you can imagine how many variations of filing systems we had. I did not want to go back and sort out all those records, so we decided on some new rules going forward, pertinent to all new files and information being created. When the network was installed, we only put in one shared drive. We encouraged everyone to segregate all necessary and timely company information currently residing on their individual hard drive and to consider how it should be organized according to the new protocols.

The biggest problem we had was our outdated, DOS-based order-entry software (similar to an MRP [material requirements planning] system), which had not been designed for a network with multiple users simultaneously extracting and saving data. Using Microsoft Access, a friend of mine—one of those technology whiz kids who boggle your mind when explaining how things are working inside that box—was able to extract data from this antiquated software's database and ultimately move it to an Excel spreadsheet that everyone could access on the network. I frequently find when the central computer system cannot perform a task, an auxiliary Excel file is necessary until a better system can be found. Using Excel's tracking feature, we could all search for and extract the data we needed from the DOS program and understand who had made any changes. My friend even included an automatic update function so the data was frequently extracted from DOS and refreshed in Excel. Now, everyone had access to our orders and the material on order. We also brainstormed some other ground rules regarding how to store and retrieve new data.

7.6 PURCHASING IS A CRITICAL ADMINISTRATIVE FUNCTION TO LOOK TOWARD IMPROVING

One area where I first focused on taking advantage of the network's abilities was in the purchasing function. I wanted Sandra to move the purchasing data over to the new shared drive in the organized format I mentioned earlier. Sandra alone had been handling this data in the same way for so long that it begged improvement, mostly because no others had been involved (often we think our own process is OK until others bring in their ideas and—hopefully—open our minds to the possibilities).

Up to this point, the only change of any substance in purchasing had been the simple tracking system for late deliveries that I implemented during my first few weeks. Although most purchasing improvements center on price or inventory reductions (usually brought about through reducing the minimum order quantity or the lead time or both), I had only about an 18-percent material cost on the average, which we tightly controlled. And although I worked to provide sufficient time for the "buyers" to collect multiple supplier quotes, I was now more interested in establishing some standard stock material. I determined this as a necessity because, although our supplier lead time was only one to two days for cutting plate material to size, I was finding we periodically had problems obtaining the minimum order size and I was beginning to see more requests for even shorter lead times from our customers. A lot of these short lead times were not possible to achieve if we had to order our raw materials by 3:00 p.m. to receive them the next day or the day after that. Therefore, keeping some "strategic" inventory would allow us to quote on those really-short-lead-time RFQs (request for quotations) if they could be cut from an on-hand stock of standard bars or sheets of material.

I provided Sandra with the sizes of fourteen different bar stocks and sheet materials I wanted to keep in stock and told her to start with a maximum of four pieces and minimum of two pieces for each of the articles. I also asked her to think about a simple reorder system. Naturally, a lean practitioner would think in terms of a Kanban system; however, I did not want to *tell* Sandra how to redesign the reorder system. Instead, I wanted to hear her ideas and then guide her in the right direction. She basically nailed the Kanban concept with her suggestion: somebody from the shop would notify her every time a complete bar was consumed, and when two of any type were consumed, she would order more (the lead time for these sheets and bars ranged from one to three days). I pointed out we should have the system standardized in case she was on vacation or the guys in the shop forgot to let her know. (Mentioning the need for vacation is always a good way to get people to buy into documentation or standardization. Knowing someone else can handle a specific task allows the person who usually performs it to take their vacation). We agreed to attach a simple (Kanban) card to each bar; as the shop guys finished a bar, they would bring the card to Sandra and she could track it on the wall with predetermined slots for the various cards. I further indicated that she needed to monitor (on the same board where the cards were hanging) how often we reordered, how often we were short, or how often we immediately required more of a particular material. My maximum of four, minimum of two had been just a lazy man's guess as a starting point, but with a little thought and data she could likely adjust that up or down for each material. I further asked her to monitor other typical materials she frequently ordered and to consider stocking some of those. This also helped reduce the administration time and effort in purchasing since orders for stock materials can be grouped together on a "blanket purchase order" and release against it instead of having to generate separate orders.

Lean principle: *Kanban is a Japanese word that essentially means a system of notification to replenish what has been consumed. This is in contrast to MRP, which uses forecasts and lead times (looking forward) to anticipate what the customer will likely consume, and advises on ordering materials and planning internal production. Unless you have accurate forecasts that do not exist in made-to-order businesses, replenishment style reordering is superior to MRP order systems. Kanban replenishment is a better option for "runner" materials (discussed in Chapter 6) and others should only be purchased or manufactured according to the customer's orders.*

You might think it is crazy for a lean guy to suggest new or additional items to stock in the raw material inventory in what is essentially a made-to-order business. But I knew that although some of our customers were price sensitive, the priority periodically became the lead time. In that case, a lead time of two to three days could take me out of the ball game on a potentially high-margin order. I would also like to clarify there is a big difference between unplanned, unmonitored, and unnecessary inventory and what I call "strategic" inventory, which is determined as necessary and is kept at a minimum by continually monitoring and adjusting it.

Lean principle: *Inventory is a necessity to compensate for the differences in the lead times and minimum order sizes required by customers and the lead times and minimum purchase quantities offered by suppliers (or the internal supplying processes). If the customer's desired lead time is shorter than the supplier's (or supplying processes), it is necessary to hold enough inventory to compensate for the difference (until you can improve the supplier's lead time). This was becoming the case for us as the customers demanded shorter lead times to compete in this profitable market segment. The inverse is also true: When the customer's lead time is longer than the supplier's, no inventory is required and you can either buy or build to order. When the inventory is there because you have planned around this and have worked to further reduce this difference in lead times, I like to call it "strategic" inventory so it can be distinguished from unplanned or unnecessary inventory.*

When organizations have significant capital tied up in inventory (which was not our case) and want to work to reduce this, not only do they need to involve the right people and departments (one of which is purchasing), they also need to use the proper measurements to focus their improvements on the root causes of the problem. Remember: inventory is most notably the result of two factors—lead time and minimum order size (accuracy of forecasts also has a strong influence). So, measurement should reflect these influences. Some organizations still refer to inventory in financial terms (i.e., "We currently have $500,000 of inventory"), which makes it difficult to judge whether there is too much and on which products to focus. Others have moved to referencing "inventory turns," which is annualized cost of goods sold/average inventory. However, the correct lean measurement is DSI (days supply of inventory, also called days sales of inventory). DSI is the converse of inventory turns but, because the units are in days, it can be directly compared to the lead time (which is also in days) for the parts involved and it becomes easy to judge whether you have too much or too little.

For example, if someone tells you that you have a DSI of twenty-five days (meaning, under normal usage you have a twenty-five-day supply on hand for that part), and you know the lead time to either purchase or manufacture the part is four days, then you have too much inventory and your target should be four days plus possibly some safety stock.

Lean principle:

$$\frac{Days\ supply\ of\ inventory\ or\ days}{sales\ of\ inventory\ (DSI)} = \frac{average\ inventory/}{cost\ of\ goods\ sold} \times 365.$$

Or, another way to look at it:

$$DSI = average\ inventory/cost\ of\ goods\ sold\ per\ day,$$

which is the converse of inventory turns but a much better measurement because the units are in days and can be compared to lead time, one of the most influential reasons for inventory. Many organizations struggling to reduce inventory do not clearly understand the reason for it and the factors influencing it. But if you know your lead times for the various part numbers and compare those to the DSI, you can have a focused discussion on what is a reasonable target for that inventory (by specific part number) and what can be done about the lead time to further drive improvements. This also links to the DSO (day sales outstanding) measurement (discussed in Chapter 3). Remember: if you could order a minimum of one piece for every part number (without cost implications) and have it the next day, there would be little need for any inventory.

Since I arrived at the stage in my lean transformation that I viewed the supporting processes from the front office as currently generating the most significant bottlenecks, I was to the point in my OSKKK strategy of working on "Kaizening Flow & Processes" in the office. Another opportunity in the front office was to train Andrea, the office assistant, to handle the purchasing (and minimize delays to our customers) when Sandra was on vacation or sick. This requirement to train someone else on the purchasing process had been previously identified on our cross-training matrix, as shown in Appendix H. As a starting point, I provided Andrea with the documentation I had made up while I was being trained by Bob, and I asked her to further detail this while she was being trained and complete any steps I had missed. Again, there is no better time to document or improve the existing written procedures than when someone is learning the process.

I was also seeing RFQs involving materials for which we had little or no previous experience. Determining how to cut and work with each material was important in the shop, but in the office it was critical that various materials could be purchased at a reasonable price with a short lead time. I had asked Sandra to document the available suppliers and pertinent information for each material. I worked with her to further develop this with a more refined Excel sheet in which we could search for primary and secondary material descriptions as well as vendor, lead time, and price. I also wanted her to continue adding information on any new materials that were being requested, whether or not we received the order. It would always be good for future reference, and building a valuable material database helped to justify the lost time on quotes for which we did not receive an order.

7.7 UNSUCCESSFUL AT SIGNIFICANTLY REDUCING THE TIME NECESSARY FOR QUOTATIONS

Quoting was another area that posed some challenges in terms of productivity. In particular, the significant amount of time that was necessary for putting together some quotes (calculating setup and run times, specifying and quoting material) could be reduced or eliminated if a similar quote that had been previously prepared could be located quickly. Bear in mind, customers periodically asked for the same or similar parts to be quoted. So, a reference system to locate quotations would be a great benefit if it was quick and simple. Like a lot of "database"-type projects, this begged the typical question of how much detail was required for quick access to past quotations. I had to think about the expected outcomes and the expected savings. At that time, our system was only to file a hard copy of the quote by customer with any attached documentation. Once the quotation file for a particular customer got too thick, it was put on my desk to sort through the old quotes and decide whether any were worth keeping, on the chance we might still receive the order. Most of our business was represented by short lead times, and the majority of quotes for which we did not receive an order within one to two weeks were lost opportunities.

The time and (potentially) money to set up this database were not the only considerations. The time to populate it with each quote and the time to search through former quotes for all RFQs with the probability of no match being found were highly likely, which would mean we would have wasted effort on both the inputting and searching. Naturally, this needs to balance against the time savings once a similar quote was found and against how often this was likely to happen. I came to the conclusion that it would be less than 10 percent of the time when we built a part similar enough to share quality information between the previous quotation and the new request for quotation. Therefore, Sandra and I decided to abandon this idea and leave that part of the quoting system as it was. I think she was relieved that she was not going to inherit the task of entering all this data for each quotation into the computer—we frequently quoted between three and fifteen part numbers per day, so there would have been a lot of data entry.

However, I still wanted to make one simple change that involved a more systematic follow-up on quotations for which we did not receive an order. We currently did it on a random basis, and I wanted a meaningful system that could help to improve the quoting process without too frequently contacting the customer's purchasing agents for feedback (after all, how often would *you* want to explain to suppliers why they did not get their order). I also figured that periodically it might provide a second opportunity to quote a portion of the order if we had come close or the buyer preferred to work with us, etc. I thought we could somehow designate for follow-up only the critical quotes that we felt were either our type of part or ones in which we had put a lot of effort. Sandra could also keep track of our hit rate with various customers, and where we had a low rate on receiving orders, she could then choose a few quotations to follow up on and feed back her thoughts to me and Jake (the programmer/estimator) about why we had not received an order. So, Jake and I began marking quotes we thought would be good candidates for follow-up. Sandra noted on her standardized work calendar that on Wednesdays she should go through the quote files and determine any follow-up to be made based on customers with low hit rates.

You might be wondering what a "standardized work calendar" is. It is a simple monthly calendar for each person in the office to mark periodic tasks for which he or she is responsible and when to follow up. Often, people plan to follow up or monitor something each week but they get busy and forget. When consulting, I frequently ask questions like "How often do you confirm the suppliers on-time delivery?" and a typical response (after a long and painful pause) is "More or less every other week." Which really means rarely, if ever. I did not want that to happen; so, my two administrative employees and I each hung a calendar near our desks, showing the day on which we planned to perform periodic (usually weekly or monthly) tasks. Then, we would mark off each task as it was completed. Naturally, some tasks fell behind a day or two; much longer than that, and I was bound to take notice and ask about it. The hardest part of this was to lead by example, as I frequently got busy and missed a task or two myself. Because I had made it one of my weekly tasks to review the other two calendars, I had to get my own things in order before pointing out anyone else's shortcomings.

Lean principle: Standardized work for managers is really a critical element of managing within the PDCA (Plan, Do, Check, Act) cycle. It puts some structure into everyone's week so they don't get busy putting out fires and forget the weekly/monthly monitoring/follow-up that they should be committed to. Usually, it is best to visually display the items to be followed up on and when they will be done so everyone is held to the schedule. Some managers like to set up this management audit on a random schedule so the various departments do not know when a review will take place and must keep everything up to date at all times, though this can cause resentment.

7.8 5S FOR SHARED COMPUTER DRIVES AND FILES

Returning to transferring all pertinent data to the network drive instead of going back through eighteen years of data on individuals PCs: We decided to start immediately creating most new data files on the network. Files that were determined to be "common" and relevant were also moved to the network drive. I had implemented a standard convention for naming and locating the directories and the files and I had established maximum levels of subdirectories, etc. I was not sharp enough to understand both our current and future storage requirements on the shared drive; instead, all my guidelines were open to change and adaptation but only after we tried the current suggestion and later agreed on the need to modify or adapt it. No two people will ever file something the same way when there is no preexisting system; therefore, others will lose time trying to locate items or finally give up and ask. My system was not perfect but, because of certain rules pertaining to the title of the directory or file (how things were worded, word order, numbering, date formats, etc.), the search function became a much more applicable tool.

I was hoping that all the ideas I was suggesting would encourage others to suggest various improvements, and slowly they began throwing out more of their own ideas. Since it is not reasonable or possible to implement all suggestions, I had to explain why certain ones were worth doing in the near term and why others were not feasible or did not seem to have enough benefit to offset the implementation costs. I was also hoping to develop "Kaizen eyes," not only in the shop floor team but also among the office personnel, and I believed from the suggestions I was getting, they were starting to see the waste within many of the processes.

7.9 OUTSIDE QUALITY ACCREDITATION

One other item I was determined to work on during this time period was to receive a quality accreditation from an outside source to help in being recognized by larger organizations as a qualified supplier. Most quality departments of the larger customers for which I was currently manufacturing parts had different processes in place to certify their suppliers. Someone from the quality team would typically audit our processes at various time intervals to ensure we had robust processes in place to meet their quality standards. We appeared able to meet their various requirements, but I also wanted to hold an externally assessed accreditation to use as a marketing tool.

My priority was accreditation for quality standards, not for environmental or health and safety standards. The ISO was what I was most familiar with and was mainstream when I had been in the automobile industry. As I started down the ISO path, I recall it was relatively inexpensive to download the manuals for the ISO 9001 (the quality accreditation) for our industry. The manuals contained surprisingly little direction on specifically what was required. The basic guide was to define the company's processes for either X, Y, or Z, and then ensure they were robust and being adhered to. When I looked into the cost of having an auditor come to our plant for review and accreditation, I was shocked. I do not recall the exact cost but it became apparent why so few small companies pursued it. I decided instead that the quality systems we already had in place only needed some small tweaks to meet the requirements spelled out in the ISO's manuals. So, we put the additional process steps and documentation in place and, instead of telling our customers we were "ISO 9001 accredited," I mentioned we were "ISO 9001 compliant." A bit of a play on words, but we were following the guidelines. We just had not spent the money for the actual accreditation.

7.10 SUMMARY

- A team leader should be brought in prior to the start of the shift to ensure all materials, information, tooling, programs, documentation, etc., have been prepared, so there are no excuses for late starts and planning can expect a productive first hour with no abnormalities encountered.
- It is worth considering where potential employees have previously worked and whether those companies are known to be lax in their policies (sometimes this is influenced by company size).
- Administrative process improvement should follow the OSKKK strategy and if there is no apparent bottleneck process, purchasing is always a good place to begin, especially for companies with a high purchasing spend.
- "Strategic" inventory is necessary when the expected customer lead times are shorter than the supplier lead times (or manufacturing lead times). In these cases, a replenishment system (Kanban) can be utilized for regularly repeating "runner" parts (also known as "A" parts in the context of ABC analysis).
- Standardized work for managers should be a visualized plan of their commitments to monitoring/follow-up. This is a necessary step of the PDCA cycle, especially in organizations consumed with firefighting.

8

Moving the Business

8.1 INDUSTRYWIDE DOWNTURN

The semiconductor equipment industry continued through one of its cyclical slowdowns. Of my seven major customers, five had noticeably slowed. Up to this point, I had only been able to diversify with one new customer in the medical device industry—a contrast to the semiconductor equipment industry in that it appeared less cyclical and price-sensitive. This industry was a reasonable size in the Bay Area so I had decided to pursue new customers in this sector. I had built about eight different parts for the new customer and only one had repeated, for a total of nine orders. It was a start but not enough to offset the effects of a major downturn in the semiconductor equipment industry.

Unfortunately, I had to let one of my operators go because even after cutting the work week to thirty-five hours, there was not enough work for everyone. One of the great lean ideologies is the value of the employees and the importance of offering them job security. But I had to face the reality that I did not see much changing in the near term. In choosing whom to let go, I had more freedom in this small, not strongly regulated business than I would have had in a large organization. So my decision was strongly influenced by the employee's ability to add value—his skills and attitude—and not based on seniority. While it is true that the operator I let go had the least seniority at my shop and the least experience in the industry, he also had the least abilities, a mediocre attitude, and, in my opinion, not much potential to be further developed.

I now find many firms—especially large ones and those in countries that are strong in protecting job security—utilizing a strategy of employing some temporary or subcontracted workers in most areas of the business to create flexibility with their capacity and to help in getting around rigid regulations. This is one way to create some flexibility within more rigidly regulated industries, allowing you to follow the business cycles. But it is never ideal because a lot of training and cost is invested in temps and then you pay the price when either there is a slowdown of work or they decide to leave for better opportunities. Also, you pay an hourly premium for temps, which could be rationalized in the short term if you hire people through agencies as a screening process for existing openings. But when you use temps to create flexibility, it usually becomes more long term and therefore more costly. There is no easy answer but, hopefully, cross-training and flexibility with your permanent workforce allows you to adjust to some of the smaller cyclical swings with flexible hours, overtime, and helping each other (this should be visualized by the cross-training matrix shown in Appendix H). In a short-lead-time business like mine, where all parts are made to a customer's order, there is little flexibility in planning or leveling the schedule; therefore, lots of flexibility in the workforce is needed to absorb these peaks and troughs in workload.

8.2 BACKGROUND FOR MOVING THE BUSINESS AT THIS POINT IN TIME

While Bob (the former owner) and I were negotiating the sale of the business, a new investor had bought the building in which Bob leased space. The new building owner had increased the rent so dramatically that Bob was worried it would affect the sale. So, he prepaid the rental increase for a one-year period to ensure the sale went through and to smooth the transition. I had accepted this and hoped that by the end of the first year the new landlord would realize he was overpriced in the market and would be willing to negotiate a reasonable contract with me due to experiencing sufficient vacancies. However, when the year was up, the building was about half vacant but he would not budge on the rent. So, with the current slowdown in our workload and the new layout opportunities a move offered, I figured it was not a bad time to shop around.

Our layout at that time was a hodgepodge resulting from years of growth by acquiring various machines and placing them wherever there was space available. Does this sound familiar? I could not go too far because my employees all lived close by and did not want to travel. And, my customers wanted us close by to maintain the high level of service and short lead times. They were accustomed to having someone there right away to pick up special drawings they needed quotes for, or they wanted to review some drawings with Jake (the programmer/estimator) or me, or they wanted to meet to discuss a quality concern.

Lean principle: In OSKKK (Observe, Standardize, Kaizen Flow & Process, Kaizen Equipment, and Kaizen Layout), Kaizening the layout is reserved as a final improvement step predominantly because many other improvements require little to no capital while yielding better returns on investment (ROIs). Though we were far from arriving at the last "K" during our first cycle through OSKKK, the business case to relocate created the opportunity for Kaizening our layout. Keep in mind that OSKKK is not a one-off process; rather, it is a continuous loop.

Key point: Any type of slowdown where employees have additional time available often represents an opportunity to work on improvements that you might otherwise be too busy to consider.

For all these strategic (or large) decisions like moving the business, I was still using my father as an advisor. Having held executive positions in companies as well as owning his own business, he had a pragmatic and logical approach. Also, having invested in my company, he had every right to offer his advice on strategic decisions like this. He was in complete agreement that it was the right thing to do and should not affect the customers if done correctly. Naturally, it is great to bounce ideas off someone you trust and who has the right background.

The search took only a few weeks and we located some industrial space in San José, only about fifteen minutes from our current location and well-centered between our customers. The price was actually less than the portion of the rent we had been paying during the previous year (remember: Bob had already subsidized the rental increase for one year). It was 250 square feet smaller than our current location, which was fine with me. I figured even with any expansion I would likely be considering we could make it work. Also, the unit directly adjacent to the one available for lease (along its south side) was being utilized for storage by one of the other businesses within this multi-unit building, and they agreed to consider renting part of the space to me for future expansion. Ironically, the adjacent business along the north side was a plating shop that handled many of the processes we currently outsourced (anodizing, alodine, passivating, etc.)—talk about a lead-time and handling improvement. The other real advantage was the previous tenant had also been a machining business who had left all the power lines, transformers, and air lines in place. The icing on the cake was the office was air-conditioned, which was not the case in our current office.

8.3 CREATING A NEW LAYOUT FROM A BLANK CANVAS

Before involving the team in the layout discussion, I wanted to ensure everyone was OK with the proposed new location. I had already taken Tom (the shop foreman) to the new site to ensure it would not greatly affect his commute. The team studied a map of the location: For some, it was closer to home. For others, it was a little longer drive. But, everyone was on board.

Planning a move and working on a new layout was right up my alley. Naturally, I wanted a lean layout—great material flow, visualized flow and visual management, reduced walking, more flexibility of tasks to be shared between the operators, keeping bottleneck processes out in the open, etc. I involved Tom and Jake in first reviewing my layout proposals and then received input from the others.

I wrote out a list of what I believed were the critical considerations (naturally based on lean principles), then included three proposals with material flow lines drawn in to get the thinking started. My list of critical considerations included the previously mentioned ideas as well as not creating islands of workers but instead incorporating work cells, the shortest flow path for large parts and frequently utilized process steps, the critical and bottleneck processes being visible from the main aisle, and finally the shared processes and resources to be centralized (certain measuring equipment, tumblers, tooling, and the programmer's desk as he frequently supported program changes and improvements).

When considering layout options bear in mind how each operator will spend his time, especially on CNCs (Computer Numerical Control) or other machines with automated cycle times, try to balance the machine's cycle time with the worker's available time. If the worker cannot perform another task (and is forced to wait on the machine), then leave out some small step of the machine's cycle and make this a secondary operation on a manual machine to fill the worker's time, thereby also shorting the machine's cycle time thus increasing machine capacity. This type of operator work balance should also be taken into account in any layout proposal (only completing it for typical parts or "runners") or when purchasing new equipment.

Lean principle: When proposing a new layout (or a layout change), it is always necessary to draw in the major flow lines. This is critical in evaluating layout options (of which there should be at least three proposals). Even if you are familiar with the processes, put in the flow lines. It is best to use thick lines for frequent trips or large/heavy materials. If your layout looks like a plate of spaghetti—especially filled with lots of long, thick lines—try another option.

I firmly believe that any manufacturing plant layout diagram that doesn't include the major flow lines is a waste of paper. Even if you are experienced in working with layouts, you want to clearly see and analyze the flow. Bottlenecks and heavily utilized processes should be well-marked on a layout, and process steps that often flow in sequence can be marked with the same color, thereby highlighting poor layouts when one color spreads throughout the entire layout. You can get pretty fancy with flow lines incorporating different colors for different types of products, thicker lines representing the movement of heavy materials or more frequent movements, and thin lines representing small parts or less frequent trips. When the flow lines and these other criteria are drawn in, you can more easily compare layout options.

Naturally, you must force yourself to draw up multiple options. At Toyota, they liked to encourage four to five different proposals. The first one or two are easy; then, you start stretching yourself and become creative. I guess I was a little lazy with only three, but I figured we would settle on some combination or adaptation of the ideas in front of us.

Key point: When creating any layout proposal, always draw in the major flow lines and mark up other considerations like bottleneck processes, U-cells, highlighting of frequently utilized processes, minimum space for WIP (work In process), and overall optimization of square footage.

8.4 A NONDISRUPTIVE MOVE

We needed to work on a plan for a nondisruptive move that would not affect our production schedule. Fortunately for the move and unfortunately for our profitability, we were suffering through a slow time in the industry. We had one thing in our favor: We had very flexible machines, many of which had similar capabilities allowing a flexible move sequence. Conceptually, we could move a machine or two and start up production at the new location while continuing to operate the remaining machines at our existing shop. An electrician could prep all the wiring and connections prior to moving each machine. Renting a second compressor and making a temporary connection into the existing air lines was also fairly simple. Therefore, we could move one or two machines and their related tooling, stabilize them and get them back into production before moving the next machine, essentially operating the two shops simultaneously. Tom could be based at the new location while I handled "regular business" (at least as regular as you can make it during a move) and hold down the fort at our old shop.

After receiving three quotes from equipment movers, we had made the choice and starting looking at the timetable. The movers figured they could easily move the majority of the equipment during four days, finishing over the weekend, during which we could move the office and remaining material, tooling, and odds and ends. So that was the plan. We went with a "seamless transition."

We had worked through the layout options and arrived at a compromised plan—as you know, every time you make a new layout, there is a compromise between various advantages and disadvantages, and rarely are there only advantages making it an easy and clear choice. We had a somewhat long, narrow building with the office and shipping/receiving at the front, so we were able to basically form a long thin "U" with a few smaller cells incorporated into it. We had only one loading dock to be used for both shipping and receiving in the new location (not the best layout but I think it is typical in smaller plants), so our options regarding ideal flow were limited. Our larger CNCs, which handled the larger material, would be located closer to the shipping/receiving area. Shown in Appendix I is a partial view of the relocated CNCs; you can see one side of the CNC machining area's "U" cell (essentially forming an "L" with some of the machines). Other processes would basically follow the process flow in as close to a large "U" shape as possible, with the start and end points meeting near the shipping/receiving area. Following the flow of our typical process steps: after our receiving inspection benches was the tumbler room, where the material was cleaned and tumbled prior to going on the machines, and again after the final machining process, prior to going to outside contractors for plating or painting, then parts were moved onto the various machines. If assembly was involved, it was usually after any plating or painting (outsourced processes), so we located the small assembly benches and equipment near shipping. This made sense because after assembly the parts were packaged and shipped to the customers.

Lean principle: The third "K" in OSKKK, Kaizening the Layout, has the following sub-steps:

- *Ensure previous steps of OSKKK have been worked on before rearranging layout (there is no point in relocating wasteful processes).*
- *Collect data: process flows, capabilities, new products, bottlenecks, OEE (overall equipment effectiveness), value stream maps, information flow, etc.*
- *Compile a minimum of three layout proposals, all showing flow arrows and complete correlation matrixes.**
- *Review new layouts to measure against all lean principles and remove non-value-added layouts to justify costs.*

---

* Refer to *Made to Order Lean: Excelling in a High Mix, Low Volume Environment* by Greg Lane for additional information.

- *Work to improve the man/machine/materials ratio.*
- *Consider new machinery only after working to improve existing machines and incorporating all learnings into specifications for new machinery.*
- *Simulate the new layout. either marking the floor (for existing layouts) or with cardboard mock-ups of the equipment (for new processes).*

From a visual standpoint, this was going to work fairly well as we could walk down the middle of the "U" and clearly understand the status through the continuously updated day-by-hour or planning boards placed on all critical machines. Naturally, the "U" shape also lent itself to flexibility for the operators to share work. We did not have a one-man-to-one-machine mentality and as we frequently had longer cycle times in the range of ten minutes to more than one hour, one man could load and deburr parts from more than one machine simultaneously. Since the longer run times were typically on the larger machines, we made more or less a mini "U" cell out of those. This left flexibility to share tasks, not only between the larger machines but basically across the entire shop (the whole shop was not that large—a man could walk through all processes within about a minute). We put the shop office basically in the center of the "U," ensuring it did not block the view (everyone in the room had visual contact with one another). In the new layout, we planned no walls for the shop office; just the programming area and common/critical measuring tools were located there with everything out in the open. Those of you thinking about noise and distractions while programming because you would be surrounded by loud machines, not to worry; a good pair of industrial headphones to block noise and a big screen to work from would allow Jake to enter his own little world of concentration.

8.5 SIMULATING THE NEW LAYOUT

Once we had settled upon our new layout, we marked out everything on the floor at the new site. This was not only to help the equipment movers to know where things went, it also allowed us to simulate and imagine the new environment in actual scale instead of just reviewing it on paper. We made a few small changes, mostly moving things a few inches one way or the other. I have found that you can get away with just marking out the floor to get a proportional feel for the existing processes; however, when you are developing new processes, you must work in three dimensions to simulate as much as possible. This is best done through cardboard mock-ups. Naturally, you try to do this as close to scale as possible and then simulate the actions and movements to take place within the processes.

Key point: On the floor of the area you will be moving an existing process to, mark out the new layout (that was developed on paper) so that you get a feel by simulating activities. If you are developing a layout for a new product, you should simulate this with three-dimensional cardboard mock-ups (made to scale) before agreeing on the equipment to purchase and the new layout. Remember: always consider the operators' work balance when making a new layout proposal and locate equipment in work cells that will best balance the machine's and operator's time.

One other point was that all of the shop services (electrical, air, data cables) in the new location came from overhead as is common or at least desirable in new construction. (The exception is when you have cranes or other machines moving overhead that do not permit this; but, this was not our case.) This leaves considerable flexibility for future layout changes, especially if you have the ability to install some extra wire and air lines that can be coiled up for the future. We preinstalled a few extra feet of flexible air line at all the air drops, then coiled and attached it to the hard piping. I also had the electrician put about fifteen to twenty feet of extra wire at each electrical drop, coiling it and attaching it to the conduit. The goal was no conduit directly to the machines, and so far the local electrical codes were allowing us to get away with it. This would not only leave us some breathing room if we didn't get it right, it would also leave a lot of options open for continuous improvement and expanding the business.

8.6 INTRODUCING PROCEDURAL CHANGES DURING THE MOVE

Another great opportunity to take advantage of when moving to a new location is to change any work practices or standardized work you have identified that necessitates improving. It might appear I was jumping from "Kaizening the Layout"—the final OSKKK step—back to "Standardization"—the second step. But remember: OSKKK follows an endless loop of continuous improvement. The first day an existing team member must drive to a new work location, he or she is expecting some new experiences and is as open-minded as that individual will ever be. I felt my team was relatively open to new ideas, and this point was constantly driven home with the frequency of changes taking place over the past year and a half. They were starting to understand what "continuous improvement" meant, but I still wanted to take advantage of this opportunity to introduce some additional changes. I first wrote down a few possible changes to be introduced and then invited Tom to brainstorm with me. The list included ideas like everyone wearing new shop aprons that contained pockets for standard tooling (e.g., deburring tools, Allen wrenches, dimensional pocket reference guides) and anything else that the operators did not like to share or leave at the workstations but required continuously. Providing everyone with all necessary tooling also helped to reinforce the idea that all team members were responsible for deburring and other tasks. Marking the floor for items like "current job" and "material for next job" was helpful as well as introducing a lot of workplace organization (5S).

When moving to a new location, it is also a good time to introduce change within the procedures; in other words, any new work standards should be incorporated as part of the move. One of the critical wastes I continued to observe (even after Tom was in the team leader position) that necessitated a change was the operators were still walking away from their machines to perform non-cyclical tasks like emptying chip bins, tumbling material whenever they felt they had sufficient parts to fill a tumbler, or performing random measurement checks that required centralized instruments in the shop's office, etc. If the cycle times were long enough that they could do this without the machine stopping and waiting, I saw no problem. But, if there was no way to reduce or improve the time the task required, then I did not want the machine waiting; instead, I wanted the team leader to handle it. Remember: you always want things balanced, but it is better to have the man waiting a few seconds for the machine than to have the machine stopped and waiting for the man. If Tom was too busy, then Jake could handle it if he was not in the middle of programming. As we started out in our new shop, I wanted to reinforce that we were all there to keep the machines running and every minute we were not "cutting chips" and making good parts was time (and money) lost. Again, this is measured by OEE. There were a few other procedural changes I introduced, but those discussed here were representative of the critical ones.

Key point: A great time to introduce changes to processes or to introduce new processes you want implemented is when making layout changes. It is the perfect time to start workplace organization (5S), and people are more accepting of changes at this point.

8.7 USING A MAJOR EVENT TO INTRODUCE CHANGE IN THE OFFICE

This concept of introducing new procedures during a transformation or big event is not unique to the shop floor. It also applies to the office. The big change for our office regarding the layout was that we were going to institute an open office. I would now be located closest to the door to the shop floor (as I was back and forth most frequently). The office assistant would be next in line with access to the shop floor as she was frequently organizing the daily shipping and performing some part-marking and packaging. Sandra (the office manager) was placed closest to the front entrance and furthest from the shop as she spent most of her time handling the extreme level of administrative processes that are associated with a small business and she also dealt with visitors. We also looked at where various office hardware (printers, faxes, copy machines) were located, based on who used them more frequently and where they were less distracting. Just as with the shop-floor layout, we also ensured everything was networked and that all new information was now being put on the network drive. Some office visualization boards were also installed, so available machine capacity (updated daily) was visible when speaking to customers. Other boards included a priority board and a vacation planning board. We also had a place for our skills matrix, which showed the current cross-training status and our plan going forward. Many of these visual improvements were duplicated in the shop office (for the shop personnel), although without walls it was a bit more difficult to find a location to hang these boards.

> **Lean principle:** *Lean office layouts are a consideration of the relationship between three factors: the flow of work through various departments, the employees, and the equipment. The primary consideration should be given to workflow and achieving straight lines for the most frequent processes without backtracking or crisscrossing. This can be further linked to aligning employees (or departments) with the value streams they support. An example from manufacturing is placing the responsible supervisor, purchaser, planner, and engineer for a particular family of products together in a small office in the middle of the production area; it will be hard to point fingers if everyone sits together resolving the daily issues.*

Overall, our move went smoothly, and after a hectic weekend we were up and running Monday with everyone in the new location. Because we kept all our existing phone numbers we had not affected our customers with a lapse in communication or on-time delivery issues. Naturally, we sent out a notice about our new location beforehand as we did not want to catch anyone off guard as it might appear we were doing something detrimental to our customers. Later, we could work through changing the mailing addresses with all customers and suppliers, but for the time being we were focusing on the orders at hand and maintaining our near-perfect on-time delivery record.

Reflecting on the move, I think it was successful because we worked hard planning and preparing many weeks beforehand. We also talked it up as a positive and made sure to clearly explain the purpose and advantages behind the changes being introduced. I also openly brought up the perceived disadvantages; for example, now the operators would be spending more time in front of their machines instead of going to the tumblers and measuring areas (as this is frequently viewed as job enhancement by having a wider range of responsibilities). I always spoke openly and worked to clarify how the advantages outweighed the disadvantages and that all improvements helped with job security, not guaranteeing it but keeping us ahead of the competition. I have witnessed a few other organizations' very chaotic relocations. I think traditionally the majority of the people are so involved with their day-to-day tasks prior to a move that by the time they sat to think through the implications, it was too late to properly plan and there was only time to react.

Now I really felt like the company's owner. The new location was created by me and my team, and little of Bob's presence was felt there. I just needed to expand into new markets and survive the latest slowdown in the semiconductor equipment industry. In this case, the move had served many purposes. It had not only reduced our fixed overhead (by reducing our monthly rent), it also allowed us to work in an improved layout that was sure to save money each day with less movement of people and material. We were also closer to our supply base and could now shorten our lead times for outsourced services like plating and painting. I could more easily visually manage the shop and, if we expanded in the future, we could also grow into the adjacent storage area. And the air conditioned office was a critical factor and a productivity improvement for those working there (after all, temperatures in California are frequently warm).

8.8 SUMMARY

- Although the OSKKK strategy relegates Kaizening the layout to the final step because of the cost implications, there are times relocation is preempted for economic or market reasons, determining a different sequence in an implementation strategy. Since OSKKK is a continuous improvement loop, you will be returning to work on the other Kaizen steps as you follow the endless cycle through this strategy.
- Flow is a critical element in any shop-floor or office layout and all layout diagrams should include flow arrows.
- Simulation—either through marking the floor when relocating existing processes or mocking up scaled cardboard three-dimensional machines/processes for new layouts—should be completed to allow everyone to visualize and simulate the new layout.

9

Accurate Pricing through Better Cost Allocations

9.1 INTRODUCTION

I wouldn't say that every detail had been worked through and resolved with regard to our move to the new location, but we had focused on the major problems and, for the most part, things were now running smoothly. I was proud of the team and happy with our new location. We were in an industrial area with a strong presence of machining and fabrication shops, which accounted for the large localized supply base. We now had a plating shop next door, a painting company across the street, and a machine tooling supplier within a block. I worked out a simple pricing structure with the plating shop, which allowed us to determine the plating costs we would incur and to include them directly into our quote instead of going through the internal effort with each RFQ (request for quotation), which specified plating, thereby necessitating subcontracting. So, we avoided the delay and administrative costs of sending out an RFQ to the plating company and receiving a price, then rolling it up in our quotation. This further reduced non-value-added work in the administrative area; better yet, it only took about thirty seconds to transport the parts to the plating shop. They promised us priority if we utilized them for most of our volume, further reducing our lead time and administrative costs to organize transportation.

Since it was a slow sales period, we were coping in the office and shop without serious issues. But, like many businesses experiencing slow times, we were only able to shed some variable costs. Our fixed (mostly overhead costs) remained about the same, so our profitability had been low for a few months. As is customary in slow times, not only were we receiving fewer RFQs but our customers were feeling more price-sensitive and their purchasing departments had more time to shop around. I felt confident that our material estimates and quoted labor times were very accurate as we still tracked all labor and material against every quote and on Fridays we reviewed those that were in excess of ±15 percent. I had methodically kept this process going as well as keeping myself in practice by completing quotes and reviewing them. Although Jake (the programmer/estimator) was handling about 85 percent to 90 percent of the quotes, I randomly jumped in to keep in practice and receive feedback. However, one cost factor with which I was not comfortable was how we charged those minutes and hours of labor—converting them from time into dollars—with respect to our indirect labor and overhead costs, which had been incorporated into our hourly shop rate.

Previously, I have mentioned that the logic behind OSKKK (Observe, Standardize, Kaizen Flow & Process, Kaizen Equipment, and Kaizen Layout) also applies to office processes. You must first observe the current situation and then work to standardize it so you have a basis from which to make improvements. In administrative processes, the key improvement comes from the first "K," the Kaizening of flow and process, which most often involves improvements based around computer systems or programs that dictate the flow of the process. Whether companies are using a larger, more powerful software package like SAP or Oracle, or a smaller one, many improvements are related to data input, output, or some type of change to the application. Most administrative Kaizen takes place within the processes (or related software). Some companies utilize the second "K" of Kaizening the equipment's productivity. The third "K," Kaizening the layout, is where many additional improvements are discovered but a more significant cost is incurred. For example, having the planner, buyer, supervisor, and possibly the engineer for a value stream sitting beside one another often minimizes a lot of finger-pointing and saves time in communicating. Now, the issue I had identified for my business was to Kaizen the process related to how we charged customers for our indirect labor and overhead costs.

I have met managers who feel that in reality they do not need very accurate product cost information because they cannot choose the jobs; they can only do what is necessary to retain the customer. I find this thinking incorrect because the customer often chooses what jobs you will be offered or allowed to quote, and if you are only taking jobs to keep the customer happy without comparing the prices to your actual incurred costs, you are walking a dangerous line.

9.2 DETERMINING MORE ACCURATE ALLOCATIONS DURING TOUGH TIMES

I indicated that when I took over the business, the former owner, Bob, had been using a straight $60-per-hour costing for all quoted labor. He felt this covered all overhead costs as long as sales reached a minimum point every month. I had adopted this rate. But earlier I began to break it down into some various other rates based mostly on the type of material we were machining, or adding an additional mark-up for some customers, though I had done this randomly and haphazardly. In other words, I had done a little observing and started changing the process without a lot of PDCA (Plan, Do, Check, Act).

During this industry slowdown, not only were we quoting and selling less but our average hit rate on receiving orders from our quotes (which previously hovered near 70 percent) had dropped to less than 50 percent. Naturally, we could drop our labor rates to keep people busy and attempt to cover our overhead but that seemed a hit-or-miss strategy and was not reflective of the indirect work that went into the various orders.

Being a lean guy, I had learned and attempted to apply some "lean accounting" in my consulting work. One methodology I had success with was a simplified version of activity-based costing (ABC). To me, ABC helps to allocate as many indirect and overhead costs as possible based on the level of activity they consume (not necessarily getting it exact but it becomes a more precise cost). I figured our material costs were competitive (we often received two or three RFQs for material, and according to all indicators we received a great price per pound) and our direct labor times were accurate. Plus, we had made a lot of improvements in setup-time reductions, we always programmed aggressively, and we used the newest technology in tooling to keep our cycle times at a minimum. Therefore, the only way I figured our competition could beat us on price was either with lower overhead costs or mistakes in their quoting. The only other differences I could see in our costs were my loan payments and my lack of experience, which I ruled out as a factor because Tom (the shop foreman), Jake, and the other operators had significant industry experience. I knew that some of my competitors, who were also approved suppliers at customers like Applied Materials and LAM Research, were larger shops with considerably higher overheads. So, how could they be underbidding me?

Lean principle: Lean accounting works to provide accurate, timely, and easy-to-understand information that supports lean activities. It helps with making correct choices regarding growth, profitability, pricing, and where to focus improvements. It will meet generally accepted accounting practices and is more understandable and directly applicable to making pricing and investment decisions while justifying lean ideologies like growing the employee's skill sets.

9.3 USING MY "MODIFIED ACTIVITY-BASED COSTING"

I was convinced that a great share of the difference in quoted prices lay in my competitors' various rates and how they allocated costs. So, as much as possible, I wanted to get my rates to reflect the "activity" level (i.e., the real office and indirect shop costs incurred) for each product, which would directly address many indirect costs and—hopefully—would better help proportion our overhead. I could not afford to continue to turn only 50 percent of quotes into orders, especially with as few RFQs as we were receiving in those days. But, on the other hand, I could not afford to lose money by making low-ball quotes and not understanding what my actual costs were on a particular job. Having previously evolved a few different rates based on the type of material we were machining, I felt I had learned something and could spread that concept into other areas, especially the administrative functions, where a large part of my overhead resided. Job shops like mine naturally had much higher overhead when compared proportionally to high-volume manufacturers. For example, we had much more indirect activity associated with each part we built (therefore, we had higher indirect costs that were being allocated arbitrarily).

The question was how to more accurately assign these costs to the various products that consumed them. Here again, I thought I would start with the direct and indirect shop activities as they related to the various parts, and then tackle the office activities, which were all considered indirect. I did not want to create too complicated a system and figured I would not be able to come up with a way to distribute all costs to specific parts. But, I wanted to reduce the large amount that had simply been generalized into the one rate we had been using. I liked the ABC accounting concept of creating some general categories and not attempting to be exact because I did not have the time or ability to get the accuracy to two decimal places. I would more accurately allocate based on the customer's and part's characteristics, which consumed time and resources in the office, and those costs or activities I could not specifically account for would be rolled into these rates. I did not plan to make things too complicated and did not necessarily advocate strictly following a detailed ABC approach. Instead, I felt I could have one rate for the office and another rate for the shop. The rates would be based on the indirect activities and costs involved and the sum of these two rates, along with the cost for direct labor, would make up the total. The total could then be summed with directly attributed costs like the materials and outsourcing. This new rate would be inclusive of all overheads that could not be based on the activity they consumed like rent, loan repayments, etc.

Lean principle: My "modified" activity-based costing (ABC) attempted a realistic means of determining the real cost of providing a product or service. It worked to accurately allocate some direct and indirect labor costs and overhead to the particular products/services or customers that consume these activities. The general methodology encourages grouping products or services by categories that affect their required activity level and then assigning weights or costs to these categories, creating accuracy but not precision.

For each area (both the shop and office), I envisioned a separate type of matrix that would take into account the principal indirect activity levels and costs incurred for the necessary tasks to produce and ship a certain type or family of parts. For example, in the shop the activity level involved (the person's or machine's time that was consumed) was influenced by the material from which the part was to be manufactured and also the specific tolerances. The operator's necessary skill level, along with checking activities and the level of programming complication, also dictated how much time was required for estimating. Trying to categorize everything could get very involved. But remember: The "modified ABC" strategy I was attempting to implement encouraged working toward being more accurate than I had previously been but not exact down to the minute (or cent). I wanted to be able to account for the majority of effort involved and to be specific about the true costs involved. In this way, I felt I could increase our hit rate on the quotes during the slow times, and during the busy times it would still help in better qualifying my true profit margin per specific part number (and customer).

Working to improve our pricing by more accurately distributing indirect costs is obviously a Kaizen to the process, the first "K" in the OSKKK strategy. The reason this became a priority at this point was based on business needs caused by the industrywide slowdown and the necessity to quote more competitively. I had previously improved some other administrative processes, then jumped to Kaizening the office layout (the third "K"), and had now come full circle to further Kaizening administrative processes. Keep in mind that the sequence of OSKKK is based on logic and cost of implementations versus the benefits, but it cannot take into account unique changes in the business environment that dictate the opportune timing of certain improvements.

9.4 STARTING "MODIFIED" ACTIVITY-BASED COSTING IN THE SHOP USING A MATRIX

It is probably easiest to first discuss the matrix I made for the shop, and then I will explain the one for the office. I will reference the first version of the matrix, though it naturally lent itself to a continuous improvement process and was still being evolved when I sold the business. A copy of the original matrix is shown in Appendix J, Part I. I simplified the two axes of the matrix, the first reflecting all direct activities influenced by the type of part (attempting to account for additional activity not already accounted for as direct labor for machine or setup times). The other axis further subdivides these categories by the indirect shop tasks likely having an influence and consuming time for a particular part (measuring/programming). I am sure you can imagine all the influences in a business and envision this going into three dimensions or more, but I kept it to a simple two-dimensional matrix and accounted for differences by further segregating into subcategories. Starting with the shop influences that were most strongly affected by the activity level required for the particular part, there was the material (the additional machining time for tougher materials was already factored in but this material also consumed more tooling, which needed to be accounted for with a higher rate). This was further influenced by the amount of deburring involved as some could be done within cycle while the machine was running versus significant deburring that would often require additional time outside of the machine's cycle. One more factor was the tolerance on the part, which affected whether additional checking and adjusting time would be required. Naturally, this additional measuring and adjusting time frequently involved Tom or Jake on the more complicated parts. And the tighter tolerances or excessive features with critical dimensions equated to additional time for the operators as well as the programmer and team leader, thereby increasing the cost. All this additional work also influenced whether one man needed to be dedicated to a machine or he could instead operate more than one machine simultaneously. The number of operators required has a direct cost correlation and the point system developed (within the matrices) helped to reflect this. The idea behind the matrix was simple: the more difficult the task, the more time it consumed; therefore, it received a higher point value (shown as +0, +1, or +2 in the spreadsheet in Appendix J).

On the other axis, I put the various categories for the indirect support taking place in the shop. Again, the various categories and subcategories were based on the time and effort required from the indirects in the shop, which included Tom and/or Jake and me. These were then also categorized into levels of +1 to +3 to account for the time or activity involved so that a total combined effort level from direct and indirect shop effort could be summed up in the matrix. Consequently, the higher the cumulative total of points from both axes, the higher the activity level required for the part; therefore, the higher the associated cost. In theory, we had already accounted for the direct person's time on the machine through the machine cycle time and setup time, but we were not always factoring in the additional direct and indirect activities and time required for the particular part.

The items affecting how the indirect people in the shop spent their time were dictated primarily by how many measurements were involved (more measurements generally equated to more difficult parts), more complicated parts generally required support to help in determining how to measure them. The next factor affecting the shop's support staff is how difficult the program was to write and debug. Obviously, simple programs usually worked immediately and, at the other end of the spectrum, the difficult CNC (Computer Numerical Control) programs required more time to develop and debug. Naturally in some cases to quantify which row or column you utilized was subjective (i.e. easy or difficult customers), but it was a starting point.

In summary, the following items were identified as affecting the activity level in the shop:

- Ease or difficulty of measurements
- Ease or difficulty in writing CNC computer programs
- Type of material (soft or hard)
- Ease or difficulty in deburring (cleaning) the part
- Quantity of difficult tolerances to maintain

9.5 HOW TO RELATE THE MATRIX TO COST

The principle in the matrix is simple: the higher the cumulative numeric value, the more effort being required from both the direct and indirect shop personnel; therefore, the customer should be charged more for this higher activity level. That is not to say improvements could not be made to reduce the effort level or time involved but, at this point in time, it was a reflection of reality (part of the goal of any type of ABC is to help in identifying areas or tasks that require improvement). Logically, a lower numeric value would be linked to a lower cost for the customer and a higher number to a higher cost. Before explaining how I arrived at linking this to financial numbers, let me clarify what I did with the related level of office-staff activities.

9.6 MY "MODIFIED ACTIVITY-BASED COSTING" MATRIX FOR THE OFFICE

I followed the same principles in the office. I created a separate matrix to reflect the variables that influenced the activity level required in the office based on the part and the customer. Across the top, I placed "Influence from the Customers" (i.e., the difficult vs. easy customers) as this affected the time involved, and it was further impacted by the level of packaging and the method of shipping. The original office matrix is shown in Appendix J, Part II. The other axis dealt with the major factors affecting the activity level in the front office. For example, any changes to the specifications (or having to resolve unclear issues with the customer's engineers) had a large effect on the time required from the front office (this was more common with certain customers and part types). Also affecting the time was the number of items on the bill of material for a particular drawing; naturally, the more items, the more time it took to purchase and receive those items. (Historically, we were progressing into performing more assembly work, and this was having a direct effect on administrative time.) The last issue affecting the office's effort level was the amount of outsourcing. Each item being sent out required obtaining a quotation, shipping, receiving, tracking, and a payment. The same logic was applied in the matrix; a higher numeric value represented more effort being required. The combined office scale ranged from a total effort level of four to nine, while the shop had more factors influencing it; therefore, the scale had a larger range from four two twelve.

In summary, the following items were identified as affecting the activity level in the office:

- Level of customer support required (changes to orders or specs, sales support, standard specifications)
- Number of items on the bill of material
- Number of services requiring outsourcing
- Customer payment (on-time, good terms and conditions)
- Level of packaging requirements

Now, this arbitrary scale had to be converted to a dollar value for a customer's quote. These two matrices in no way took into account all of our overhead costs or all the tasks necessary to operate the business—they only helped to relate more accurately some major influences on how our direct and indirect time was spent in relation to processing various jobs according to the characteristics that most directly consumed our time. (Though the rate I was to utilize had to account for all the fixed overhead costs that were not accounted for in the direct and indirect activities within the matrices, those would be more arbitrarily rolled in). In terms of "official" activity-based costing, this was not a complete analysis or plan for how to reallocate all of our costs based on their activity level, but I knew it was better than simply utilizing one rate or the few general labor rates I had previously put in place, therefore I refer to it as "my modified activity-based costing."

9.7 RELATING THE MATRICES TO HOURLY COSTS

Based on the typical hours of work we would usually sell, I knew that in slower months a rate of $60 per hour had traditionally covered most of our costs, including the various overhead charges. Therefore, I wanted to use that as a basis and somehow distribute it more accurately, based on the direct and indirect activity levels I had determined in the matrices (previously I had only been trying to account for direct labor and left both indirect and fixed costs arbitrarily distributed). I did not see how it was possible to fairly distribute many of the other overhead costs (though this would likely be pursued in full-scale activity-based accounting). Historically, the $60-per-hour rate had satisfied the overhead costs and I felt this was the best I could do at that point in time. I knew the costs incurred for direct labor including benefits averaged about $20 per hour, so I could assume the other $40 per hour ($60/hour shop rate − $20/hour direct labor cost) covered all indirect and other overhead costs. This was the proportional part I needed to more accurately distribute. I had determined that about 60 percent of our overall costs (excluding direct material and direct labor) resided in manufacturing and the other 40 percent were in the office (salaries, overheads, and other directly assignable office costs). Therefore, I decided to split the remaining $40 per hour rate, attributing 60 percent ($40 × 0.6), or $24 per hour, to shop-floor activities and 40 percent, or $16 per hour, to office tasks. Then I linked this figure to the numeric scale in the shop and office, respectively. I linked the $24 to the shop matrix's middle value (#8) of the scale and felt that increasing or decreasing $2 for each point was relatively representative of the costs we incurred. This is shown at the bottom of the chart in Appendix J, Part I. Naturally, this method of assigning costs was still based on the labor hours associated with the job but since we knew (through our continuous feedback system) that these were accurate, it seemed the best baseline to utilize at that point.

The remaining 40 percent of our costs (including administrative labor costs) were assigned to the office matrix. In this case, the remaining $16 per hour ($40/hour × 40% of distributed costs) was assigned to cover all administrative costs other than direct materials; it was also evenly distributed on the office scale. The middle point (#6) was therefore linked to the $16 per hour, again with an increase or decrease of $2 per hour being assigned to the effort levels above or below #6, respectively. When I totaled both the shop and office matrices and combined this with the $20-per-hour direct labor rate, I arrived at a minimum hourly rate of $48 per hour ($12/hour from the office + $16/hour from the shop + $20/hour for direct labor) assigned to the parts requiring the least activity from direct and indirect labor or a maximum of $74 per hour ($22/hour from the office + $32/hour from the shop + $20/hour for direct labor) for jobs consuming the most indirect effort from both the office and shop. This was quite a difference from a blanket rate of $60 per hour for all jobs but was much closer aligned to our true activity levels.

Naturally, this could be further developed and refined to include considerably more variables but I felt it was a good starting point. It was more reflective of the actual costs we incurred with each job and I hoped this would help us in winning more work. I was not sure how our competition determined their hourly rates or how sophisticated they were in allocating all their costs within their quoting processes but I figured we were better off than before. Even though we could now easily associate a variable labor rate with each job after we had calculated the actual setup and run times, we still had to adjust this for the customer and the current market conditions. The important point is that we now had a more accurate cost figure that reflected reality in allocating our indirect and overhead costs. So, when we were confronted with a choice about how we should price to win a job, we could more accurately determine our profit margin and make a better pricing or repricing decision. That by itself would allow us to compete better. Pricing jobs with an hourly rate from $48 per hour to $74 per hour was a considerable difference that we had not previously accounted for. And I was sure it had cost us some business at the low end of the scale when we applied our $60-per-hour general rate and we probably had a poor margin or lost money when we won business for which we really incurred costs of nearly $74 per hour. Now, we might not receive as much work for the difficult jobs but we were likely to make a more stable margin on the work we did win. Time would tell if we were on the right track.

To summarize what had been done to this point: I discovered an easy way to better account and relate our pricing based on the activity levels of our indirect labor that various types of parts consumed. This method also helped in better proportioning some of our overhead costs. I still had not determined a better way to allocate some of the fixed costs to a particular part number, but traditional ABC accounting does offer some suggestions in this area.

Key point: *Indirect costs can be proportionately better allocated to the products that consume indirect time based on the activity level, as demonstrated using a simple matrix.*

In the end, the market determines the price based on the various suppliers' quotations (this will be influenced by which suppliers the customer is aligned with, the type of part, the number of competitors, etc.). Difficult-to-manufacture parts and rush jobs frequently commanded a higher price because they demanded a higher level of activity, and certain customers were less price-sensitive (though all still demanded superior quality, and some were pickier than others regarding subjective issues like surface quality or cleanliness). In any case, I now better understood what my true costs were, based on how the various parts and customers consumed my team's time.

9.8 HOW OTHERS OFTEN ALLOCATE COSTS

In my consulting work, I find most companies either content with applying traditional accounting allocations or uncomfortable challenging them; therefore, they easily accept the profit margins based on whichever methods the accountants choose to utilize for allocating the various indirect and overhead costs. This is likely caused by a variety of factors, but I firmly believe most manufacturing managers and executives feel uncomfortable with the idea of challenging the accounting methods (unless they are accountants themselves). I find they might ask their controller to look into lean accounting but do not fully understand the implications within their current system. Another factor I feel plays a major role is the high cost of materials in many businesses, which creates a feeling of keeping the focus on material costs and not worrying about the accuracy of direct and indirect costs. I often find manufacturers with whom I work have material costs near 50 percent of total cost (or the sales price) and periodically it exceeds the 50-percent mark. In my case, material averaged 18 percent of sales so we had a high value-added portion and it was critical to quote this correctly.

Direct labor today often accounts for only 7 to 10 percent of sales value in some manufacturing industries. Therefore, managers often consider this of lower importance in relation to how critical it is to estimate and assign it correctly, though the problem is that many accounting systems allocate most or all of the indirect and overhead costs based on these direct labor hours (as I was doing). Remember: the total indirect and overhead costs frequently account for nearly 30 percent of the sales price. So, if you are allocating those costs based on poor direct labor hours and not assigning them based on time (or activity), you can end up misallocating a large percentage (30% + 7%) of your costs, losing considerable business based on incorrect pricing estimates. I have demonstrated simple methods to more accurately account for the indirect time, though the fixed costs are considerably more complicated to correctly allocate.

Not being an experienced accountant myself, I am sure many could poke holes in my methodology; the truly analytical person would say it was oversimplified but I figured it was a better reflection of reality than what was previously in place. And later I was able to further learn and improve this methodology. In a way, there were some easy measurements to determine the success of my new pricing strategy; I would immediately start to notice if my hit rate on orders received climbed above 50 percent for the jobs I was quoting, then I could also compare my end-of-month profitability to previous months. Naturally, I was not just hoping to receive more work in a troubled and competitive market; I was really hoping to improve my profitability, the number one goal of every business. I had to factor in the slow market and lower sales because obviously I received more overall profit in very busy months. But, at least I could look at the recent profit compared to the new profit as I introduced this new labor scale ranging from $48 per hour to $74 per hour. I felt good about realizing the pitfalls in an oversimplified costing system and felt I was making step-by-step improvements. Time would tell.

9.9 KEEPING THE TEAM LEADER FOCUSED DURING THE SLOW TIMES

Naturally, during the slow times we were not working overtime. However, Tom was still coming in a little early to prepare the machines, materials, and any paperwork so all the operators could start on time. Even during a slow period, it was better to pay a little overtime to one man and avoid having many others get a slow start. These were also ideal times for cross-training, preventive maintenance, and other items we had put off during the busy times. As I mentioned earlier, I even had a cross-training matrix showing our current status and our training plan. So, it was easy when someone had a little time available: First, they checked the cross-training list to see whether any of the tasks for which they required experience were currently taking place. If not, they checked a "things to do list" I kept updated to keep people productive and put improvements in place. (An example of the cross-training matrix is shown in Appendix H.)

I have seen many plants where a "things to do list" does not exist. So, when things slow down, the operators also slow down—adopt a slower pace—because they fear that they could be laid off or lose their job if they do not appear busy. Though my tracking system in which operators recorded their actual times compared to quoted times prevented them from slowing their pace, I figured it was better to list the things we needed to do so that, instead of slowing down the pace to look busy, operators understood there was work waiting. I wanted everyone to feel there was always something to do that added value and prepared us for busy times. Basically, it worked although it was by no means perfect. But, as I support other companies, I often find this list is not available (maybe it is in someone's head), at least it is not out in the open for all to reference. Often, these nonlean plants seem too busy firefighting to take advantage of this excess operator time when it becomes available. I learned this technique from Toyota, which always organized a few areas/departments in the shop (i.e., making new tips for the welding robots) where supervisors could send operators who had no work. And then the area would not be responsible to account for those labor hours. It is simply a matter of recognizing that it is hard to guarantee eight hours of work every day for every employee without having lots of flexibility and management organization to deal with the varying demands placed on people's time.

Key point: Again, it is vital to have a cross-training matrix (with a development plan for each employee) visually displayed and up to date, along with a list of tasks (improvements, maintenance items, etc.) that need to be completed so you can motivate operators to switch to value-adding tasks during slow periods. This is critical for every company.

9.10 INCREASING PROCESS CAPABILITIES TO REDUCE OUTSOURCING

We also did what most others do in tough times—we tried to stop outsourcing any products we had the possibility to manufacture in-house. For a year and a half, we had been trying to quote all drawings we received. However, we often did not have the in-house capability to make some of these parts, or in some cases we could manufacture them but not with the most efficient and competitive equipment for that type of part (i.e., we only had manual lathes, not CNC lathes, for making certain round parts). So, we had subcontracted those to other shops when we received the order (we would typically charge 15 percent to 20 percent above the subcontractor's price); but, in this price-sensitive market, we stretched our capabilities in every way possible to manufacture most of these parts in-house.

I had begun leaving the business for short periods—approximately one week per month—to do some lean consulting work. I knew that with more of these standards in place, the business would run better utilizing less tribal knowledge and rely more on established processes even for difficult tasks like quoting. As I mentioned, one of my goals was to get the business stable and standardized enough for it to run on well-defined processes instead of requiring an on-site "master" firefighter—me—to help coordinate the other firefighters.

9.11 STANDARDIZING THE BUSINESS PROCESSES ALLOWS TIME FOR PURSUING OTHER OPPORTUNITIES

It was about this time that the dot-com boom was taking place, and living in the San Francisco Bay area put me right in the middle of it—eBay and Yahoo had their headquarters only a few miles from my business. I had many friends who were getting swept up in the dot-com boom and later one or two made their fortunes from it before the bottom fell out.

I came up with a concept for a Web site and got a friend—a high-tech guru—interested in working with me in the development. The idea was based on none other than the machining and fabrication businesses. During this period, it was becoming typical for customers to send their technical drawings out for quotation via the Internet. In some cases, it was better for machine shops to receive the AutoCAD file directly as they could import it and build their CNC program around its geometry instead of redrawing the complicated parts in their own software. The Web site idea came from several directions:

- Customers were sometimes not sure of the different services, qualifications, and limitations of the various shops.
- Customers also wanted to ensure their drawings would be kept confidential and to know which suppliers held the correct certifications (i.e., AWS [American Welding Society], ISO 9001:2000, etc.).
- Customers were usually unaware of other suppliers who could provide competitive quotes for various types of parts.
- Many CNC and sheet metal companies did not have the capability to open electronic drawings in the various formats in which they arrived (e.g., AutoCAD, Mechanical Desk Top, Inventor).

The opportunity that the Web site could provide for the supply side—the various machine and fabrication shops—was to bring customers and suppliers together. My idea was to create a type of marketplace Web site where customers could submit their drawings to all suppliers—"open quote"—or to "approved suppliers" in an organized and secure format. Suppliers could receive the necessary information and the drawings in a format they could access. Technical questions could be posted anonymously to a forum or comment board visible to all those quoting on the job and the customer would only have to answer each question once. (Keep in mind this was quite a while ago, before any similar Web sites existed.)

My friend and I built a prototype Web site to display the principles and some typical menus. I started meeting with some of the purchasing people at my larger customers to get their feedback on the idea. I would show them how to log on to the Web site and how to send a few drawings out for bid. It was going well, and we were busy taking in the feedback we had received and making modifications.

However, my bubble was burst when I met with a buyer who said she had been visited by someone with a similar idea about a week prior to my visit. She even gave me the man's name and the name of the company. Dismayed, I ran back to the office where my buddy and I did some quick research on the Internet. Between our research and the information a few friends could gather through the grapevine, we discovered that the concept had been in development about ten weeks and the company had just received $6 million in venture capital and now had five people engaged full time. We were in no position to go further as we basically had no money and both had full-time jobs. I guess the only consolation was that my idea was at least worth $6 million to some venture capitalists; unfortunately, I was not on the receiving end of that money—always a day late and dollar short, the story of my life.

I guess the most applicable business lesson when developing a new product or concept is to quickly determine whether there are competitors and what they are working on. That's probably taught in the first year at business school and anyone who didn't learn it academically would say its just common sense. I will say, however, that at the time it was not easy to know which dot-com sites were under development as everyone was keeping their ideas secret, and I just stumbled across the fact that somebody was working on a similar concept.

One saving grace might be that I have monitored the situation for years and I have never seen that Web site nor heard of anyone in the industry using it, which either means it was not such a great idea or it was not executed correctly. Oh well, at least I tried to earn the title "entrepreneur."

I have mentioned taking this diversion since it was made possible by standardizing the business processes to the point that I felt comfortable enough to temporarily put my focus elsewhere.

9.12 SUMMARY

- Lean accounting, specifically activity-based costing, can help to better allocate direct, indirect, and administrative costs to the specific product or service that is consuming that activity. My "modified" version is one way to arrive at various labor rates to account for the ranges of activity levels involved.
- A matrix utilizing various subcategories can be helpful in grouping activity levels based on certain characteristics of the part and the customer.
- Most companies function with lots of costs being arbitrarily allocated, making the accuracy of any specific product's profit margin very questionable. Although my version of activity-based costing is by no means exact, it would likely be more accurate and allow better decision making if properly applied.

10

Up-Front Delays

10.1 THE MEASUREMENTS CONFIRM SUCCESS

We seemed to be bringing in more work and the measurements indicated it was at least partially due to our new pricing structure. Since we had switched our hourly rates from a flat $60 per hour to a range of $48 per hour to $74 per hour, our hit rate on quotes was averaging over 60 percent, compared to averaging less than 50 percent previously. It was still slow times in the industry we predominantly supported so the improved hit rate was helping to increase our sales, thereby increasing our profits. It also seemed our profit margin was stabilizing, which was another measurement of our new pricing structure. The final measure of success I utilized was randomly looking at periods where we had a few high-labor-rate jobs running (i.e., $74/hour), and monitoring how busy (or how stressed) the office staff and/or indirects in the shop were, compared to normal. This was basically a subjective measure and I was probably slightly prejudiced, wanting to prove my point. But, it certainly appeared that when we had a few more jobs with higher labor rates, the indirects (both shop and office) were busier. So, the higher labor rates truly reflected a higher activity level among indirects, thereby proving we were better cost-estimating our indirect time.

10.2 CONTINUOUSLY DEVELOPING PROTOCOLS ALLOWS MORE AUTONOMY FROM DAY-TO-DAY OPERATIONS

Standardized systems like establishing criteria for using a variable labor rate continued to put more structure in the company, not only requiring fewer judgment calls and less tribal knowledge when performing various tasks but also they increasingly allowed me to be removed from the day-to-day operations. As I mentioned in the previous chapter, I had started to consult, which kept me out of the office about one week per month and forced the others to manage all aspects of the business (though I often had my mother watching the money a little more closely during those periods). You know that old saying about a boss only being as good as the people under him or her? Well, I was trying to evolve this, not only through minimizing good people running around with heads full of tribal knowledge but further by putting standard processes in place that drove results while not completely relying on knowledge, experience, and/or personal judgment. In other words, making an attempt to have an established protocol for most situations.

One of the wastes I was continuously working to eliminate in my business was the delays, the things that kept us from cutting chips on a machine. It may sound simple: After we got the order, we bought the material and any special tooling; then, we wrote the CNC (Computer Numerical Control) program for the machine. And when the job came up in the schedule, we manufactured the part. Still, there were many reasons why this might fall apart, and a good place to focus was where problems and delays were encountered in the up-front processes. For example, imagine if we had the ability to foresee problems—estimating problems, purchasing problems, problems with the drawings or technical specifications, problems with quality specifications, problems with the program, tooling problems, etc.— and resolve these issues before it was too late. If we could do that, we would make large improvements on the lead time. Life would have been much easier if I had always been able to provide the actual value-adding process with everything—good quality material, drawings or specifications with no issues, clear quality standards, an achievable schedule, a qualified employee, and fully functioning machines and tooling—on time. Well, dream on—or maybe not. With standard parts, those we had been manufacturing for some time ("runners" or "A" type parts), we were able to eliminate most of these issues. We were able to minimize many of these disturbances for most runner parts when repeat orders were received. Though since at least 40 percent of our work at any point in time was for a part we had not previously manufactured, we needed to work toward eliminating these problems on all jobs. I found better planning was essential: If we could arrive at a point where we'd actually be performing capacity planning instead of chasing materials, many of these issues would be taken into consideration.

10.3 PLANNING ONLY BASED ON AVAILABLE MATERIALS IS COSTLY

We had in place many of the traditional systems to avoid the classic problems; for example, the inspection of incoming materials, the writing of the programs at the earliest possible time to help in identifying issues with the drawings (missing dimensions or specifications). And we had begun visual capacity planning after materials were available.

The use of capacity planning is one critical difference between my business and many of those that I support. Some companies are so stressed with chasing late materials that when they all finally arrive, the job is quickly released to manufacturing without any capacity planning. Some of you might even be familiar with jobs being released with only enough material to complete the first few operations steps and the hope that the missing materials will arrive before they are needed for the later process steps. This releasing of orders only based on material availability is obviously dangerous because the work order might arrive at an overloaded process or a bottleneck. And if nobody in production had been made aware of the constraint, they could not take any proactive steps to minimize the bottleneck and maintain the lead time. Consequently, this newly released order immediately increases the size and delay of an existing bottleneck. Naturally, in these cases the lead time through the business becomes whatever time is necessary instead of a planned time and is usually dictated by the bottleneck (basically following the "theory of constraints").

The ideal situation to work toward is to have a weekly overview capacity plan in place for all bottleneck processes based on the material's anticipated arrival. After the materials have arrived, those orders should then be released for detailed capacity planning not to exceed twenty-four hours at a time. The twenty-four hour limit cuts down on the amount of time you will have wasted if you experience problems during the day—and we all do—and your plan is thrown off and needs revisions. When this happens, you'll only need to revise the plan for those unfinished jobs that had been previously scheduled within the twenty-four hour period instead of some longer period—say, rescheduling an entire week. A rule of thumb that has worked is to only post a detailed plan for a process one day in advance (in a three-shift operation, plan three shifts ahead). I would like to capture this as a key point because we were doing it and receiving a competitive advantage, but I know many others who do not perform this planning for a variety of reasons.

Lean principle: The theory of constraints is a management approach that focuses on the importance of managing constraints. A constraint (also known as a bottleneck) is something that inhibits you from getting more out of a process. All businesses have a minimum of one constraint. The constraint within the flow of your business is determined by the process or step with the smallest capacity. Since lean entails increasing capacity (aided by capacity planning), the theory of constraints is a management methodology that compliments lean thinking.

Key point: To improve on-time delivery and process effectiveness, once per week, prior to receiving all materials, a weekly overview capacity plan should be developed for all bottleneck processes based on the materials' anticipated arrival dates. Then, after the materials have arrived, those orders should be released for detailed capacity planning (not to exceed a 24-hour plan). This ensures you can anticipate and minimize the effects from these bottleneck processes.

10.4 CAPACITY PLANNING BASED ON LEAD TIMES

We were essentially a JIT (just-in-time) business in the sense that we only built when we had an order and we released the job to production primarily based on taking the customer's due date and subtracting the lead times for internal and any subcontracted process steps planning that the customers will receive it exactly on the promised date. This type of planning requires that you know your specific lead times and task times for each process and ensure they are maintained or risk being late to the customer. In our case, this also entailed managing the flow through external processes like heat-treating, plating, painting, etc., where we maintained a close relationship and followed up with our suppliers to ensure those lead times were achieved. The trick with lead times is to realize when they were starting to exceed that which was originally planned and take action to minimize this. The problems we encountered were typically at the second, third, and fourth process steps, when work started to queue up at that process and create a bottleneck. We needed to either anticipate this in our planning or identify it in real time and become proactive. Throughout the years that I owned the company, we maintained between 98- and 99-percent on-time delivery to the promise date, but this required hard work, the ability to identify the bottleneck early, and a lot of flexibility within the team (i.e., overtime, cross-training, running processes simultaneously, etc.). This also occasionally required we negotiate a "promise" date with our customer upon receipt of the order instead of just agreeing to their "request" date. Our capacity planning was accomplished through the day-by-hour boards, as shown in Appendix D.

Lean principle: Lead time is simply the time between instructing something to begin (i.e., placing an order) and receiving the finished good from the process/supplier. It is a key focus for any company working to improve profitability. This is a focal point in value stream mapping, process mapping, and reducing inventory. Remember: there are various lead times, like customer lead time and manufacturing lead time, and various terms in lean like throughput time, total product cycle time (used in value stream mapping, which is slightly different than lead time). Make sure you understand the start point, stop point, and contents of what you are working to improve when dealing with any form of lead time.

Key point: To maintain on-time delivery and keep the flow moving, you need to first know your lead times (both internal and external), and then plan accordingly. Further, you need to monitor where the lead times are not being maintained and quickly treat those processes as bottlenecks and take appropriate actions.

10.5 IDENTIFYING AREAS WHERE WE WERE ONLY BEING REACTIVE

We knew how to be proactive in some areas although I was continuously looking to identify where we seemed to be only reactive. Naturally, this is critical as only reacting without solving the problem at its root cause means it is likely to repeat. However, since there are rarely sufficient resources available to resolve many issues at their root cause, you must have a method to select those that will ultimately lead to the most profitability upon their resolution. One area where it was easy to become proactive instead of reactive was with suppliers that were often late. Instead of accepting that a part had not been delivered by the due date, we determined that any supplier with a history of being late more than twice would be contacted basically each day after placing an order to see whether it was still progressing to plan. It may sound crazy to call each day but remember: we were a short lead-time business; therefore, we were frequently working with materials that were due in a few days. Even for exotic or special materials, we were frequently paying to expedite as our customers rarely ordered with long lead times. (Naturally, this begs the question, "Was the entire industry disorganized?" But, it appeared that our customer's customers who purchased the machines to etch the computer chips all worked in a very dynamic and quickly changing industry.) That is not to say that we never experienced few weeks lead time for materials, but this was the exception and in these instances we would only call a problem supplier once—one week before it was due. Naturally, this does not always get a part in on time but at least nobody could claim they had not received the order, and this constant communication would make us aware it was going to be late and everyone—including our customer—could plan accordingly.

10.6 AVAILABLE TIME UTILIZED TO DOCUMENT PROCESSES

Whenever the indirects had enough free time, I tried to have them write out the steps (either a standardized operations sheet or a process map) for any process we had not previously documented. This may sound extreme but I found that people would rather "be" busy than "look" busy.

Remember: the office is an even-more-difficult environment to provide eight hours of value-adding work for everyone each day he or she shows up. I had shown everyone how to draw process maps (basically flowcharts) and we only did it by hand; therefore, it was not too complicated. There is always the possibility that employees—thinking about job security—will not document all the process steps or will leave out some shortcuts (or improvements) they have discovered. But, some documentation is always better than nothing.

Process mapping (like value stream mapping) is also a great help in identifying where standards are lacking or opportunities for improvement lie. I noticed that these types of "keep busy looking for improvement" tasks never got done when I was out of the office, and of course I knew it wasn't because suddenly everyone was busy. I assumed it had more to do with me continuously pushing people to add value whenever I observed otherwise. I found you can push people toward their best productivity if they see the boss always working hard and adding value. And you need to provide them the knowledge and structure to identify non-value-adding tasks, and to create a format that encourages them to make suggestions (an example of mapping techniques is shown in Appendix M).

Lean principle: Value stream mapping and process mapping are great facilitation tools to focus different perspectives through examination of the processes based on data gathered at the place the work is performed. Value stream mapping is used to analyze the flow of materials and information (related to customer orders and purchasing of materials) currently required to bring a product or service to a consumer. This is a higher-level map (not necessarily expanding each process into detailed steps). Process mapping (sometimes referred to as VSMi) is a flowcharting method that uses general symbols to show the flow of a process, typically utilized in administrative or office processes. This is used for mapping in greater detail and takes into account processes with parallel steps and decision points (a graphic representation is shown in Appendix M).

Any other recurring delays that we noticed in releasing jobs would be tracked with a simple tick list on someone's desk or up on one of the boards. After a few weeks, I was either convinced it happened often enough to merit looking at for a more permanent solution, or it was nothing to lose sleep over, as I already had enough items both in my professional and private life to keep me awake at night. So, I did not want to add items to the "worrying" list that only occurred infrequently.

10.7 LEAD TIME REDUCED THROUGH "STRATEGIC" INVENTORY

Another area that was previously mentioned in helping to shorten lead time and avoid delays was stocking a wider selection of raw materials. Naturally, it was critical to have the correct type of material in stock, though in cases where the stock material was too large, we had the ability to cut it to size (which incurred additional cost but, if cutting to size shortened the lead time and helped secure the order, it can be justified). On the other hand, stocking too small a size of a material would never help as there was no such thing as a "material stretcher" in our business. A bit of experience and data helped in choosing which materials to stock and I did not view it as excess inventory. Instead, I considered it "strategic" inventory, meaning I not only had it there for a reason, I also regularly reviewed and adjusted it to ensure I had the correct type and quantity on hand. Instead of viewing all inventories with suspicion and considering them a negative, I tried to separate what was on hand because of poor planning versus what had been strategically acquired to improve the business's profitability. This is critical, and I would like to note it as a key point because I often feel lean transformations focus on reducing all inventories instead of separating out strategic inventory.

Key point: Any inventory that is in place to reduce lead time, improve on-time delivery, and is regularly reviewed to ensure you have the correct material and quantity on hand should be considered "strategic" inventory—a lower priority for reduction. On the other hand, inventory that is a result of poor planning or is not helping improve lead time or on-time delivery should be a high priority for reduction. Remember: inventory is necessary to compensate for the difference in the customer's lead time and the supplier's lead time. So, the focus should be lead-time reduction, thereby reducing the need for inventory.

One other item that I kept more stock of than the previous owner was commonly used machine tooling (i.e., end mills, taps, drills). It was easy to determine which tooling had the highest consumption frequency and to stock levels of those tools based on their lead time while considering how various order quantities affected price, reducing administrative costs and lost time because the operators did not have the tooling when required. There was essentially no chance of this tooling becoming obsolete and resulting in a write-off. I even considered systems offered by tooling suppliers where they stocked and replenished a toolbox for you at their own expense and invoiced each week based on what you consumed. I determined this method would be more costly for us as I received generous discounts on tooling by going directly to the wholesaler, although the lead time was longer (which I was usually able to accommodate with my planning method). I was able to justify the cost of the higher inventory expenses. Many companies with whom I have worked have found that a supplier's automatic replenishment system actually results in savings over having the process internally managed. That was not my case (as my administrative costs were probably lower than that of other companies), but it is worth looking into. Lean people typically call the system that sets levels of consumables and automatically replenishes them "consumable Kanban," and I would recommend implementing it wherever possible after determining whether it is less expensive to manage internally or externally.

Lean principle: Consumable Kanban is setting up an automatic replenishment system for consumable items (tooling, gloves, chemicals, packaging material, small hardware, etc.) to reduce all the administrate costs, carrying costs, obsolescence costs, etc. Again, Kanban is basically determining minimum and maximum points that trigger an automatic replenishment in the easiest fashion. Kanban is ideal for consumables and materials that have regular usage, especially those that are frequently ordered (meaning they incur high administrative costs) and/or have a high inventory level. Remember, many companies experience a high administrative cost to process each purchase order. Kanban reduces this cost by using a few blanket purchase orders.

10.8 PRIORITIZING PROBLEMS DURING BUSY PERIODS

Many of the refinements I have been speaking of all sound nice to implement if you have the time and resources. It probably appears I had things running so smoothly that I came into the plant, got a cup of coffee, read my email, and then went looking for improvements to make. I wish that would have been the case; instead, I had days I still spent firefighting from the moment I walked in the door or times when a phone call got me out of bed early. Other times, I found myself either filling in for someone who was not there or jumping in to support a seriously overloaded bottleneck process. Those of you familiar with small businesses know that the fewer employees you have, the more hats you are likely to wear. And these small businesses are often fighting the same problems day in and day out because everyone is too busy to resolve the real issues. Instead of randomly and blindly making the time available to work on problems, I always tried to only focus on repetitive problems and periodically I had to do this on overtime. Of course, my personal overtime hours included no cost (just as yours might be free of charge) but, during busy times, Tom (the shop foreman), Jake (the programmer/estimator), and some of the operators might even be asked to stay to work through a problem that was plaguing us or to implement something we could not find the time to handle on straight time. I am still convinced it was better to pay time and a half than to lose time reworking parts or being forced to wait because all the material, tooling, or information was not available to perform a job.

10.9 THE LACK OF HANDS-ON EXPERIENCE IS VERY COSTLY

I indicated that we tried to write our CNC programs as early as possible, often the same day that we received the order. This was critical because often we were working on prototype or newly released parts; therefore, the drawings were often missing information or contained errors. I would like to say that most of these problems were caught during the quoting process. But, during quoting you do not review the drawing with the detail that goes into writing the programs necessary to manufacture the part. However, what the quoting process often demonstrated was the lack of practical training and experience the customer's design engineers had. I feel comfortable making this statement because I am an engineer and had previously worked as a mechanical engineer doing design work. I was now on the receiving end of the design work, though at this point in my career the job at hand was trying to figure out how to manufacture the parts. Many of the mistakes I saw had to do with tolerances. For example, sometimes it was as simple as a sheet metal or fabricated part that had been drawn within a template for a machine part and the general tolerances specified in the title block were for a high-tolerance machined part, not for a simple sheet metal cover panel. In many cases, the part could be manufactured to the tighter tolerance (with some difficulties) but it took more time, frequently it had to be run on a better machine, it required more quality checks, and would likely incur some scrap. All this equated to a much higher cost for myself or for my competitors, most of which we would identify at the quoting stage and pass on to our customers. The other option would be to question the tolerance. The two predominant reasons this was not often done were that the buyer did not want to go through the work of contacting the engineer and requesting they change the tolerances, or they did not want the anticipated delays that would come with any changes. We also knew that their incoming inspectors would reject any parts not within tolerance (without questioning why such a tight tolerance was being applied to a simple cover panel, for example). So, we had to choose between three options: maintain these incorrectly specified tight tolerances, get it corrected, or not quote the part. These problems with tolerances are just one example. However, most engineers feel that any feature that is marginally critical should have a tighter tolerance called out than necessary and this will ensure the manufacturer achieves close to what they need. But, they often do not consider the cost implications or that the manufacturers generally achieve or exceed any tolerance specified.

Some think these issues are covered by DFM (design for manufacture) or DFA (design for assembly), and naturally these are valid process steps to go through. But they normally do not catch problems or issues with fabrication drawings relating to tolerances or missing dimensions. Tolerancing problems are representative of issues that just drive the cost up but remain buried in the design of the part. It is typically the subcontractors who might notice this, but they realize pointing it out will cause delays in the best of cases. Or, it might encourage overworked purchasing agents to buy from a competitor who has submitted a price that includes this extra cost instead of taking on the extra work and delays to save costs by getting a tolerance changed. The only time buyers called me back was when my competitors and I had all no-quoted a part because of a difficult/impossible tolerance or other callout in the drawing. At this point, they were interested in resolving the problem. During my time in the business, we probably had more than seventy-five of these occurrences. And every time that it escalated to the point where it was necessary for me to speak with the engineer, he or she said it would be no problem to make the recommended change. Often, the engineer currently responsible for the part was not even aware of the reason it had been designed and drawn that way. However, in all these instances only once or twice did engineers have the time or ambition to change the original drawing—they would only commit to faxing me a "red line," in which they would note the change and sign it. This meant the problem would come up again when either someone else built the part or the incoming inspector referred to the original drawing. This is just one example of where the "official process" of changing a drawing must be so long and painful that the workaround appears easier. But, in the long run this problem is likely to bite you in the butt a few more times. This is also an example of not actually solving a problem because you have not arrived at the root cause. Identifying the cost of each occurrence and quantifying how often this happens would likely lead the respective companies to mapping the current state and identifying improvements. This issue was brought up again as it continued to plague us and should again be highlighted as an improvement point for companies that hold responsibility for design work.

Lean principle (from Chapter 1): DFM (design for manufacturing) and DFA (design for assembly) are two lean ideas that work to bring the designers and manufacturing team together during the design process with the aim to improve manufacturing productivity. Keep in mind that typically 75 percent or more of the product's cost is determined during the design phase.

10.10 MY PERSONAL EXPERIENCE OF
GENERATING COSTLY DESIGNS

When I started as a design engineer fresh out of the university (actually designing new manufacturing process equipment), I was put straight to work as a design engineer for production equipment. Like in many companies, new employees needed to be "productive" right away, and there was no time for me to be further developed or to learn the business in a hands-on fashion. Productivity was judged by how well you handled projects, mostly on time and to budget, though all budgets are relative to how detailed they are and how stable are the influences.

During this period, I got to know (socially) the main fabricator this particular manufacturing company used. This level of comfort with a supplier is normally looked down upon but since I had no influence over sourcing decisions made by the purchasing department, I don't think it hurt much. What I learned one night over a few beers with Rex (the owner of the fabrication shop) was more practical and cost-effective than a lot of years experience without this feedback. He was joking about working long hours the past week and then indicated that most of that time had been spent on a piece of production equipment I had recently designed. He went on to say that he was not too bothered because he had included most of these hours in the quotation and factored it in the cost. I was a bit surprised because I felt it was a fairly straightforward fabrication for a shop like his. He indicated that the tight tolerance called out was consuming the majority of these additional hours. The next words out of my mouth were, "What tight tolerance?" After he stopped laughing (I assume because he expected this response from me), he asked whether I had not noticed that in all the design's title blocks, a ±0.005-inch tolerance was being called out and I had specified all dimensions to three decimal places. Being young and naïve, I answered that I had not even noticed the tolerance in the title block. And I'm sure he repeated this "over the water cooler" and it received a few hearty laughs there as well. To put it in perspective for me, Rex went on to explain that a single human hair was roughly 0.005 inches thick—and that really sunk in. I had not really ever thought of what that tolerance meant in practical terms and now I was sitting in the bar thinking that there was nothing in the entire fabrication that needed to be accurate to within the thickness of a human hair. I asked if I could revise the drawings and we could receive some type of cost savings. Rex was a good guy and told me he would work with me. The next day, I went to my boss and explained what I had learned, assuring him I would not make the same mistake twice, and he encouraged me to do what I could to save money on that job.

Looking back, either Rex was just being a nice guy or his ulterior motive for buying the beers was that maintaining those tolerances was really starting to make the job difficult and possibly a money loser. By offering a price reduction in exchange for reasonable tolerances, he would likely not incur further scrap and losses from any rework time. Either way, I learned a lot and it has always stuck with me. Owning my business allowed me to reflect on how many engineers had never learned the same lesson.

My belief is that if all mechanical design engineers responsible for machined or fabricated parts spent at least a few weeks working in a machine or fabrication shop, the company would really benefit. When I worked at Toyota, all new employees—especially those without experience—received hands-on training before starting in the office or the shop. This is the traditional approach Toyota takes and a reason for their reduced lead times and cost. Naturally, this principle is applicable for all areas and disciplines.

10.11 SUMMARY

- Standardizing protocols for all processes leading to quality problems or additional costs should be a priority for managers trying to avoid daily firefighting.
- Value stream mapping or process mapping (for administrative processes) should be taught as a tool to objectively evaluate current processes and identify improvement opportunities.
- Developing a schedule should not be based only on the availability of materials but also on the lead times and capacities of the processes involved (machines and people). This will necessitate that a PDCA (Plan, Do, Check, Act) cycle is continuously updated with new processes and lead times.
- Inventory that reduces lead time to help meet customer expectations should be considered "strategic" inventory and viewed as a tempo-

rary improvement until other solutions are implemented to reduce the lead times.

- Upstream or downstream processes that are influenced by your activities/responsibilities are areas where you should receive hands-on training; this will allow you to better provide what is needed, often leading to significant cost savings.

11

Making Money during the Good Times

11.1 INTRODUCTION

After a few years of hanging on during a significant industrywide sales slump, it seemed the "dreams" for all of us tied to the semiconductor equipment industry were coming true. For some time, the chip-making equipment industry had been developing new technology around etching on 300-mm diameter silicon wafers instead of the 200-mm diameter wafers that had been the standard. The chip makers (e.g., AMD, Hewlett-Packard, IBM, and Intel) were preparing to invest and would receive many benefits, like significant cost savings and higher yields, from the 300-mm advances. But, there were also disadvantages, like the cost of the new tooling, the time-consuming and complex requalification of existing part numbers on the new tools, more bowing and bending with the 300-mm wafers, and various other problems that come along with new technology. We had been producing some prototype parts for the 300-mm wafer machines and were now starting to see a heightened level of activity to get some of this new technology into production.

11.2 IMPROVING PROCESSES DURING SLOW PERIODS PAYS OFF

Taking advantage of the workforce's available time to make improvements during slow sales periods can really pay off when things trend back to the upside. I was not only excited about the potential profitability and the chance to grow the business, I was also feeling a little smug, knowing that all the process improvements I had put in place during the slow times were about to really pay off. I was also hoping to be rewarded for hanging on to my key employees during the downturn as we were now in prime position not only to take full advantage of their skills but also, with our improved documentation and standardization, we could quickly train any new hires.

As normal when transitioning from the prototype to production stage with highly technical products, the order quantities started small and there were immediate requirements for a wide range of part numbers to build these complex machines. I am not sure how many different fabricated and machined part numbers an etching chamber has but it appears to be in the thousands. We were starting to receive small production orders for most of the prototype parts we had previously worked on and were also busy with various other first-builds on new parts. It was a period when we tried to quote almost everything including both fabrications and machined parts that could not be manufactured in-house (outsourcing was required).

The office was busy and I kept thinking of the payback that would come from all the improvements to the flow of the administrative tasks. These improvements freed up more time for the staff to quickly provide additional quotations to our customers, obtain prices from more than one subcontractor, and request more than one quotation on all materials. Naturally, this led to increased sales with significant cost-saving implications.

The simplified lean implementation strategy of OSKKK (Observe, Standardize, Kaizen Flow & Process, Kaizen Equipment, and Kaizen Layout) does not dictate where the primary focus should be (e.g., the shop floor or the administrative processes); instead, OSKKK dictates that the primary focus should be on bottlenecks. (See Appendix L, which shows the actual sequence as we went back and forth between shop and office improvements based on the needs of the business or the bottlenecks.) Since I had shifted the focus back and forth between the shop and the office depending on the perceived constraint, I would now receive the full benefits coming from the entire business having an increased capacity.

11.3 PROBLEM-SOLVING SKILLS DEVELOPED DURING THE SLOW PERIODS BEGIN TO PAY OFF

Probably the most important thing I had partially gotten in place was the development of my employee's "Kaizen eyes" and increasing their problem-solving skills. This is not to say that I had spent any significant time developing the operators or setup men but at least Tom (the shop foreman), Jake (the programmer/estimator), Sandra (the office manager), and Andrea (Sandra's assistant) had begun the process of "learning how to see," so to speak. This left me with significant resources to deal with all the new problems that we were sure to face if the business rebounded and grew as quickly as it appeared to be doing. It would have been great had I also spent more time evolving the setup men and the operators, but at least I had always tried to ask questions and let them reach their own conclusions. I had also encouraged Tom to coach the operators—though he still enjoyed the quick and direct solution of telling people what to do—but I understood this would take time, as dictating was the easiest and most comfortable for him as it is for many of us.

Another reason for our less-formal problem-resolution method was that we were small enough for it to be almost impossible to avoid going to where the work was done when confronting a problem. Often, many companies are criticized for quickly coming to solutions while sitting in meeting rooms or shying away from the details and only being results-driven. In my case, I only utilized a little structure to get people to specifically define the problem and identify its root causes since most of the team was already familiar with the details of many of the processes for which they might be working on a solution. I only needed to ensure they did not jump to conclusions without progressing through the proper thought processes or analysis and miss out on the root cause. I prided myself on being able to perform any task in the office or the shop and made sure I did it with just enough frequency to keep from getting rusty or forgetting the details. As I have said, "the devil is in the details," and unless you try performing the process, it is unlikely you can guide its improvement, especially by only demanding that the measurements are improved. There may be times the problem-solving skill level of your direct reports are sufficient to implement working solutions, but keep in mind how expensive it is to implement the wrong solutions. I am always interested in managers who only demand results and do not get involved in the details because they must believe their staff are very skilled and they themselves do not add any value in the problem-solving process. If they only stomp around demanding improved results (financial numbers), how can they be sure they are really adding value to the company? Although I had arrived at the comfort and confidence level that allowed me to accept work as a consultant one week per month, I still believed I was adding value the other three weeks by guiding and developing the problem solvers and resolving a few issues myself.

Lean principle (from Chapter 4): Problem solving in lean terms involves a structured approach basing the solution on data gathered through observation. Normally, this requires a minimum of five steps (as discussed in Chapter 4) or could involve more complex statistical methods like Six Sigma or a structured approach to engage and develop those involved like A3.

When working to identify opportunities in larger organizations, those involved with the processes should be guided through value stream mapping for processes involving a physical product or through process mapping for administrative and office processes (see Appendix M for clarification on these applications).

11.4 THE LEADER KEEPS IN PRACTICE

I periodically challenged those who performed daily tasks in the shop and office to determine who was faster—them or me. For example, I would compare the time it took to set up similar jobs (similar number of tools, measuring points, etc.) on one of the machines. We had an agreement that any significant mistakes disqualified that individual and the other won by default. This ensured a high quality level but also made the point that standardization supported productivity. I set up the challenge for two reasons: (1) to keep my skill levels up and (2) it was motivating and encouraging to the operators to create a little competition. I always drove home the point that speed wasn't important if you lost it on quality—but it was fun. Actually, I lost more than half the time, which obviously made my team happy. But, I did continue to earn their respect, especially on the occasions when I won.

As the number of incoming orders increased, we immediately returned to a forty-hour workweek. After months of short workweeks, now I was offering overtime and had plenty of volunteers. Tom was always the first to get overtime and the last to lose it because I always needed his skills overseeing the shop, preparing the machines, and watching the quality. It was not long before Jake was also putting in some extra hours writing all the new programs that were required. As it became obvious that we needed an additional setup man, our concern was in finding someone with experience with our type of machinery so the new person could quickly become productive. As I indicated earlier, this was usually not a problem as we had equipment that was common within our industry and many were familiar with the controls. But, these were not normal times—our competitors were also ramping up quickly and looking for qualified people.

Tom threw out a suggestion about hiring his brother, who had previously worked there—he was familiar with the business and Tom said he was a very hard worker. If his work ethic was anything like Tom's, that would be a real attribute, but then I remembered some strange advice from the former owner, Bob. He had recommended not hiring Tom's brother if it was suggested, apparently Tom's brother had previously worked there and come to blows with Bob over attendance issues. Being pressed to satisfy my customers and take advantage of some potential sales records, I decided to take the chance.

Bert, Tom's brother, seemed honest enough in the interview, admitting that he had "screwed up" with his attendance while working for Bob. I explained our rather demanding attendance policy—a combined total of three times late or absent in a rolling ninety-day period meant immediate dismissal—and Bert said that would not be a problem for him. Also, Bert felt he would be comfortable working for his brother, and Tom had promised me that he would recommend firing Bert immediately if he got out of line—no hard feelings. In this case, I believed Tom since he had never put up with any unacceptable behavior and I imagined he would not make an exception for his brother.

Bert got to work quickly and was really adding value. He was an extremely hard worker like his brother (I guess it runs in the family) and appeared to be a team player. His biggest fault was that he jumped into all tasks so quick and hard that he periodically missed a detail in the setup, which cost a bit of scrap or extra adjusting time.

Within the next month, we took on another operator, and this growth pattern continued for some time. I was so busy that I was starting to shy away from committing to too much consulting work as I was continually managing/supporting our overloaded shop and office processes.

11.5 DIVERSIFICATION WOULD HAVE BEEN HELPFUL

Sudden growth spurts are not ideal in most situations and we were stretching ourselves to cope. We really had our hands full with six out of our seven largest customers being in the same industry. We would not have gone through these wild gyrations in sales levels had we been able to change our portfolio of customers through diversification. I continued working to evolve customers in other industries but up to this point I had only succeeded with one new customer in medical devices and two in the microwave/radar manufacturing industry. So, about 70 percent of our sales volume still remained in the semiconductor equipment industry. Wanting to be a better salesman was not going to get the job done. So, I had tried a few different independent sales reps who specialized in machined and/or fabricated parts and did not have a conflict of interest by also representing one of our competitors. Although none of the experiences were negative, they never really brought in any significant requests for quotes, and the few jobs we landed through them were not highly profitable. We were scraping the bottom of the barrel, so to speak, with these types of jobs.

11.6 THE NEED FOR A SECOND SHIFT

About six months into the production phase of the 300-mm etching machines, we were running out of capacity for one shift. We had many of the tools in place that had proved helpful in increasing the existing shift's capacity. For example, we were now excelling at capacity planning and monitoring against that plan. We had also made strides with setup reductions and increased machine feeds and speeds up to the limits of new and superior tooling. Therefore, a second shift was next in the cards.

Operating a second shift was always a point I wanted to arrive at. Actually, I dreamed of a three-shift operation, as most owners would. The downside is that without competent people to manage the various shifts, an owner could find himself dealing with problems at all hours. We also found ourselves in the typical growth dilemma in which we did not require the capacity of a full second shift but were left to justify the extra associated administration costs.

Ideally, Tom would manage the second shift and in the short term I would manage the first shift. We could immediately move a few people and some work to the second shift to help create a balance. The problem was that Tom had a very large family, actually nine kids, and wanted to be at home with them in the evenings. In the end, it was Bert who was willing to run the second shift, and he appeared to have sufficient skills.

The plan was that Tom would work a little overtime to make sure the second shift had a smooth start and in the near term I would handle phone calls during the evening and deal with any problems outside Bert's comfort level. The plan was two fold: (1) allocate only the less-complex jobs to the second shift, (2) schedule more work than they have capacity to handle so if they reached a point on any job in which they could not solve the problem, they could leave it set up on that machine and move to another machine. Because the second shift would not be operating all the machines, it would be possible to leave a particular machine set up when a problem arose and move to another job. Then, the problem would be resolved the next morning. Naturally, the second shift had to clearly communicate the problem so Tom or I could quickly resolve it the next day.

The second shift ran about as smoothly as could be expected. Bert had two of the better operators with him in the evenings and was tackling the easier jobs. I periodically received a phone call at home and occasionally I went into the shop when there were enough problems simultaneously that the operators did not have another job to work on (no use paying people to stand around).

The second shift began immediately after the first shift ended, which was not ideal for a number of reasons: The first shift had no catch-up ability for problems. The first shift basically could not work overtime to make up for shortfalls in completing the planned production for the shift, which in turn could affect on-time delivery. The main reason we went this way was because Bert felt more comfortable with a direct handover and he and the other operators did not want to work too late since the public buses ran infrequently after midnight. Also, we were not sure how long the second shift would last based on the customers' demand so we wanted to make any transitions back and forth as painless as possible.

While I worked with Toyota I learned they normally planned a gap between their shifts allowing them the ability to make up for any lost production, almost always achieving the shift's planned production goal. Therefore, if it appeared they were not going to reach it, all affected departments were notified—two hours prior to the end of the shift—of the required minutes or hours of necessary overtime (always in increments of six minutes). As condition of employment, an employee had to be available to work up to two hours of overtime each day. This allowed them to maintain their schedule and on-time delivery whether adapting to temporary increases in customer demand or recovering from various minor production problems. (Obviously, major disruptions could not be compensated for in the two hours between the first and second shifts and typically necessitated working on Saturday.)

Even though I was not able to implement a gap of time between the shifts, I want to capture it as a key point (when either you are operating something less than a three-shift, continuous operation or assuming you do not incur start-up losses after a process has been shut down).

Key point: *Allowing a gap of time between shifts allows the option for overtime accommodating for either temporary increases in customer demand or to make up for production losses. This should help in maintaining a high on-time delivery.*

We were also working most Saturdays during this period and I was hitting Starbuck's for more coffee and donuts than I care to think about to maintain everyone's caffeine and sugar levels. You can't maintain a long-term plan of increased working hours by keeping a workforce hyped up on sugar and caffeine, but nobody knew for how long those 300-mm etching machines were going to be selling. Ours was not the type of business whose customers provided forecasts, and the one or two we received were about as useful as that famous paper used in the bathroom. So, my plan was to take in all the business that we could manage while maintaining our high quality and on-time delivery levels, supplementing this with overtime and the second shift. I was sampling my team to check if working on Saturdays was starting to impact their private lives, but everyone was happy with the overtime money that they had lived without for a few years. My warning was not to get used to the extra money as it could end at any time.

The other option was to slow sales down by raising the prices. Like anyone else, we had the option to raise prices to the point where our supply (or capacity) was balanced with demand. The danger is that up to 60 percent of the parts we were manufacturing would receive repeat orders and it was likely these new 300-mm machines would be the standard for years to come. So, it was in our best interest to try and stay competitively priced while securing many parts into our portfolio. These repetitive purchases also applied to the parts we were currently outsourcing, some of which could be made in-house (though on less-than-ideal machines) during a slowdown to help in profitably utilizing excess capacity when necessary. Also, keep in mind that we had a higher profit margin on repetitive parts as we then had a debugged program and saved time on the adjustment phase of our setup with the methodologies previously discussed.

There was other good news during this profitable period: I was busy paying down the balance on my bank loan. Although the term was for five years, I had set a goal of paying it off in four mostly due to the 11 percent rate and the vision I had that I was paying for luxury cars for the bankers, and with this boom, it was looking possible.

11.7 THE ENTREPRENEURIAL SPIRIT PAYS FURTHER DIVIDENDS DURING THE BUSY TIMES

During the slow period, we had extended our capabilities, not really through investment but—in desperation, to stay profitable—we took on jobs that we might not have previously considered. Some were just difficult to machine, but most required additional operations that would not have traditionally been considered our "core" competency. In reality, some of them required creativity and courage in finding a method to produce them to the quality level required. But, since I was an engineer instead of a machinist managing a machine shop, I had no preconceptions of what machinists did and did not do; therefore, there were no roadblocks in my mind and every drawing we received for quotation was fair game if I could figure out how to manufacture it without significant investment. I would like to say that Tom and Jake supported me in this direction but, unfortunately, they were more traditional "machinists." And although I was making progress at opening up their minds, their big leaps of faith only came each time we took on a non-traditional job and were able to manufacture it without significant pain. These were confidence builders and the next similar item that came along was not such a stretch of their imagination and was likely more profitable. That is not to say that we didn't have a few losers on which we really struggled to perform these non-traditional operations, and we periodically would decide not to take on more work with similar characteristics. Examples of the type of work we expanded into included some heating and forming operations; we also got into a bit of metal rolling (mostly into circular shapes), working in exotic plastics and rubber materials, and also the fusing together of plastics utilizing chemicals. While none of these new areas were by themselves significant, every bit helped during that slow period and during the busy times the customers were funneling more of this type of work our way. During this market upturn we could also charge a higher rate for these specialized services as there were not many other open-minded competitors wanting to experiment and learn these new processes. Whether or not a higher price was justified, our new variable pricing structure led us to charge a higher rate for this type of work because significant time (activity) was involved from the indirects in the office (locating materials and tooling) and those on the shop floor (developing the necessary manufacturing processes). Considering how this new pricing applied to these products further helped in proving to me that this attempt at ABC costing was likely moving in the right direction.

11.8 STRUCTURED PROBLEM SOLVING MINIMIZES OPINIONS

Unfortunately, this quick sales growth was a natural cause of tension, especially between the employees and me. This was on top of the natural tension that exists between a boss and those who report to him or her in any working relationship. In my case, I was trying to get as much production out as possible, not only for short-term profitability but on the chance some of those parts would become repeat orders as the new 300-mm etching machines became the industry standard. Helping to keep the tension in check were the overtime hours and job-security that accompanied this growth. So, no matter how hard I pushed to get product out during the day, nobody worried that if they worked harder during their shift, they would lose any overtime. Again, we all understood overtime was not the long-term solution but a way to deal with this increased volume while the second shift evolved. One key component I used to resolve tension during this period was data gathering. This helped remove any emotion between myself and the team. So, when a problem was encountered—and many were springing up during this period—if it was caused for any reason other than not following standardized procedures, we waited to see if it came up again before making a big deal out of it, which helped us in not continuously fighting the wrong battles.

Lean principle: *Discussions based around data are something I consider a lean principle. Instead of discussions where participants indicate "it happens a lot" or "it happens all the time," simple data gathering (i.e., tick lists) can be used to help prioritize the problems and guide the discussions. One of my favorite sayings in this regard is "In God we trust, all others bring data."*

Tom and I were mentally keeping track of the issues. When we noticed a pattern, we either started a tick list to see how often it happened or we tried to informally apply some simple but structured problem solving to get to the root cause instead of just firefighting with our gut instincts. Lean practitioners might prefer that we utilized a more structured problem solving or completed an A3 (an eleven-inch-by-seventeen-inch, one-page structured problem-solving guide). We were not formally completing A3s as I had often done while working for Toyota, which meant we were not going through a comprehensive dialogue and back and forth iterations to clarify, find the root causes, and plan a trial solution for one of the possible causes. Unfortunately, we did not go through this type of A3 process, which could have helped me evolve as a leader and my employees grow into potential leaders and better problem solvers. But, we had a simple structure everyone followed. This allowed us to keep everything based on fact.

As I mentioned earlier, we were small enough that anyone involved in resolving problems was likely already intimately familiar with the related processes. Also, I had driven everyone to be process focused, meaning that when a problem occurred he or she would think about what went wrong in the process and often questioning whether a process even existed for that task. We were then inclined to either modify the existing process or create a simple but robust process so the problem would not repeat itself. It was difficult not to just jump in and tell someone what I thought the solution was and what needed to be done (actually, this took place more than I would like to admit). Being small and having worked hard to set in motion fact gathering and process-based principles, I had a relative basis from which to successfully resolve issues without using a more structured method to resolve problems. But, in larger organizations my experience has shown this structure is a necessary step for learning and development. Although I only used some of the simple analysis tools like the five whys, fishbone diagrams (man, method, machine, materials), and a few times completed a simplified written format (five steps) to resolve our significant/larger problems, I regret not developing myself and my team further in this regard.

I would like to capture this as a key point. A structured method helps an organization grow and develop employees without creating significant tension between the boss and the employees.

Lean principle: A3 is a problem-solving tool (a fact-based tool that leads to effective solutions) but can also be utilized as a management process. Unfortunately, during this period I did not make the time available to further my skills and manage with this tool, though in hindsight it might have helped, especially in the development of Tom, Jake, and me.

Key point: To resolve problems in larger organizations, a structured method is needed that allows facts to be gathered through observation where the work is performed, and to generate more than one proposed solution leading to trials and a follow-up method. This structure will allow you to develop the team into taking ownership and responsibility while evolving everyone into logical thinkers who are detail orientated. A written problem-solving format (known as an A3 at Toyota) is recommended. OSKKK can also be utilized as a basic methodology for resolving issues.

If you are still not convinced of the benefits of at least periodically getting involved with the details, compare the financial results from two of my previous employers, Toyota and General Motors. Toyota managers generally are involved in the details, often using A3s to focus their efforts. GM managers generally concentrate on the financial numbers and shy away from involvement in the details. You know the rest of the story.

11.9 PROBLEM SOLVING REQUIRES LOOKING INTO THE PROCESS DETAILS USING A STRUCTURE

Even during the busy times, when I became involved in solving a problem (not to say I was always involved), I had to get into the details to be able not only to realize the root causes but also to try countermeasures that were likely to work in the long term. Although it is a necessity to jump into the details, a structure is needed to guide problem solving so those with a technical understanding of the process do not assume they know the solution without working to arrive at the root cause. I think I have a good scientific head that applies logic to resolving problems, but I know you must dive full force into the nitty-gritty details to find the real solutions. I learned the business from the bottom up—maybe too quickly for some people's taste—but I understood how each process worked and I either felt confident enough to discuss any problems that came up or I went back into the process using a simple five-step problem-solving approach to arrive at a solution.

In most large businesses, managers do not see the need or do not feel they have the time to learn the various tasks, and in complex/technical industries this may not be feasible. But, a manager at least needs to get into the details when resolving a problem unless the manager feels there is nothing additional he or she can offer by involving problem-solving skills or coaching abilities.

The managers at most companies that I support as a consultant are content to run from one issue to the next, usually only demanding results from the metrics and assuming their subordinates have the abilities to figure out how to get the problems resolved. Often, I am left to run a workshop without the managers (who appear too busy managing the results), and so I get into the details with those assigned the task of resolving the problems. Frequently, nobody in the room has a problem facilitation methodology to follow (hence, the need for a consultant) but most feel they already know the cause, some have their own solutions in mind, and others feel the problem cannot be resolved. Usually it is interesting to note after working on the first step (which is to specifically define the problem) how many do not understand the entire process and there is rarely sufficient data to focus the group or the analysis. Often the workshops require a break while those involved go out to better understand the processes and gather the facts or some data. No matter how often I request some of this data to be gathered prior to the beginning of a workshop, it is rarely completed with enough detail to start a thorough discussion. If the managers instead would coach employees through a logical problem-solving approach (i.e., A3), they would create a team of future leaders while simultaneously developing their own skills. However, after many years in consulting, I still find that most are too busy attending meetings to sit patiently and dive into the details and evolve their team's problem-solving skills.

Well, enough talk about how the industrial world should function—back to life in my busy machining business. By now, we had been operating profitably for more than a year in this growth market and I had achieved a record of sales and profitability within the company's twenty-three-year history, actually almost doubling the previous owner's best year. The loan was now paid off, which would allow me all kinds of freedom to consider expansion. The second shift had actually not lasted long, and sales remained high. But, as we were performing more additional operations like assembly and some of those new bending and plastic fusing jobs I previously mentioned, the machines were no longer the bottleneck. We went instead to a staggered shift, meaning Bert and two operators started their day two hours later than everybody else, giving us ten hours per day of machine time before going into overtime. Everyone was able to stay busy either running a machine or assembling or performing various other operations. I was not disappointed with canceling the afternoon shift as we remained at about the same level of sales and profitability, and I was not required to pay a shift premium. Now, my phone never rang late at night, although the early morning calls still periodically interrupted my sleep and that oh-so-wonderful peace of mind. I viewed those phone calls as what you get when you're involved in the details, care about the productivity, and are not able to implement standard processes to deal with every conceivable situation.

11.10 EQUALITY IN ENFORCING YOUR OWN POLICIES IS CRITICAL

I ended up having to let Bert go because of attendance problems. Of all the employees I had to fire, firing Bert was the most difficult for me. He was a great worker with sufficient machining skills, and he was basically my second most-productive employee, next to his brother Tom. He made a lot of money for the company, had a great attitude, and was a real hustler at keeping things moving. However, I had adopted Toyota's strict attendance policy and had to enforce my own rules to remain fair. When Bert exceeded the limit of the combined three times late or absent within a rolling ninety-day period, I actually considered relaxing the policy just so I could keep him on. But, I knew that as soon as I started bending the rules or making exceptions, it would be unfair and I would lose respect from the entire team. I prided myself on being strict but fair, so Bert had to go. When I called him in the office to tell him it was his last day, he did not even argue. He said, "I knew the rules and screwed up." He walked out knowing the blame was his alone and Tom (his brother) supported this decision 100 percent. Tom actually used a little stronger language describing his brother's behavior by saying "he fu___ up and needs to pay the price." Ironically, when I later sold the business the new owner also ignored my warning and hired Bert. I do not know how long he lasted with the new owner, but it had the makings of a script for a soap opera.

11.11 SUMMARY

- Lean's most lucrative improvements frequently come from profitably selling the capacity created via improvements.
- Significant problems should be solved with a structured approach instead of jumping to conclusions. Either a basic problem-solving

approach or the A3 methodology should be used just like OSKKK is followed when transforming a business.

- Sudden growth is hard to cope with; but standardized processes that minimize training time combined with a cross-trained workforce provide the best chance to take advantage of this.
- Discussions based on generalizations like "it happens a lot" cause a machine-gun approach to Kaizening. Instead, focus on recurring problems, even if this requires you to go back and quantify their severity with simple data-gathering tools like tick lists.

12

Expanding into New Products

12.1 INTRODUCTION

As it goes, the good times don't last forever. After almost two years of record sales levels resulting from the introduction of 300-mm diameter wafer-etching machines, the industry was once again slowing down. It appeared that a lot of the chip makers who were planning to switch from 200-mm to 300-mm diameter wafers had already done so, and there was talk around the industry about a long slowdown. By the way, I heard most of my industry gossip from the metal and aluminum sales reps that called on us. Some days they appeared to me like old ladies running around with plenty of time to gossip. Normally I was too busy to give them much of my time and only really took the time to discuss any quality problems on the occasions when they arose (out of tolerance material, late deliveries, material damaged in transport, etc.), though when things were slow I found myself with more time and suddenly was willing to listen to a bit of gossip.

12.2 THE LOGIC BEHIND EXPANDING INTO SHEET METAL FABRICATIONS

Now that I had paid off my bank loan, I was determined to expand the business. This was further driven home by the fact that I had time on my hands and needed to find more work or new products to offset my overhead costs and remain profitable. I had previously purchased a new, larger CNC (Computer Numerical Control) machine to expand our capabilities and capacity into manufacturing larger parts. I had also replaced some older equipment with newer CNC machines. The logical expansion I now envisioned was into sheet metal fabrications since for some years we had already been providing these products to some of our customers (though we were outsourcing this work). I figured if we already had some demand in this related market with a few of our clients and were getting away with a 15-percent markup during the good times, with our available floor space all we needed was equipment and the know-how to manufacture these parts in-house.

This is where that same naïve drive that gave me the confidence to buy the business came into play. I figured if I had been able to quickly learn the machining business, I could sort out sheet metal fabrication—what could be so difficult, right? The big difference was going to be that instead of having a trained staff with many years of experience to teach me the business, I was going to have to stumble through it on my own and then teach my team. Once again, I was going to have to convince my employees I wasn't crazy. But, at least the employees who had been with me from the start figured that if I could buy a business in which I had no experience, learn it quickly, and make continuous improvements, wouldn't I be able to figure out how to punch out some metal shapes, and bend and weld them before sending them out for paint and silk-screening? No big deal, right? I already had my strategy to go forward in this new business—naturally it was also OSKKK (Observe, Standardize, Kaizen Flow & Process, Kaizen Equipment, and Kaizen Layout). However, the observation step would be difficult since there were no existing processes to watch and our subcontractors would probably take a dim view of being used in that way.

Well, I didn't have as much at risk as it might appear. My plan was to buy some simple pieces of used equipment to get started in the business, and if it went well I could expand things once I really understood how to manufacture the parts and knew what the local market demanded (i.e., the best equipment to fit our niche). I was also planning to start only with easy parts and work my way into the more complex parts. I could begin any time as repeat orders were always trickling in for the previous fabrication/sheet metal parts we had supplied. And, I could start with some of the simple ones instead of subcontracting them. I also had the option to hire someone with sheet metal experience but as we were not going to follow all the traditional sheet metal processes (e.g., using a punch or laser cutter to cut the geometry), this had its limitations. The ace in the hole was that instead of investing in a big CNC punch or laser cutter and learning to program it, I thought we could start by cutting the geometry on our existing larger CNC machining centers. Although not specifically made for this, I assumed I could develop some vacuum fixtures to hold the sheets of metal in place (if that didn't work I could go with electro-magnetic tables) and use machine tooling to cut the geometry. I knew it would not be as fast as a punch or laser cutter but the batch sizes were normally small in our industry; so if we could keep our setup times short, meaning comparatively less than that of a punch, it should work. I also thought we were very good on setups, and if we could develop some quick fixturing we would be well on our way.

Out I went to buy a basic book on forming sheet metal parts. My plan was to buy a used shear and start with a manual press to form the metal. A manual press would only allow me to bend light-gauge metal but I figured it was a start and, if successful, I could quickly buy a larger press (known as a press brake). Welding equipment would also come later. One other item that would be required was a hardware press as most sheet metal had requirements for various small pieces of hardware (nuts, studs, etc.) to be pressed in place. The consumable hardware was easy to obtain though it required a few ton press and the associated tooling.

I had some discussions with my father (my advisor and fellow investor) and he also felt this expansion was the right step. He thought the risk was minimal, assuming we ensured a high level of quality. The advantage, he noted, was that, as long as we started early and had sufficient lead time, if we encountered a major problem and were not able to manufacture the parts, we could always go back and ask our subcontractors to make them. Naturally, this might affect our on-time delivery (the promise date), which was currently at about 98 percent, but this was the biggest downside other than possibly investing some time (which we had) and money into some equipment that might not provide sufficient payback if we failed.

12.3 PREVIOUS EXPANSION CONSIDERATIONS RESULTED IN LITTLE IMPACT TO THE CURRENT LAYOUT

A few weeks later I found a used equipment auction that offered a shear that could handle the size and gauge metal we would likely be working with. At the auction, my father and I found the selling prices were staying fairly low but most of the equipment was old and outdated—until the point when the shear went up on the auction block. As luck would have it, everyone appeared to have been waiting for that shear. Opening bids moved up quickly into the thousands though I persisted until we finally walked away as the winners. The convenience of these types of auctions is that heavy-equipment movers are milling around offering quotes on transport of the purchased equipment. The shear was delivered a few days later and the electrician arrived soon thereafter to complete the connections (naturally, all connections were made flexible for any future layout changes).

When I first decided on the expansion, we had previously planned for our layout to include the additional space for the equipment we were likely to purchase. The layout's limits were the space available and the lack of knowledge/experience of which type of equipment would really be required. When we had moved to our new location, I already had this type of expansion in mind and the foresight that we wanted all existing equipment together to reduce travel distance. This had resulted in an open area near the shipping–receiving door. It was also critical that this area be near the door as the raw material for sheet metal was typically provided in four-feet-by-eight-feet or four-feet-by-ten-feet flat sheets of aluminum, steel, or stainless steel. You did not want to be moving these sheets all the way to the back of the shop before shearing them into smaller pieces. On the other hand, the existing business of machined parts normally started with smaller purchased material already cut to size or bar stock that was cut to size near the receiving door. So, it was easier to transport this smaller material throughout the shop.

Knowing the products into which you might expand is critical when planning any layout so you can prepare for future expansion. Many businesses seem to spread out their current equipment to fill the existing space, feeling more comfortable using the space and not being cramped together (though this typically leads to poor 5S—workplace organization). By envisioning future expansion and leaving an area open as a continuous reminder of the possibilities, our growth was further simplified. I would like to capture this as a key point.

Key point: The best layout is to keep all current processes close together (taking into account all lean/flow considerations) and leave all open space grouped according to where you believe future expansion will take place. This minimizes current travel distances and seeing this open space continuously reminds everyone of the growth opportunities.

A picture of the original equipment and layout we put in place for shearing and bending of sheet metal is shown in Appendix K. Again, within this area we took into consideration all the previous layout points that had been reviewed when we moved to our new location (discussed in Chapter 8). We had additional space in a separate area to set up welding equipment and hardware installation in the future. Any assembly or further operations could be performed on our existing assembly benches. The only equipment purchase that would cause serious layout concerns would be a CNC punch or laser machine to cut the metal—these machines required more space than we had available. I would need to look into renting part of the unit next door, which was being used as a warehouse for a neighboring business. (You might recall that when we moved to this location, the leaseholder of that unit agreed to rent some of the space to me if the need arose.) Though all this was way down the road since I figured I could use our larger CNC machining centers to cut the geometry for the time being and when the volume or the order quantities reached a point where we were not competitive, then we would consider investing in a punch or laser.

I was also busy designing and testing vacuum fixtures to hold the sheet metal in place on our CNC machining centers. As previously mentioned, a great advantage of a machine shop is many types of parts and fixtures can be built, which allowed us to do all this in-house. My engineering background was coming into play in designing these fixtures and specifying the vacuum systems we needed to purchase. We had machine time available to work on producing these fixture plates, and after manufacturing about the third prototype we had enough vacuum pressure to hold the aluminum parts and a few of the lighter gauge steel parts in place. The biggest problem was linked to where we had to drill holes and make cutouts because once we created a hole in the sheet metal, we lost the pressure from at least one of the vacuum points (zones) in that area and the parts periodically started moving. We worked on some variations utilizing different fixtures to cover the eventualities and separated the vacuum pressures into different zones within the fixtures. This gave us some flexibility but also required that we change fixtures more often than I had anticipated, increasing changeover time and reducing our ability to compete. In the end, we settled with a growing number of vacuum plates that also incorporated some adjustable mechanical clampdown points. This got us started and actually held an advantage over many sheet metal punches; for example, when we additionally clamped a part down, we could mill and drill through thicker and harder materials than most CNC punches could go through, opening up a niche market within the heavier gauge materials.

Working in these heavier gauges (this niche market) was a consideration for the size of press brake we would later purchase. To manufacture parts in this unique niche now required a press that would allow us to also bend these thicker gauge metals. This would open a market niche that the average sheet metal business did not have and could be a potentially profitable one for our non-conventional approach. This is another point worth capturing.

Key point: *When developing new processes, make sure to understand what special capabilities you can add that will allow you to serve unique markets that support potentially higher profit margins.*

After the shear was up and running, we found it was a very easy tool to operate and it required almost no training. I had also purchased a small manual bending press that could handle up to 16-gauge material. This would be a starting point and later we would purchase a used press brake with sufficient capacity for the heavier materials. The first bit of difficulty was in determining the overall dimension of the sheared material by taking into account the "bending coefficients" that were required. When you bend metal—depending on a combination of the type of metal, its thickness, and the bending radius of the tooling you are using—you must subtract a coefficient (these are provided in various tables) for each bend after summing the lengths of the various edges involved. It is not worth going into any more detail, though this was the first step that required a bit of experience. So we pulled out some prints for our customers' lighter gauge simple sheet metal parts that had previously been outsourced and started experimenting.

12.4 FILLING THE FIRST ORDER

After a bit of playing around and throwing a lot of small bent pieces into the scrap bin, we figured we were ready to try filling our first order. We had learned that our shear held very tight tolerances, which made us extremely happy. On the other hand, the manual bender was difficult to use and did not hold accuracy very well. Both Tom (the shop foreman) and Jake (the programmer/estimator) had been experimenting along with me and were quite excited to learn these new skills and bend metal after spending most of their lives only cutting it. After waiting almost two weeks, we received a purchase order for a previously subcontracted simple sheet metal part—fifteen pieces of a simple bracket. We went to work and soon had the parts manufactured within tolerance. Other than a bit more time and scrap than would have been competitively acceptable, we had done it and were on our way. For the time being, neither Jake nor I were ready to start doing any quoting for these parts until we had a bit more experience, but we could certainly build in-house any repeat orders for which we had the capabilities and grow into more complicated parts with more bends, more hardware, and tougher geometry.

Regarding preparation of quotes for newly fabricated parts being requested, we finally ended up cheating a little. Jake and I would take our best shot at coming up with times and costs and we simultaneously sent it out to our subcontractors for quotation. We then compared our numbers to theirs and tried to understand the differences, though this was difficult because we could only see their final cost in dollars and could not determine where the difference could be within our labor times, labor rates and material costs. We adapted our standard quoting process to incorporate the differences for sheet metal parts (including a slightly different labor rate) and tried to include all the possible tasks for a sheet metal part on a single page, even services like welding, which we were not currently doing. Now, we had one quote page for machined parts and one for sheet metal fabrications. The sheet metal was only in its infancy and likely would go through a lot of iterations as we learned and continuously improved the process. But, for the time being it helped guide us so we did not forget to include any costs. We only used our subcontractors' quotes as a checking system in the short term, and within a few months we had enough confidence to quote on our own. For our sheet metal quoting process, our "observation" was done by comparing our quotation with those from our subcontractors, than we were able to evolve a "standardized" process, which would later be followed by continuously Kaizening the process, always mirroring OSKKK.

We quickly arrived at the point where we needed to purchase a proper bending press, known in the industry as a press brake. I determined that between a twenty-five-ton to thirty-five-ton press would ensure we could bend the thicker materials, many of which the local sheet metal shops could not produce as they lacked the capabilities to punch the holes or shapes in these materials. I located a press that would do what we needed on eBay. The seller was located on the East Cost, which would add time and transportation costs to get it to California, but none of the local equipment brokers had anything meeting my requirements and price range. As with the shear, the price went a little higher on the eBay auction than I would have hoped for, but I came out the winner. I found an equipment transporter and things were put in motion. Once again, the electrician ran some flexible power lines and we had already allowed sufficient space in our layout (this is the press brake shown in Appendix K). So, the installation went smoothly. We had also purchased the hardware press and stocked it with what we were finding to be some of the most commonly demanded hardware. This small hardware often had to be purchased in 500- or 1,000-piece lots (not an ideal minimum-order quantity) and some part numbers had a few days lead time.

Since this hardware was not an expensive item, we set up a simple organization system and reordered through a basic Kanban system (frequently referred to as consumable Kanban). As most of you have learned, these small items should be treated as consumables and a simple replenishment system that reduces administration costs should be utilized. Supplier-managed replenishment systems (where the customer is not involved in managing the inventory) are a great option, but this was not available to us.

The press brake arrived without tooling so we started purchasing some common dies. Each new tool required a learning curve and frequently we had to come up with a custom set of bending coefficients for the various materials we were using it on instead of simply using the coefficients from the sheet metal handbooks. The vacuum plates combined with the flexible clamping were working fairly well at holding the sheets of material in place, and we were getting quicker on our setups and faster at verifying the measurements according to the print. While programming the parts, Jake and I learned early on we had to indicate the bending coefficient being utilized on the setup sheet so that whomever was verifying the dimensions could subtract out this number (i.e., 0.045 inches/bend) when verifying the dimensions. Other than this complication, most of the steps were the same as on the machined parts. The only other additional step is where there were square the corners on the rectangular punched holes called out. We were cutting this with a small end mill so the corners had a minimum radius, which required that the operators additionally use a specially designed file to manually square up the corners.

12.5 INVESTING STEP BY STEP

From the incoming requests for quotations, those that required welding were still being outsourced and we had not yet started aggressively pursuing our customers for additional sheet metal work until we acquired more experience. Slowly, more complicated parts containing more bending work were being manufactured in-house and our tooling for the press brake and hardware press was growing. Now, our biggest limitation was welding. We finally reached the point that we required the ability to weld aluminum, stainless, and mild steels to expand and meet the required specifications demanded by our customers. Welding the various types of material to the required quality levels were not skills we could quickly learn in-house. Therefore, my idea was to hire a part-time welder. I could also use that person to help advise what type of welding equipment I should purchase based on the type of work we were currently outsourcing. I knew terms like MIG and TIG welding but was not sure which of the capabilities were required. Also, I had yet to be confronted with a request for any welding certifications on the work I was doing (I assume because most of it was not "safety critical"). But I was sure this was likely to come up.

I quickly learned that what I required was TIG (tungsten inert gas) welding equipment. TIG uses a shield of inert gas, usually argon, to shield the process from the atmosphere, resulting in no slag spraying out all over the part and almost no porosity in the welds. A TIG system using DC (direct current) electricity can weld stainless and mild steels, and a unit using AC (alternating current) electricity can weld aluminum. MIG (metal inert gas), also known as wire feed welding, has two disadvantages: it produces lots of spatter and creates porosity in the welds. Though MIG is much easier to use, it would not produce the type of welds required for the work I wanted to perform. So all I needed was to find a used TIG with both AC and DC electrical capacities and a welder who knew TIG welding inside and out, could obtain the necessary quality levels, and was willing to work part time. How difficult could that be—right?

While discussing a complication with some work I had subcontracted to a sheet metal shop down the street, I mentioned to the owner that I wanted to buy a used TIG machine and find someone to help me on a part-time basis. He told me he had just replaced one of his TIG machines with a new super-duper machine and wanted to sell the old unit, which had both AC and DC capabilities. It got even better when he indicated his primary welder, who had twenty years experience and was one of the best he had ever come across, was always looking to pick up additional work. I immediately bought the TIG welding machine and took the contact details for his welder. By the way, I did inform him that I was planning to enter the sheet metal business with limited capabilities, and would build the smaller and simpler parts in-house but still send out any larger or more complex parts. I also put in a sales pitch for doing work in thicker gauges that he did not have the capabilities to punch through. Later on, I did periodically receive subcontracted work from him for heavier-gauge sheet metal parts, which just goes to show that although I disliked the sales side of the business, maybe I was developing a flair for seizing on new opportunities.

The TIG unit arrived and Emilio, the welder, was not only interested in working for us part time, he also volunteered to fabricate a welding table and order the necessary start-up supplies on his own time. I could not accept his offer to perform some work without receiving pay, but we agreed on a pay rate. And while he was getting my little welding shop in order, we agreed on a simple system to notify him when I required welding on a particular afternoon, I would leave a text message on his cell phone during the day and at 3:00 p.m., when he finished his shift, he would come and do my welding. In the beginning when I was learning the welding symbols in the drawings that I was quoting, he would tell me how long it would take him to weld those particular parts. He had no problems reading prints and estimating times. And just to add a little icing on the cake, he had a friend with similar skills. who could do the welding when Emilio was not available. As we all know, you don't want to put all your eggs in one basket, and I could not put my business in a position where we might temporarily be without welding capabilities in a quick-turn industry. After meeting with his friend, we set up a similar arrangement and contact system. This functioned very well the entire time I owned the business.

The point to reinforce here is that you need at least two qualified people to perform every task within your business—anything less is too risky. Therefore, you should have some type of cross-training matrix visible to ensure you meet the minimum requirement of two trained employees for each job in your shop and office. Although many try to keep track of it in their head, it should be documented in a matrix that visually displays all employees and all the tasks performed within your business, further indicating who is qualified (and maybe to what level, on a scale of one to four) for each task. You can also show your future training plans in a different color on the same matrix. An example is shown in Appendix H.

Key point: A necessity for all businesses is a skills/cross-training matrix showing the current training status of all employees (office and shop floor) in relation to all tasks. It should further indicate any planned training to make up for shortfalls anywhere there are fewer than two competent people trained to perform a particular task. This should not be managed in someone's head but should be visible for all to see.

12.6 OSKKK TAKES TO LIFE WITHIN OUR NEW PROCESSES

Now we were able to manufacture in-house many of the jobs that had formerly gone out to subcontractors. We were also doing our own quoting for sheet metal parts and were continuing to evolve a standardized quoting process specific for sheet metal work and fabrications separate from our quote sheet for machined parts. Because we now had a little experience with these parts, we started the same tracking of actual hours against quoted hours that we had been utilizing for machined parts. Since we were less experienced and encountered more problems with these parts, we had a much larger variance between our quoted times and actual times. I was reviewing these on Fridays with both Jake and Tom, not only to understand what we could learn for future quoting but also what we had to do in our processes to remove some of the waste and reduce the time required. Again, this feedback loop (PDCA: Plan, Do, Check, Act) in the quoting process proved critical in driving improvement, and it is especially prevalent on new products or those for which you do not have a lot of experience.

12.7 ONCE AGAIN, A PDCA CYCLE IN THE QUOTING PROCESS PROVES CRITICAL

I continue to come across companies that estimate labor times for a new project, determine the material costs plus any development or indirect costs, and after determining the final price they are periodically confronted with a customer or market that demands a lower price. Instead of just working backwards from the market price and adjusting their hourly rates and/or profit margins to determine whether this new target price is acceptable, they start changing their estimated hours to fit in line with the new target price suggested by the customer. Normally, they cite anticipated efficiency improvements as the justification for reducing the estimated hours. But, I have found this to be a mistake. It most often takes place in organizations that do not have a robust labor-quoting system, or feel the labor is only a small and negligible part of the entire quotation, or do not really trust their quoted hours. These are the same firms that typically do not have a good track record of making improvements in working methods to reduce these labor hours. Instead, I recommend internally developing the quoting skills for labor hours by instituting a PDCA loop for the estimators, which should result in more faith in quoted labor hours. Then, when faced with determining whether or not to agree to a customer's target price, work backwards to calculate the hourly rate (in dollars) associated with the target price:

$$\frac{(\text{Target price} - \text{material costs} - \text{other costs} - \text{required profit})}{\text{quoted hours}} = \text{hourly rate you will receive}$$

and decide whether this is acceptable. I experienced instances where a customer gave me a target price with the option to take it or leave it; in these cases, I would back-calculate the new hourly rate and decide whether there was enough profit left in the job.

Now back to our newly acquired ability to weld in-house. Another advantage we discovered was that when machining an expensive part and too large a hole or cutout was made or when we removed too much material, Emilio could often fill in our mistake with some of his wonderful welding and we were able to re-machine the existing part instead of having to purchase more material and start over. I assume this was done by others in the industry but I am sure it is not something most companies admit takes place.

Lean principle: Balancing machine cycle time with the operator's cycle time when specifying new equipment benefits from lean thinking. Even within a made-to-order business where machine cycles are likely to vary depending on the various products being built, average cycle times can be estimated (for typical parts), and what the operator does within that cycle should be considered before investing too much in automation. For example, I find many companies invest in additional auto load robots and conveyor systems on the same machine on which they also pay an operator to stand and wait for the machine to cycle. This was also a consideration as I purchased equipment for the sheet metal business. (See Figure 12.1.)

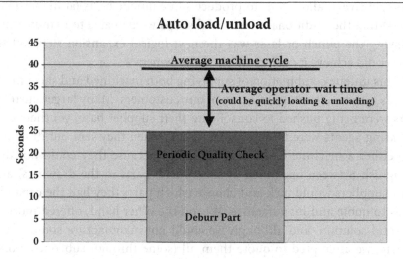

FIGURE 12.1

12.8 AGAIN, ENGINEERS' LACK OF HANDS-ON EXPERIENCE IS COSTLY

After a period of manufacturing these sheet metal parts, I again found (like I had discovered with machined parts) that the engineers often did not design parts that were easy to manufacture, and therefore they unknowingly increased the costs. I observed this in many forms. For example, there were often difficult tolerances to maintain (especially when a few bends were involved) or no place (fillets or cutouts) to allow room for the weld along with difficult areas to bend when it would have been more cost-effective to weld two pieces together. Again, this demonstrates the necessity and cost justification for engineers to acquire hands-on experience in manufacturing if they are designing fabricated products. Or, at least it demonstrates a need for a "design for manufacturing" process to be put in place.

Over the next year, we grew the sheet metal business to somewhere around 30 percent of our total sales volume. We slowly progressed to more difficult parts and added some simple equipment to roll round shapes. During my time as the business owner, we never did purchase the CNC punch or laser cutting machine. We continuously improved cutting the geometry on our CNC machines and, although it limited the size of material we could work with and the batch sizes for which we could remain competitive, it allowed us to produce some unique parts (at higher margins) that the traditional sheet metal shops were unable to manufacture. Buying the punch or laser was the next logical expansion step, but we never did achieve it during my tenure as owner.

This unique combination of supplying both machined and sheet metal parts was an advantage to many of our customers. Many larger customers were being pushed to consolidate their supplier base, yet their purchasing agents were frequently frustrated when they sent out drawings to either a machine or sheet metal shop (because they could not distinguish between machined or sheet metal parts in the drawings) and the suppliers would pick and choose which parts they had the capabilities to quote and manufacture. We, on the other hand, offered more of a total solution, and although we could not manufacture some of the parts, we attempted to quote them all (some through subcontractors).

It was preferable for the overworked buyers to receive from one supplier a complete quote package with competitive prices and—ideally—short delivery times for all the drawings they sent out. Therefore, we continued to work our way into that idealized "preferred supplier status" with some of our customers. Again, having customers with overloaded buyers who are not technically savvy is a situation for all suppliers to take advantage of by adapting their services. These buyers also rarely have the time or inclination to visit their suppliers; therefore they do not recognize their in-house capabilities. The best situation is not to have your own purchasers overloaded (always having time for obtaining competitive quotes and managing suppliers) while putting in place methods to take advantage of your customer's busy buyers. Having worked with many companies' purchasing departments, I have found incredible amounts of time lost on non-value-added activities and little time devoted to critical strategies like sourcing new suppliers. Remember: if 50 percent or more of your cost goes into purchased materials, a lot of opportunities lie within this department (and having the time available to obtain the best pricing, lead time, and quality leads to great payback).

I think many companies expand into related products after they have determined an opportunity exists. The example from my business holds the most interest for companies that do not develop their own products. But, even for those firms responsible for development, some of the lessons learned here are valuable. For example, wherever possible, try to establish a presence in the market before making any significant investments (like temporarily subcontracting some or all of the steps) while evolving as an established supplier for these items. Minimize investments where possible until you have learned a bit about the product and market. Look for easy-entrance products to get into the market and later develop the skills and capabilities for providing the more difficult products or services. That's what I learned evolving my business into a new market, and as things slowed down in our industry, this diversification really helped. To put it in perspective, over 400 similar businesses (machining and sheet metal companies) in California alone went bankrupt during this time period, but I feel we survived this turbulent period because of our focus on the continuous elimination of waste along with our expansion into sheet metal.

12.9 SUMMARY

- Expansion into similar and complementary products is a logical step.
- Job shops can minimize the risk of growth into new areas by first outsourcing these new parts while simultaneously developing the in-house capabilities.
- Existing layouts should not be allowed to expand into all the available space; instead, they should consume the minimum space required (helping 5S and flow) and leave the open area free of debris to remind everyone of the growth opportunities.
- Minimize investment by balancing the average machine's cycle time with operators' task times, not overinvesting in automation while an operator is being paid to wait on the machine.

13

Business for Sale

13.1 INTRODUCTION

Although we were not experiencing a boom in the primary industry we served, we were holding our own. The addition of the sheet metal capabilities had positioned us uniquely in the market—we were one of the few shops that offered not only machined parts but smaller sheet metal and fabricated parts. Our customers continued to find this attractive as we could competitively supply more types of parts, reducing their supply base and the effort involved in obtaining quotations and in the purchasing and receiving processes. Also, the fact that our on-time delivery remained near 98 percent kept us in the "A" tier of their respective supplier management programs.

The sheet metal side of my business was in its early growth stages; we were learning where our strengths and weaknesses resided and thinking in terms of which direction we could further grow this area. Our non-conventional methods of cutting/punching the part on a CNC (Computer Numerical Control) machining center instead of punching out the geometry were allowing us to work in a unique market niche for heavier-gauge formed parts where there were fewer competitors. With all this going for us, plus knowing that the cyclical nature of the semiconductor equipment industry likely meant it would bounce back soon, and with our increased capabilities we would potentially be more profitable than ever, why on earth would I consider selling the business?

The reason for selling lies in my personal life and not in the state of affairs with the business environment. It came down to an agreement between my wife and me. Bottom line: we decided it was a good time to move to Spain, my wife's country.

The lean consulting work I had stumbled into through my previous employer had expanded to a point that I felt could grow into a livelihood based out of Spain. I had been consulting almost one week per month and just by word of mouth had expanded past having Delphi Automotive as my sole client. I figured if I was finding more consulting work without looking for it, I could likely find enough work in Europe if I aggressively pursued it. With the decision made, it was time for me to learn how to sell a business.

13.2 DETERMINING THE PROCESS STEPS FOR SELLING A BUSINESS

To sell the business, I thought I probably just needed to reverse the steps I had gone through to buy it five years earlier. Since I had not started the business and grown it from my garage, I likely had less emotion involved in selling than the former owner. I just needed to figure out where to start and the elements involved. I did a bit of brainstorming with my father, who had previously owned and sold a larger business, and we thought that I should first do some research and read up on current methods for selling a business. A few of the books I bought proved to be less helpful than I had hoped and also functioned better than prescription sleeping pills, but I found a few worthwhile bits of advice that helped me to rough out a plan.

I am basically opposed to using middlemen who add little value or bring almost no practical experience to the table; therefore, putting a business broker between me and potential buyers offered few advantages in my mind. I recalled the young salesman (for the business broker) who was involved when I bought the business: he added some experience in the process steps of buying a company but had no background in the industry and the previous owner was the one answering most questions. Therefore, I felt if either the Internet or advertising in other media would bring me together with potential buyers, I could handle the rest.

Before I could list the business for sale, I had to first get some financial records in order and then come up with a method to determine an asking price. My father and I discussed using an analysis that involved a bit more than just a valuation based on earnings. Since neither of us were accountants by profession, we decided to seek professional help.

13.3 DETERMINING AN ASKING PRICE

We found a local CPA (certified public accountant) who had experience in evaluating sales prices for companies; although most of his experience came from service, financial, or retail companies, we decided he was the best fit. We provided him with the previous five years of tax returns along with our financial records. He worked with the same financial software that we used so it was easy for him to pull the necessary data directly from the computer files. After a few meetings to fill in the blanks, we determined to fix a selling price based on a combination of earnings and a market valuation (weighted more toward the earnings). Although assets are a consideration, most potential buyers are more concerned with future profitability. In our case, the matter regarding assets has more to do with the age and condition of the various machinery in terms of when additional investment may have been required. Remember: we were selling the company for the value it held as an ongoing business (the real value is in the goodwill—the customers, processes, employees' skills, technology, past earnings, patents, etc.) and we were not looking for an asset sale.

The accountant's analysis was based on taking the yearly income (adding back any owner's salary) and subtracting the costs to hire an experienced business manager to replace me. Then he took an average of the remaining income from 1999 through 2002 and divided it by his anticipated rates of return—15 percent, 18 percent, and 20 percent—to determine a price range. He also completed a projected income analysis for the next three years and completed the same steps with the same desired rates of return, giving us three more potential asking prices. His advice was to choose a starting price from among the six numbers he provided. The idea was to look at the business as an investment with a certain factor of risk, making the assumption that it would not be owner-operated, and then depending on the rate of return wanted on the investment (the accountant assumed an investor would demand a rate of return between 15 percent and 20 percent), which then determined the asking price. My

196 • Mr. Lean Buys and Transforms a Manufacturing Company

father and I were more comfortable using the valuation from the last three years of earnings as those were actual numbers and it was roughly the same type of valuation method we used when buying the business. Forecasting sales numbers going forward is best left to the potential buyer, and although we would share this part of the analysis, they could play with the "what-ifs." We simply felt more comfortable basing our asking price on the historic reality.

13.4 A MARKETING PACKAGE

Once we had a starting price in mind, it was time to put together a marketing package. To align with the selling process I wanted to put in place, I put together a package that had to be released in steps, first providing enough detail to interest potential buyers without providing the name of the business. Afterwards, a potential buyer could sign a non-disclosure agreement, after which we would provide a second package containing more financial and product detail, general terms and conditions (e.g., I would not finance more than 10 percent). If interest continued, the potential buyer would have to send me some company or personal background along with financial statements—bank account statements, stock statements, or letters of credit from a bank, etc.—to prove the ability to pay. If I found this acceptable, then we would meet at a neutral location (restaurant, coffee shop, etc) and I would provide the buyer the third and final marketing package, which contained detailed financials and a few years of tax returns. During this meeting, I planned to answer questions and after giving the buyer time to further review the third package of information, I could set up an after-hours appointment for the buyer to visit the business. That was my concept, and I went to work putting the packages of information together.

I also set up a separate email account and bought another cell phone, both of which were only to be used by potential buyers when making contact. This would help in maintaining anonymity for the business, ensuring that no calls or emails were intercepted by the employees and the name of the business was not accidently disclosed. This is critical to minimize the employees' and the customers' anxieties.

13.5 ADVERTISING

Now, I was ready to start my advertising campaign. I planned to start on the Internet, and as I recalled from when I was trying to buy the business, some "business for sale" Web sites (open market style) were available where potential sellers could list their offerings and potential buyers could either search or periodically run ads stating the criteria for the types of companies they were interested in purchasing. I found that since the time when I had purchased the business, the Internet had really grown in this area. There were so many choices of where to advertise that I had to spend many hours just trying to qualify and rank the various Web sites. I used criteria like how easy they were to find on search engines, what types of companies they specialized in, the amount of daily traffic they had, how easy the site was to use, and the cost to place an ad. I started with running ads on two of the larger sites and clearly stated that I wanted "principals only."

What would turn out to be a long process had finally begun. I learned some of the tricks that brokers used to try and weasel their way into getting an exclusive listing for selling a company. They started contacting me immediately after my listing was posted (although I had stated "principals only"). They claimed that they represented a client who was interested but wanted to meet with me before introducing the client. My answer in the early stages was always that I was not interested in working through a broker and would see how things went for a few months before considering any broker intervention. At that point, I was not willing to pay the 10-percent commission that business brokers were looking for until I deemed it necessary. I was also convinced that an "exclusive listing" was not a route I wanted to follow as I thought it really would limit my reach and tie my hands in terms of being proactive.

13.6 THE FIRST NIBBLES

Finally, inquiries did arrive from investors, from companies in related industries looking to expand, and from private individuals. My procedure was very simple and the first steps could be done though email or fax if necessary. If they were still interested after the first general marketing package, I would email them a boilerplate non-disclosure form for them to sign and send back, then I would email out the second part of my marketing package. It seemed to contain enough information to interest some of those potential buyers to go the next step. However, because of the different formats on those "business for sale" Web sites, I ended up answering a lot of inquires that only clarified for some buyers that this was not the business for them. Therefore, as I expanded my advertising, I chose only those Web sites that allowed enough description and details (like maximum 10-percent seller financing) to eliminate the casual interest of the typical "tire-kickers," which helped in minimizing the waste of my time by taking the first few steps with those who were not serious.

13.7 CONSIDERATIONS OF OWNER FINANCING

Owner financing is an interesting subject—a bit like a double-edged sword. Obviously, the larger the percentage of the sale price a seller is willing to finance, the more risk they are willing to share. If you indicate that you will finance a fair portion of the asking price, then it can be said you are stating confidence in the business's longevity and certainty in the buyer's ability to manage the business. On the other hand, if you will not become involved in the financing to some extent, it makes a statement about your faith in the business's future. When I bought the business, Bob (the former owner) did not offer any financing and I did not push the issue. But, in retrospect I should have requested some financing to secure his interest in the success of the business. The problem I now faced was trusting a potential buyer's ability to learn and successfully manage the business as I had done. I figured that offering 10-percent financing showed a bit of confidence in the business. But, I felt I could not justify offering more as I did not have an in-depth understanding of the potential buyer's ability to make the correct management decisions. All the process standardization I put in place would also help in supporting the business's success and place better odds on me recovering the 10 percent I financed. I was also reflecting on all the security a bank could ask for that a seller could not (with seller financing). For example, in my case the bank had required me to assume personal responsibility for the value of the loan by having first rights to all business assets. I had to commit to securing all personal assets and agree to potential future garnishments against me, plus a life insurance policy that would cover the value of the loan in the event of my demise. Any seller financing was always going to be subrogated to the primary lender if things went belly-up and I would likely only have rights to any business assets that remained after all bank debt was accounted for.

Lean principle: Process standardization should be considered an asset when expelling the effort to develop the standards and also later when selling the business. You have minimized reliance on tribal knowledge and often decreased the skill level necessary to complete certain tasks.

As the months rolled on without any offers, I increased my advertising with additional Web sites and started running newspaper ads. Also, when brokers called indicating they represented a potential buyer, I began offering up to a 5-percent commission if they were to secure the sale. But, I stuck to not listing with any agencies and absolutely no exclusive listings up to this point. I had met offsite with a few potential buyers to answer their questions. About four months after listing the business, I had only hosted two after-hours visits of the plant and neither seemed the ideal candidate and no offers came forward.

13.8 LOWERING THE PRICE

I did what most in my situation would do and started lowering the asking price as I was mentally ready to move on to the next stage of my life. The new price created a slight increase in traffic; therefore, more requests for additional information were coming my way. Most potential buyers appeared impressed with my three-stage organizational approach of distributing material a step at a time to help in establishing an interest level before both sides really started sharing critical financial data. Back when I was buying the business, I had determined that banks working with the Small Business Administration basically liked to see 30 percent or more as a down payment; so, when I looked over a prospective buyer's financial data it was fairly easy to approximate the cash they needed to qualify for conventional financing.

As a seller, I wanted to appear confident without appearing like I thought I had the world's best business mind or had pursued every possible avenue to expand and improve the business. Remember: every buyer has their own improvement ideas and is thinking how they can profitably grow the business. My angle had been the implementation of lean along with a little common sense, and although I felt most of the "low-hanging fruit" had been harvested, I was salesman enough not to advertise that thought. I did not believe all the lean avenues had been exhausted but the next steps would require significantly more effort. I also felt that many growth opportunities still existed (including many outside the scope of my idea to further expand in the sheet metal area), and left it to my salesmanship to plant these ideas in the minds of the prospective buyers.

13.9 THREE SERIOUS BUYERS

It was probably seven or eight months since I had listed the business before some serious prospects came along. Three were worth getting excited about: The first was the owner of four separate companies including one that sold small aluminum enclosures to house various electronic configurations that invariably required outsourced machining. The second was an aggressive investor who had bought and grown various businesses and had accumulated millions in equity. And the third was an individual with the financial means and a sales background who wanted to get out of corporate America and run his own company.

Many long discussions followed with the first prospect, and he even set up a pilot program where his team was subcontracting to us some of the machine work for his company's small electric enclosures (the entire pilot ran without any problems). Unfortunately, after all the discussions and effort he was not able to put together an offer as quickly as the other prospects. Obviously, his desire was vertical integration through which he could provide additional sales (and increased profitability) to an existing machining company like mine. Plus, he could also reduce his lead time as he would control the planning and priorities instead of relying on outsourcing the machining of his electronic boxes to someone else.

After about nine months, three separate offers came in within the same week: The first came from the aggressive investor. The second came from the individual who wanted to get out of corporate America. And surprisingly, the third came from another individual who seemed a little offbeat and did not ask the right questions or display the level of interest that the others had. But, lo and behold, out of the blue he also submitted an offer. I referred to him as "Mr. Left-Field."

13.10 EVALUATING OFFERS

Evaluating offers is probably another subject of which entire books are written, and it was also one of the many areas where I lacked experience. Whenever I require some knowledge about a process with which I am not familiar, I start by seeing what is available on the Internet. Based on reading a few articles, I determined the criteria to use and also a list of the pitfalls to watch out for. Naturally, price is likely the most important starting point. However, drawing an analogy to selling your house: if the buyer making the highest bid is not offering to put much money down in good faith or has included a lot of stipulations in their offer, you would likely consider more than just the price.

This was basically what I had in front of me:

- The highest offer, which came from the aggressive investor, was written with more big "lawyerly" words than I could make sense of, and there were many escape clauses. I remember that it had so many clauses that would allow his investment firm to back out that it seemed more like a fishing expedition than a genuine offer. One of the many stipulations that could render the offer null and void was that his investment firm wanted to meet beforehand with our two largest customers and discuss our services and their future sales prognosis. As far as I am aware, speaking with customers prior to the sale is uncommon. And it was too dangerous for me to contemplate. First of all, the customers could become anxious about the sale and start looking for more "stable" suppliers. And, I would not be in control of this meeting so I had no way of knowing what else could be brought up. On top of that, the investment company had written in other clauses for which they could back out of the deal and I would be left patching things up. For these reasons, along with many of the other scary clauses all favoring the buyer, I did not accept it even though it was the highest offer.

- Next in line in terms of price was from "Mr. Left-Field." It seemed to be missing details and serious thought and only offered a mere $10,000 down as a good faith deposit upon the offer's acceptance. This offer also set off alarms inside my head. One issue was the small deposit being offered as "good faith" along with the fact that it appeared he wrote the offer himself without seeking any legal advice or thinking through the details. Although he had displayed enough in assets to qualify with the 30-percent down payment, I figured he would either not receive financing, or if I agreed to finance 10 percent, the business would not last long enough for me to recover my money. Although in the end you may be thinking that just selling it and getting your money out is the most important thing, I really wanted to see the business do well. This is especially true in terms of the livelihood it provided for the employees. It was important to know they would be looked after and I did not feel this man would be able to do it.

- The lowest offer was put together by the individual's lawyer, and it was straightforward and appeared to be the most sincere. My father commented how the third offer appeared most similar to the offer he helped me construct almost six years earlier when I purchased the business. Therefore, the lowest priced offer was the one I accepted.

13.11 OFFER ACCEPTED

I had already found a title company to handle the transaction (similar to a title company that handles home sales but this type of firm works with all the legalities of buying and selling a business). We agreed to use the title company I recommended and further arranged to split this cost. The "good faith" money was put in an escrow account held by the title company. We were both provided with a list (different lists for the buyer and seller) of what needed to be prepared and completed prior to signing. There are considerably more details and legal requirements than those involved in the sale of a home but it's just a matter of punching your way through the list. The buyer and I agreed on a target date of approximately one month as we each felt that was the period necessary to complete our respective tasks. He had his lawyer draw up the sales contract based on the terms in the signed offer. I had my lawyer look it over and, after the lawyers batted the document back and forth and held conference calls at about $300/hour, we finally reached a sales contract with all the "i"s dotted and "t"s crossed and were on the final countdown toward the big day.

The terms of the sale included a "non-compete clause" of at least two years, meaning I could not open a similar business in Northern California during that period. I had also agreed to stay on and manage the business for six weeks during which I would train the new owner. His background was in technical sales but his plan was to hire an experienced general manager to run the business while he went out and beat the bushes to increase sales. As my plan had been to implement lean to grow the business, his angle to grow the business was through superior salesmanship (where his expertise and experience resided); I wish I knew the final results (lean vs. salesmanship). The idea was that during the six weeks of training I would help interview and hire an experienced manager. In the meantime, I was busy building and shipping what I could prior to the signing date at which point the buyer would own all raw material, finished goods, and open orders left on the books. With certain customers I could not ship early but where possible I was going to maximize my profits with early deliveries on those few items where longer lead times had been granted. I would then own all the accounts receivable for everything shipped until the handover date.

The employees were not informed until after the papers had been signed and, of course, "the money was in the bank." It was a Friday afternoon when we signed, and although I suggested we break the news together, the new owner told me I could do it alone and he would not be in until Monday morning. I was a little surprised as this is when the employees need the most reassurance that things will continue in more or less the same fashion. So, this pep talk usually came from the new owner detailing how he planned to operate and usually included some improvement ideas. I remember when buying the business that I was very concerned with how I handled this discussion to minimize the employees' anxieties. Therefore, although this time it was not me assuming the reins, I decided to wait until Monday morning when he was there so we could make the announcement together. Watching the team on Monday morning, I think Tom (the shop foreman) took the news the hardest as we had worked closely together over the years. During the next couple of weeks, I tried to assure him that I really respected his skills and dedication and enjoyed our time together but explained again how it was time for me to move on. I also tried to reassure him that the business was secure and even explained that I had financed some of it so my interests were also at stake.

13.12 DRAWING TO AN END

It was often pointed out to me that the process of selling a business of this type without previous sales experience or involving a business broker was risky. In the end, I did all right, and although I likely made some small mistakes, I do not believe I would have found a buyer quicker or someone willing to pay more using a broker. I would have just been out 10 percent of the sales price. I think in this case hiring a broker is a heavy price to pay. With the mainstreaming of the Internet, more options are available for bringing together parties with similar interests. Therefore, I would like to capture this as the last learning point, not necessarily a lean idea but a basic concept.

Key point: When you are required to perform a process for the first time that can also be handled by an outsider, first understand the difficulty and steps involved and compare this to the cost, time, and skills you have available for the task. Don't get sold into thinking you can't do it without prior experience until you at least understand what is involved and what benefits that prior experience will likely bring. Learning new processes makes us all better people.

As I was writing this book almost six years after the sale of my company, I knew that the business was still rolling along. I have not kept close tabs on how the business has been progressing, though I am happy to say I received every penny back from the portion I financed. I would like to believe part of the ongoing success was from some of the more robust and standardized processes we put in place during my tenure. Because things were standardized and documented, I know it was easier for me to train the new owner than it had been when I received my training from Bob.. More often than not, I was able to refer to standardized and document processes as I handed the business over. And I was almost jealous when reflecting on how simple it was for the new owner compared to the anxiety and late nights I had gone through until I had some of these critical procedures in place.

Naturally, there is an emotional side to buying, improving, and then selling a company. Overall, I am happier in life, having removed some of the stresses associated with being an owner, especially those for which you have minimal control or influence over, such as the upward and downward shifts of the primary industry you serve. On the flip side, there are things I miss, like the feelings of excitement when we secured a good order, or profitably growing the business, or in implementing improvements that had an impact on the bottom line. It is also difficult to walk away from the natural kick you get from being completely responsible.

13.13 SUMMARY

- When confronted with overseeing a process for which you have no experience, be sure to learn existing process steps from various perspectives before deciding how you will outline and handle the specific process.
- Standardized processes should be considered a business asset as they help ensure ongoing profitability without complete reliance on maintaining the same workforce over the long term because of their tribal knowledge.

14

Reflections

14.1 INTRODUCTION

One of my biggest fears in writing this book was that readers might not see how my experience of implementing lean methods in a small business can be applied elsewhere. However, after years of supporting lean implementations in mostly medium-sized companies (typically made-to-order businesses or service companies, including small subsidiaries of larger corporations), I have found again and again that many of the strategies I utilized in my business are imperative, and the same basic issues exist requiring similar solutions. Although areas within my lean transformation were fairly traditional and you may have already implemented some of these steps, I also hoped that other discoveries are likely unique to job-shop environments and might provide some new avenues to explore in your lean journey.

Despite having had my share of failures (e.g., never implementing a successful bonus system or structured problem solving), I learned from each of them but will continue to draw my learnings from some of the underlying principles and philosophies that proved most successful.

14.2 LESSONS LEARNED

To recap: I bought a company with no background in the industry and implemented lean principles as they were called for by simply following

OSKKK (Observe, Standardize, Kaizen Flow & Process, Kaizen Equipment, and Kaizen Layout). Utilizing this strategy drew about thirty-nine various lean ideas or tools (noted in the textboxes) into the discussion to help improve my business. It would have been difficult on day one to determine exactly which lean ideas would be necessary and what the priority should be. But, by following the common sense of the OSKKK methodology, I pulled in the necessary tools as they were required and it all fell into place. I proved, at least to myself, that implementing lean can lead to profitable growth as well as increasing the profit margin of most existing work, even in a job-shop environment.

You can start an OSKKK strategy in either the shop, the office, or both as dictated by the needs of the business. The priorities are likely different for every company and vary over time depending on many factors. I could have never predicted the ups and downs in our industry and the opportunities they would offer. During busy times, most of our improvement efforts focused on increasing capacity in both the shop and the office. Bottlenecks were not limited to the shop but often cropped up in the office, also leading to opportunities. The slow periods presented opportunities in terms of the team members having the time available to make changes. I was confronted with the choice of reducing costs (through downsizing) in the short term or implementing improvements that would be most profitable during the next sales upturn. We utilized a combination, always choosing first to stay busy implementing improvements during the slow periods, and only downsizing as a last resort.

Furthermore, I found that I could not be rigid in my implementation of OSKKK for either the shop or office, especially when major opportunities presented themselves. I needed to be flexible enough to adapt my plan and take advantage of these events. For example, the combination of a pending rent increase and a slow business period led me to jump to the last step of my implementation plan (Kaizen Layout) by moving the business to a new location, improving the layouts of both the shop and office in the process. I knew OSKKK was flexible enough to allow me to adapt to this change in the business environment.

The sequence I ended up utilizing to learn and transform the business (shown in Appendix L) demonstrates the flexibility of the OSKKK approach to adapt to our continuously changing business environment. It became clear from my learning and Kaizening sequence (as well as my mother's sequence in the office) that the observation and standardization steps always came first and that Kaizening the flow and processes was where most of the improvements were concentrated. The chart (Appendix L) captures our final sequence (not our plan) and shows that Kaizening the equipment and layout came later for the most part, generally prioritized based on events taking place within our business environment.

The opportunity for me to learn a business from the bottom up and take time to familiarize myself with most processes made me a much better change agent than most managers I encounter. Many try to manage from the numbers, in the worst cases comparing mostly historic financial results to the budget (which is only someone's best guess based on recent information). Toyota had taught me that "the devil is in the details" and allowed me time to learn the processes I would later be held responsible to oversee. Toyota was well-rewarded for this investment of my time. This demonstrates the importance of taking time for observation as promoted by the first step within OSKKK. So, the lesson I learned is not to be too obsessed with managing by the financials or too busy firefighting; nothing beats taking proper time for observation before jumping to conclusions.

I tried to make PDCA (Plan, Do, Check, Act) the basis for most of my actions and not just utilizing it to guide problem solving. We are all natural problem solvers though you need a method (like PDCA, structured problem solving, suggestion systems, etc.) to bring out these natural problem solving abilities/desires; remember you can force people into performing a task, but you cannot force them to be interested. Honestly, most of us can only say we "try" to utilize PDCA since it is sometimes difficult not to just tell somebody what you think the solution is and instruct them to implement it. With the minimal meetings we held, I was able to ask more questions at the work areas, letting people better identify and analyze the specific problems or issues (Plan). Then, after they developed and implemented solutions (Do), I could (Check) on the results to see whether they were achieving the desired goal. Most of the time, all this took place informally but if the desired goal was reached, I made sure the full-scale solution was implemented and documented (Act). The idea of putting some structure in my week (standardized work for managers) and making this auditing/review schedule public knowledge by displaying it on a board above my desk was helpful in structuring this approach and forcing me to lead by example. This was further enhanced by my focus on the details and encouraged me to go to Gemba (the real place, usually referring to where value is added) to observe instead of working out solutions blindly.

14.3 USING THE CORRECT MEASUREMENTS IS CRITICAL TO ACHIEVING RESULTS

Probably one of the most critical factors was the trial and error of learning the correct measurements that drove the business to achieve a high level of profitability. Oddly enough, none of the measures that helped in daily management turned out to be the financial numbers; those were a result of focusing on the correct business metrics (i.e., periodically monitoring more timely indicators like lead time for certain customers). In my made-to-order business (job shop), it was critical to measure the actual times and material usage against the quoted numbers that represented the customers' expectations. In addition to truly understanding where I made and lost money, I became better at pricing, which during industry downturns became quite a competitive advantage. Lead time is another critical measurement for almost all shop-floor and office processes, and is even more significant in quick-turn industries. Other important measurements for machine-based processes like ours were OEE (overall equipment effectiveness) and DSO (days sales outstanding), which helped improve our cash flow (reducing the necessary working capital). On-time delivery—holding to our promise date—was also extremely critical in the fast-turn industry we supported; this was frequently more critical than the price. Although this book might not have focused on the issue of quality, it was an underlying assumption in everything we did. Higher-priced companies can still keep a dialogue going with their customers but nobody speaks with poor-quality suppliers. For me, DSI (days supply of inventory) was not a critical measurement as we carried little inventory (although DSI should be the metric used instead of inventory turns). But, for many medium-sized companies this and other measures like labor productivity, sales per employee, and employee turnover are all relevant. In my mind, the right measurements are critical for at least two reasons: the wrong measures lead to the wrong behavior, and using the right measurements with an understanding of what influences them will guide your team to focus their limited resources on the correct priorities.

Another point in using lean measurements and implementing lean principles is to help bridge the gap between the owner's (or executive's) focus on profitability and the operator's understanding of what he or she can do to help improve the stability of the business, thereby guaranteeing job security. Examples of this: when I converted the percentage improvement in OEE to dollars to clarify for Tom (the shop foreman) why he was more valuable as a team leader. And, when I used lead-time measurements (in days) showing how long it took us to convert some raw materials into finished products so all the operators could see how reducing days of lead time could help to earn more money.

14.4 CROSS-TRAINING IS A CRITICAL PART OF SUCCESS IN HIGH-VARIATION COMPANIES

Producing a high mix of part numbers with a wide variety of tasks shared among a few people made cross-training vital, not only in the shop but often more so in the office. Visualizing the current status of our cross-training (as shown in Appendix H), coupled with a training plan, allowed us to manufacture a wide variety of products with a small team. It also helped in maintaining our high rate of on-time delivery. Having a training plan linked to a wage system that paid more for higher skill levels encouraged cross-training by ensuring that when team members had available time they were motivated to use it productively.

Remember: Employers should ideally provide eight hours of value-adding tasks each day for *all* employees. Since this is nearly impossible, employers need to provide tasks (i.e., cross-training, task lists, etc.) to make the best use of slow times. If they do not, and if expectations are not set related to output, most employees will have no recourse but to spend this time trying to appear busy. Companies also need to have at least two people trained on each task so they can help during the peak workloads or fill in when someone is absent.

14.5 TEAM LEADERS INCREASE PROFIT THROUGH HIGHER OEE

A related strategy that proved to have a high rate of return was making Tom the team leader. What I learned by designating a team leader was that, by measuring the OEE beforehand and comparing it to the improved

OEE afterward, I proved that it had been the correct decision based on the cost versus benefits. This proved Toyota's concept of having "specialists" (team leaders) available to handle the problems instead of encouraging everyone to resolve their own issues was the right idea. In addition, we should not be obsessed with the number of direct versus indirect employees but look instead at the value each position adds.

Another key point is that a team leader is the first line of defense in terms of problem solving. Once Tom became proficient as a team leader, I was less involved in firefighting and had more time for the check and act portions of PDCA. Allowing team members to struggle with problems until they decide they need assistance and only then notify their supervisors (who are already preoccupied with their responsibilities) results in a company continuously needing extra time allowances to deal with problems haphazardly. Companies that operate this way are forcing themselves to accept about a 70- to 80-percent affectivity level from the entire organization. Instead, they could be targeting and measuring a level in the ninety percentiles while providing the support to achieve this (i.e., team leaders).

To encourage various improvements within your business, I recommend you quantify or convert what a one-day (or 1-percent) improvement for certain measurements will add to the bottom line. For example, you could quantify that a 1-percent OEE improvement for machine A equates to $X per year, or a one-day reduction in DSI equals $X per year, or a one-day reduction in DSO equals $X per year. This helps put these measurements into terms everyone can relate to and will increase motivation for improvement as well as keeping the team focused on the improvements with the largest impact.

14.6 MANAGING PARTS DIFFERENTLY

As we were not fortunate enough to be a "widget" manufacturer producing only a few part numbers with subtle differences, we could not manage all parts in the same manner. Therefore, the idea to classify our parts as either "runners," "repeaters," or "strangers" (also known as an ABC analysis or stock vs. non-stock parts) was very helpful in how we quoted and manufactured the parts. It is true that we were essentially a job shop and could not say for certain whether any particular part would receive a repeat order (although we had a good idea depending on the type of part, the customer, and the way in which we were asked to prepare the quotation). For example, after determining a part was likely to repeat (a runner), we usually did not include a cost for programming (as that might not be competitive and the programming was a one-time cost). I also required the shop to document all the setup procedures for potential "runner" parts so that if and when they repeated, we could profit from the previous experience. Quotes for parts that were unlikely to repeat (strangers) included the cost for developing the program, and usually we would not take the time to document the setup or prepare a setup fixture. It took some experience to allow us to classify orders in these groups, but we were right more often than not. And, by having different processes for these classifications, I am sure we were more profitable. If you design and build your own products you would categorize and manage parts in a similar fashion, classifying them as either stock (for runner parts) and non-stock (stranger parts) as your lead times would differ for these categories.

14.7 ACTIVITY-BASED COSTING PROVES HELPFUL IN SECURING MORE ORDERS

A critical discovery was the inaccuracy in our prices resulting from using a single and simplified shop rate of $60 per hour, thereby evenly allocating most indirect costs over all products (like spreading butter). After learning the business and taking into account that we had almost as many indirect as direct employees, the scope of this problem became apparent. There were many benefits realized by understanding most of our actual costs more accurately in direct relation to the part numbers (or product families) that consumed these costs. At the forefront was the better understanding of our true profit margin, especially when very competitive pricing was required. A simplified application of activity-based costing was utilized to reach a range of labor rates that better reflected the activity level required for the various types of parts. However, since the basis for applying various labor rates are in most cases direct labor hours, it was critical to first get these times accurate. We had worked on this through our feedback cycle with our quotations. Having a system that continued to refine the accuracy of the direct labor hours was our basis to proceed with this simplified version of activity-based costing.

I did not have the time or ability to associate many indirect and overhead costs (i.e., some indirect labor functions, rent, taxes, etc.) to a specific part number, but I had learned many of the characteristics of the parts and/or customers that affected how much effort/activity was required by each. From this basis, I was able to redistribute the $60-per-hour figure much more appropriately between the shop and office depending on the effort/activity required by the type of product or the particular customer. This breakdown (shown in Appendix J) created a new pricing range—from $48 per hour to $74 per hour (still based on direct labor hours)—assigned to a particular part and based on how the characteristics of the part and/or the customer affected the activity level of our shop and office. This entire concept of lean accounting is so critical, especially in competitive markets. To better relate actual costs to the products consuming them in real time, apply some of these lean accounting techniques (i.e., activity-based costing) instead of only compiling numbers each month based on government requirements (meeting generally accepted accounting principles) and trying to use only this historical data to manage your company.

A final element that I feel was critical to my success was basing my problem resolution on data. Although I was disappointed at not implementing a more formal problem-solving process, I avoided continuously firefighting by not taking on every issue and working only on those that repeated most often. I further drove some structure into our discussions by stopping the team when the conversation turned to "it happens a lot" and instead asked that a few weeks of simple data gathering (often with a tick list) take place before we put any more of our time or resources into resolving a particular issue. I also fought the urge to make a quick determination of what the root cause was and then direct someone on how to implement "my" solution. I cannot claim that I was always successful at guiding my team through a structured analysis and letting them have input to the solution, but more often than not we resorted to using the lean ideas. Having a team leader with an understanding of problem solving added to our success.

I would also like to believe that many of the processes and much of the standardization I put in place remained after selling the company. I believe that the documented processes coupled with their links to profitability earned them the right to remain in place through two changes of management in six years. The Toyota Production System (TPS) that was integrated into all Toyota's processes ensured that management changes were not followed by major process changes.

We all know this is not true in many companies: The systems and processes are not structured with a management system, therefore they are often changed based on the manager's ideas and his or her personal style. They are continuously searching for a winner in profitability but willing to sacrifice other items to get there. Each management change brings with it different priorities, usually different systems, beliefs, and definitely a new personal style. I wish I knew what has happened to the systems I developed but I would hope to find many still in place. I would also like to compare my before and after results having utilized lean to transform the business versus the new owner's sales focus for making improvements and increasing profitability.

14.8 A PROCESS TO EXAMINE YOUR BUSINESS

After reading this book, I hope you are inclined to verify whether some of the opportunities presented exist within your company. One way to start would be to select a product or service you provide that many of the employees would judge to be difficult (a "pain in the butt") and try to account for all the direct and indirect employees' time and the materials and the resources consumed. This would include all the time involved from the first customer communication through the administrative processes, all the way through packing, shipping, invoicing, and collecting the money. Naturally, you would need to assign hourly labor rates and try to proportionally account for all the other overheads that cannot be directly assigned. You should also observe the direct labor hours utilized and compare them to the quoted or standard hours for this product. I feel that by playing detective with a sample of one or two products (going to Gemba), you would get a feel for how accurate your estimates are and understand whether the projected profit margin is realistic. Naturally, your investigation should entail observation of as many of the process steps as possible, usually resulting in the identification of many Kaizen opportunities. This should lead you into undertaking OSKKK, and provide a starting point. Remember to prioritize actions for the processes that you consider bottlenecks. This would also be a good time to review your definition of a "bottleneck" and how your team determines where they are currently located and how to react to them.

This is only scraping the surface, but I would be surprised if you did not come away identifying many opportunities and engaging fellow team members in discussions that will also leave them considering the opportunities. You will likely come away understanding some shortfalls in your quoting process, planning process, and value-adding processes as well as in the accounting allocations toward determining your profit margin. Before you go off relating these discoveries to wider implications for the business and jumping into some program or action plan, you need to think about how this might take focus away from current business initiatives and you end up with a "machine gun Kaizen" approach. Therefore, I am only recommending that you consider this step as a starting point to help convince yourself and the organization of the opportunities. Then, you need a process such as strategy deployment to help in prioritizing your limited resources and aligning your improvement tasks to the current business priorities.

Lean principle: Machine gun Kaizen is a negative term that describes how you should not go about your Kaizen implementation. It is the idea of individuals randomly performing many smaller Kaizens without a plan linking them to the overall strategy or the metrics. This can be detrimental in utilizing your limited resources on incorrect priorities. OSKKK helps in avoiding machine gun Kaizen, but deciding where to implement OSKKK must be linked to the company's strategy and positively affect the key metrics.

Another thought for examining your own business: Look at the tasks I went about learning and improving during my lean transformation (listed in Appendix L), and for those same tasks that exist within your business, you should question which are standardized and have previously had their flow and processes Kaizened. You can then prioritize which of these most directly influence your profitability or cause your bottlenecks, and then begin to improve them possibly utilizing some of the improvement ideas I discovered during my transformation.

Since the purpose of this book was to tell my story as it happened and not to recommend a specific strategy or an exact method to implement lean in a high-mix, low-volume environment, you should use it to draw your own conclusions. At this point, I refer you to my book, *Made-to-Order Lean*, in which I share some ideas and a methodology to implement lean in this type of environment. I also encourage you to search for publications containing experiences of other lean practitioners implementing in these specialized environments.

While I am out working with a variety of manufacturing and service industry clients, I continuously find new ways to adapt what I know as the Toyota Production System. As these principles are continually learned and explored, I am always amazed by the number of new opportunities discovered and the creative solutions that are found. My strongest recommendation is not to get hooked on the lean tools presented in most books (as they are usually taken from high-volume examples) but instead to explore the underlying principles and adapt them to your situation.

I wish you success in your journey of continuous improvement.

Appendix A

OSKKK Methodology

1. OBSERVATION

For all operations

- Take the time to see what is happening in the work area by watching multiple cycles of the same process.
- Watch more than one person performing the process and note where standardization is lacking, especially where it affects quality or productivity.
- Document by writing the individual process steps in the sequence they occur.
- Identify the origins of variation in both flow of information and flow of materials.

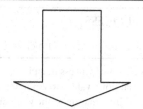

2. STANDARDIZATION

For materials, motions, tasks, and management; defined as the current optimized sequence of the process steps followed by the team members to ensure quality, safety, and productivity

- Prioritize where standardization is most critical to the organization based on observations or data.
- Observe all team members' various methods for performing the task and decide on the current standard (based on that which is best for quality, safety, and productivity).
- Have all team members work to the current standard while improvement ideas are being discussed.
- Input 5S (workplace organization) to promote simplified and productive standardization to be put in place.
- Work to minimize/eliminate problems and interruptions to the process using problem-solving techniques.
- Ensure all flows and decision points in the process have a standard methodology.

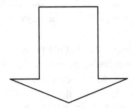

3. KAIZEN OF FLOW & PROCESS

Information and materials first; least cost to implement ($)

- Understand and map process flow (process mapping).
- Understand and map material flow (value stream mapping).
- Improve flow of material and information to the work area.
- Identify all non-value adding time in both information and process flows, then work to eliminate or minimize it.
- In business processes and material flows, work to reduce throughput time.

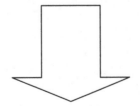

4. KAIZEN OF EQUIPMENT

Medium cost to implement ($$)

- Look at setup time (SMED; single minute exchange of dies) and work to reduce it.
- Look to improve feeds and speeds (reduce machine cycles).
- Use OEE (overall equipment effectiveness) as the measurement to drive improvements.
- Understand operator workload in comparison to machine cycle times, eliminate forced waiting.
- Look for total predictive maintenance (TPM) improvements.
- Look to simplify machines.

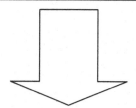

5. KAIZEN OF LAYOUT

Most cost to implement ($$$)

- Ensure previous steps of OSKKK have been worked on before rearranging layout.
- Collect data: process flows, capabilities, new products, bottlenecks, OEE, value stream maps, information flow, etc.
- Minimum of three layout proposals, all showing flow arrows and complete correlation matrixes (details found in Made-to-Order Lean).
- New layouts to consider all lean principles and remove non-value added work to justify costs.
- Should work to improve the man–machine–materials ratio.
- Any new machinery should be considered only after working to improve existing machines and incorporating all learnings into specifications for the new machinery.
- Simulate the new layout either marking the floor (for existing layouts) or with cardboard mock-ups of the equipment (for new processes or products).

Appendix B

Documentation Techniques

Figure B.1   Always start with observation.

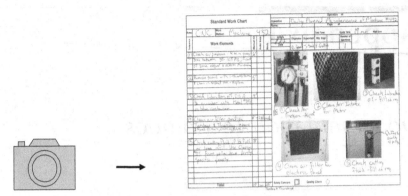

Figure B.2   Next, use digital camera to document shop floor tasks.

Figure B.3   Videos with a running commentary are an easy backup plan for both the shop floor and office.

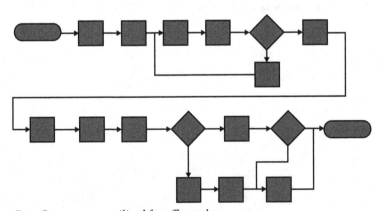

Figure B.4   Process maps utilized for office tasks.

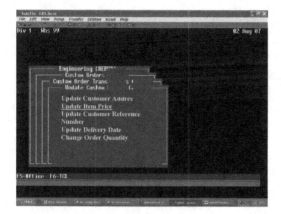

1. On Update Customer Orders menu select "Update Item Price"

2. Enter new price in "Value" line

Figure B.5   For computer tasks, use screenshots with clear instructions.

Appendix C

My First Attempt at Standardizing the Quoting Process

Quote & Tracking Sheet: *Machined Parts*						Quote #: *3341*	
Customer: *ABC Inc.* Part: *713-224981-B* Qty: *16* Due date: *3/7/02*							
MATERIAL					**CNC PROGRAMMING**		
Material estimate 1	$7.02 ea.	Supplier name	*Reliance*		**Est. (hrs.)**	**Act.**	**Charge/overhead**
Material estimate 2	$6.80 ea.	Supplier name	*Jorgenson*	Op. 1	*0.33*		—
Material estimate 3		Supplier name		Op. 2	*0.25*		—
				Op. 3	*0.25*		—
Enter hourly rate:	$60			Op. 4			
Any add. markup:	$0.00			Op. 5			
OPERATION 1						Total	0
	Est.	**Act.**	**Qty.**	**Cost/pc.**	**Problems**		
Setup time (hrs.)	0.33		*16*	$1.24			
Run (minutes)	3		*16*	$3.00			
Extra measure, deburr, fixture, etc.							
OPERATION 2							
	Est.	**Act.**	**Qty.**	**Cost/pc.**	**Problems**		
Setup time (hrs.)	0.25		*16*	$0.94			
Run (minutes)	2		*16*	$2.00			
Extra measure, deburr, fixture, etc.	2		*16*	$2.00			

OPERATION 3							
	Est.	Act.	Qty.	Cost/pc.	Problems		
Setup time (hrs.)	0.5		16	$1.88			
Run (minutes)	8		16	$8.00			
Extra measure, deburr, fixture, etc	2			$2.00			
OPERATION 4							
	Est.	Act.	Qty.	Cost/pc.	Problems		
Setup time (hrs.)							
Run (minutes)							
Extra measure, deburr, fixture, etc.							
OPERATION 5							
	Est.	Act.	Qty.	Cost/pc.	Problems		
Setup time (hrs.)							
Run (minutes)							
Extra measure, deburr, fixture, etc.							
Subcontract	Lot price	per pc.	Total (w/15% markup)				
Plating estimate	$55.00	$3.44	$3.95			Total per part:	$31.81
Painting estimate						Any 1x setup	—
Silkscreen						Expedite charge	—
Clean room pkg.							
Stress relieve			**Note: Actual times noted during mfg. in areas**				

Appendix D

Example of the First Day-by-hour Board for the Bottleneck Machine

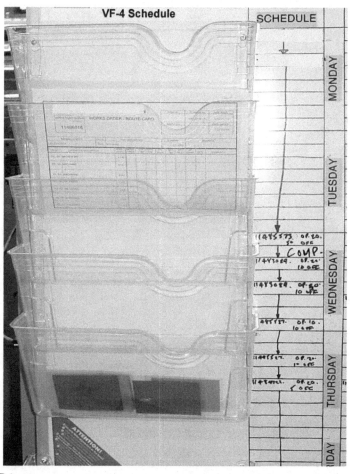

Figure D.1

Appendix E

Real-time Pareto Chart

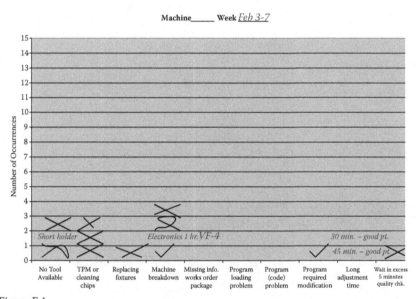

Figure E.1

Appendix F

Overall Equipment Effectiveness (OEE) for Bottlenecks

PART I

OEE is a useful measurement because it is based on the premise that all losses on machines can be quantified. It is not possible to obtain an OEE of 100 percent because all losses are counted (includes considering setup time as a loss). The idea of looking at this cumulatively is that, even if all the individual numbers (availability, performance, and quality) are 90 percent (which might seem acceptable):

$$90\% \times 90\% \times 90\% = 73\%$$

therefore, a good part is coming off this machine only 73 percent of the time.

$$\text{OEE} = \text{availability (\%)} \times \text{performance (\%)} \times \text{quality (\%)}$$

$$= \frac{\text{operating time}}{\text{planned production time}} \times \frac{(\text{ideal cycle time} \times \text{total parts})}{\text{operating time}} \times \frac{\text{good parts produced}}{\text{total parts produced}}$$

When substituting, this can be mathematically simplified to:

OEE = (Good pieces × ideal cycle time)/planned production time

I recommend using this simplified equation to start with; in addition, you should separately calculate a quality number (which is likely already being measured for other purposes). Part of the reason for the simplified calculation is that some organizations struggle with how to separate downtime into either availability or performance. An easy rule of thumb: the longer downtimes (i.e., greater than five minutes) are "availability" issues and the shorter downtimes (less than five minutes) are "performance." Though often there are few benefits derived from this effort, more importantly is for each bottleneck machine to develop specific categories for downtime and track those while calculating OEE with the simplified equation.

Here is an example of how I have gone about doing it with the operators using the simplified calculation each day:

OEE: Calculation				Week: March 2-6			Machine: VF-4	
Date	Shift	Part number & operation	Ideal cycle time (CNC-prog.) Minutes	Qty. Good pieces Quantity	Productive time = (good pieces × ideal cycle time) Minutes	Quality Good parts produced Total parts produced in %	Planned production time Minutes	OEE in % Total productive time Planned production time
2-Mar	First	716-774112 op 1	3.5	16	56	76/81 = 93.8%	7.5 hours X 60 min = 450 min	273.8/450 = 60.8%
		716-774112 op2	4.8	16	76.8			
		716-774112 op 3	108	16	28.8			
		304557 op 1	4.3	8	34.4			
		304557 op 2	2.6	8	20.8			
		440-322109 op 1	5.1	6	30.6			
		440-322109 op 2	4.4	6	26.4			
	Total			76	273.8			
3-Mar	First	554690 op 1	9	12	108	70/72= 97%	7.5 hours X 60 min = 450 min	344.8/450 = 77%
		554690 op 2	4	12	48			
		713-770321 op 1	4	19	76			
		713-770321 op 2	4	19	76			
		988431 op 1	4.6	8	36.8			
	Total			70	344.8			

PART II

In addition to calculating the OEE each day (directly at the machine), the operator also fills out a real-time Pareto chart (categories developed specifically for each bottleneck machine). This should provide a baseline for where to target your improvements.

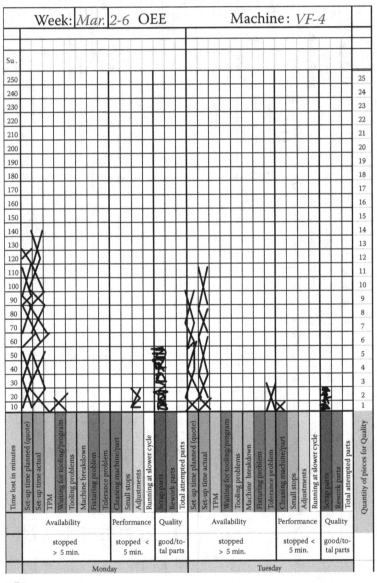

Figure F.1

Appendix G

Typical Team Leader Responsibilities

A team leader—generally promoted from within the team—is an hourly employee who has many of the following responsibilities:

- Provides assistance to primary operator
  - Answers calls for assistance
  - Troubleshoots tooling problems
  - Determines when maintenance is necessary and who should respond (whether the team leader can handle or more technical support is necessary)
  - Performs changeovers (prepares tools, material, etc.)
  - Ensures material including consumables is available and reordered as required
  - Checks quality
  - Handles defective material
  - Measures and tracks results
  - Provides emergency relief
- Provides coverage for operator absenteeism and vacation
- Follows and procures material when needed
- Available for overtime and helping administer overtime
- Assists area supervisor to ensure proper "rotation" concepts
- Performs training and maintains training documentation (updates cross-training/skills matrix)
- Supports monitoring and improving OEE (overall equipment effectiveness)
- Performs quality audits

- Oversees TPM (total predictive maintenance) and monitors conformance to TPM procedures/schedules
- Provides input to root cause analysis
- Provides documentation for machine problems/downtime causes
- Assists supervisor to ensure proper scheduling of production (schedule day-by-hour boards)
- Assists supervisor to maintain department supplies and indirect materials

Appendix H

Cross-Training or Skills Matrix

Manual & CNC Machining Matix

Documented Procedure	Risk
Load/unload and basic deburring	G
Basic measuring with calliper & micrometer	G
Understanding of tolerancing & deter. out of tolerance	G
Able to make minor offset adjustments in machine	G
Set-up of offsets for tooling in machine	G
Set-up of tooling	G
Setting up fixtures	G
Picking up 0 offsets	G
Load program from computer library to machine	G
Understand and correct G-code in program (line-edit)	Y
Able to change diameter (geometry) offsets	Y
Utilize all measuring equip. in Q.C. area	G
Manual & off-line tapping	G
Manual lathe - set-up	G
Operate manual milling machine	Y
Set-up manual milling machine	Y
Basic programming	R
Set & run 2-D angles on manual milling machine	R
Conceptualize and develop 3-D programming	Y
Estimate set-up time	R
Estimate run time (machine cycle time)	Y
Engraving of part numbers	

Employee	Dates for training/notes
1 Tom	
2 John	
3 Jake	
4 Bert	By August 2001
5 Julian	TBD
6 Alfred	By June 2001
7 Conney	
8 Kenny	
9 Greg	on-going

Status of cross training: G G G G G G G G G Y Y G G G Y Y R R Y Y

G Low Risk
Y Medium Risk
   High Risk

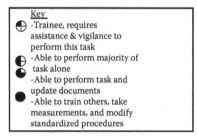

Key
⊕ -Trainee, requires assistance & vigilance to perform this task
◐ -Able to perform majority of task alone
◑ -Able to perform task and update documents
● -Able to train others, take measurements, and modify standardized procedures

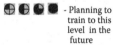

- Planning to train to this level in the future

Figure H.1

Appendix I

New Layout with Some CNCs Set Up as an "L" Cell

Figure I.1

Appendix J

*Initial ABC Costing Matrix
for Shop and Office*

PART I

		Shop Activity Rating											
Direct Shop influences / Indirect Shop influences		(+1) Soft Material (aluminum, plastic, etc.)						(+2) Hard Material (steel, stainless, tungsten, etc.)					
		Easy Deburr (+1)			Heavy Deburr (+2)			Easy Deburr (+1)			Heavy Deburr (+2)		
		No tight tolerances (+0)	Few tight tolerances (+1)	Significant tight toler-ances (+2)	No tight tolerances (+0)	Few tight tolerances (+1)	Significant tight toler-ances(+2)	No tight tolerances (+0)	Few tight tolerances (+1)	Significant tight toler-ances (+2)	No tight tolerances (+0)	Few tight tolerances (+1)	Significant tight toler-ances (+2)
(+1) Easy measurement (1–30 measure points)	wEasy to program (+1)	1 + 1 + 1 + 1 + 0 = 4	1 + 1 + 1 + 1 + 1 = 5	1 + 1 + 1 + 1 + 2 = 6	1 + 1 + 1 + 2 + 0 = 5	1 + 1 + 1 + 2 + 1 = 6	1 + 1 + 1 + 2 + 2 = 7	1 + 1 + 2 + 1 + 0 = 5	1 + 1 + 2 + 1 + 1 = 6	1 + 1 + 2 + 1 + 2 = 7	1 + 1 + 2 + 2 + 0 = 6	1 + 1 + 2 + 2 + 1 = 7	1 + 1 + 2 + 2 + 2 = 8
	Medium to program (+2)	5	6	7	6	7	8	6	7	8	7	8	9
	Difficult to program (+3)	6	7	8	7	8	9	7	8	9	8	9	10
(+2) Medium measurement (31–50 measure points)	Easy to program (+1)	5	6	7	6	7	8	6	7	8	7	8	9
	Medium to program (+2)	6	7	8	7	8	9	7	8	9	8	9	10
	Difficult to program (+3)	7	8	9	8	9	10	8	9	10	9	10	11

(+3) Difficult measurement (51+ measure points)												
Easy to program (+1)	6	7	8	7	8	9	7	8	9	8	9	10
Medium to program (+2)	7	8	9	8	9	10	8	9	10	9	10	11
Difficult to program (+3)	8	9	10	9	10	11	9	10	11	10	11	12

Conversion of Shop Activity Rating to Hourly Cost

Shop Activity Rating	4	5	6	7	8	9	10	11	12
Hourly Shop Cost	$16	$18	$20	$22	$24	$26	$28	$30	$32

PART II

Office Activity Rating

Office Activity Rating		(+1) Easy Customer (on-time pay, good terms, etc.)		(+2) Difficult Customer (not on-time pay, poor terms, etc.)	
		(+1) Easy ship & pack requirements	(+2) Difficult ship & pack requirements	(+1) Easy ship & pack requirements	(+2) Difficult ship & pack requirements
(+1) Minimal or standard customer support requirements (few changes, easy sales support, standard specifications, quantity, etc.)	(+1) Short bill of material (1–5 items) + no outsourcing	1 + 1 + 1 + 1 = 4	1 + 1 + 1 + 2 = 5	1 + 1 + 2 + 1 = 5	1 + 1 + 2 + 2 = 6
	(+2) Medium bill of material (6–15 items) + outsourcing 1–2 services	5	6	6	7
	(+3) Long bill of material (16+ items) + outsourcing 3 or more services	6	7	7	8
(+2) Increased customer support requirements (frequent changes, extra sales support, additional specifications, quantity, etc.)	(+1) Short bill of material (1–5 items) + no outsourcing	5	6	6	7
	(+2) Medium bill of material (6–15 items) + outsourcing 1–2 services	6	7	7	8
	(+3) Long bill of material (16+ items) + outsourcing 3 or more services	7	8	8	9

Conversion of Office Activity Rating to Hourly Cost

Office Activity Rating	4	5	6	7	8	9
Hourly Office Cost	$12	$14	$16	$18	$20	$22

Appendix K

*Initial Equipment and Area Layout
for Expansion into Sheet Metal*

Figure K.1

Appendix L

Sequence Utilized for Learning the Business and for Implementing Lean

Tasks	OSKKK				
	Observe (Document)	Standardization	Kaizen of Flow & Process	Kaizen of Equipment	Kaizen of Layout
CNC machine operation	1	6	42, 84	66, 85	78, 86
CNC machine setup	3	7	45, 55, 61	66, 86	
CNC programming	7	10	11, 83, 84		
Workplace organization (5S)	4	5	44		78
Interviewing	8	9			
Machine TPM		59		60	
Identify shortage of skills	14	15			
Actual vs. estimated times	19	20	21		
Problem-solving development			48		
Team leader development		49	50, 57	64, 67	
Overtime management		53	54		
Bonus system/suggestion system		56	64		
Machine productivity improvements				63	78
External quality accreditation		77			
Stocking of tooling, consumables		82			
Shearing/bending sheet metal	87	88	90	92	
Welding					

SHOP

OFFICE	Quoting machined parts	2	12	13, 28, 52, 58, 74, 79		
	Quoting sheet metal parts		89	91		
	Input customer orders	C, 22	G	23, 79		
	Setting hourly rates for customers	16	17	18, 43		
	Pricing for materials	F, 29	72	73		
	Purchase orders	A, 30		69		
	Purchasing/receiving job materials	B, 31	I	32, 70, 71, 81		
	Payroll	E				
	Invoicing	D				
	Planning (capacity)	25	26	27, 34, 51, 80		
	Planning (materials)	24		33, 80		
	Bookkeeping	H				
	Monthly closing of the books	M, 38	O, 39	P, 40, 65		
	Packaging	K	N			78
	Organizing shipment	J				78
	Producing the work order package	35	36	37		
	Collecting customer payments	Q, 41	R			
	Standardization through visualization		75			78
	Workplace organization (5S)	S	T	U		78
	Computer system/network			68, 76, V		

Key: 1 through 92—the sequential order in which I learned and implemented changes; A through V—the sequential order in which my mother learned and documented the office tasks.

Appendix M

Different Applications of Value Stream Mapping and Process Mapping

Value Stream Mapping
- A **high level snapshot** from door to door of a business
- Follows material flow & some information flow (order entry)
- Helps to identify improvement opportunities
- Does **not** incorporate decision loops or parallel processes

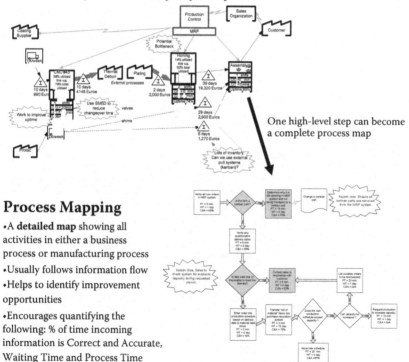

One high-level step can become a complete process map

Process Mapping
- A **detailed map** showing all activities in either a business process or manufacturing process
- Usually follows information flow
- Helps to identify improvement opportunities
- Encourages quantifying the following: % of time incoming information is Correct and Accurate, Waiting Time and Process Time
- Incorporates decision loops and parallel processes

Figure M.1

Index

About the Author

Greg Lane began his lean journey after earning his bachelor of science in mechanical engineering from the University of Wisconsin in 1986 and his master of business administration from the California State University in

1989. He was one of the few selected for a one-year training program conducted by Toyota's masters and centered in Japan. He became certified as a Toyota Production System (TPS) Key Person and returned to the United States, where he trained others in the NUMMI (New United Motor Manufacturing, Inc.) plant, a Toyota–General Motors joint venture in Fremont, California.

Since his training in 1992, Greg has continued his lean learning by working on implementing lean around the world, supporting large and small companies alike. In 1998, he began to focus his lean endeavors on meeting the specific needs of high-mix, low-volume manufacturing and service providers. Although his work is geared to companywide improvements, Greg has also focused on individual departments—purchasing, engineering, finance, and planning—to improve efficiencies, reduce lead times, and reduce costs.

While working as an independent consultant, Greg purchased and operated (for six years) his own manufacturing company, which specialized in fast turnaround on high-mix, low-volume parts. He used TPS to grow the business and nearly double its sales, and sold it at a profit to concentrate on supporting others in lean implementation.

Though his recent concentration has been with high variation and low-volume applications, Greg started in high-volume environments and his experience includes everything from test, repair, defense, and overhaul businesses as well as many non-manufacturing companies such as service providers. His previous book, *Made-to-Order Lean: Excelling in a High-Mix, Low-Volume Environment,* explained how to adapt certain lean principles for made-to-order businesses. He has also developed training manuals and materials in use by lean practitioners as well as publishing articles in various engineering periodicals.

Greg is a faculty member of the Lean Enterprise Institute in the United States and a senior advisor to the Instituto Lean Management in Spain. He has worked in twenty-four countries supporting lean transformations and speaks English, German, and some Spanish.

Greg and his associates are always interested in helping others in their lean journeys, especially when challenged with nontraditional applications. They can be reached at glane@LowVolumeLean.com or more information can be found at www.lowvolumelean.com.

Printed in the United States
by Baker & Taylor Publisher Services

Printed in the United States
by Baker & Taylor Publisher Services